the cinema of SEAN PENN

DIRECTORS' CUTS

Other selected titles in the Directors' Cuts series:

the cinema of CHRISTOPHER NOLAN: *imagining the impossible*
JACQUELINE FURBY & STUART JOY (eds)

the cinema of THE COEN BROTHERS: *hardboiled entertainments*
JEFFREY ADAMS

the cinema of CLINT EASTWOOD: *chronicles of america*
DAVID STERRITT

the cinema of ISTVÁN SZABÓ: *visions of europe*
JOHN CUNNINGHAM

the cinema of AGNÈS VARDA: *resistance and eclecticism*
DELPHINE BÉNÉZET

the cinema of ALEXANDER SOKUROV: *figures of paradox*
JEREMI SZANIAWSKI

the cinema of MICHAEL WINTERBOTTOM: *borders, intimacy, terror*
BRUCE BENNETT

the cinema of RAÚL RUIZ: *impossible cartographies*
MICHAEL GODDARD

the cinema of MICHAEL MANN: *vice and vindication*
JONATHAN RAYNER

the cinema of AKI KAURISMÄKI: *authorship, bohemia, nostalgia, nation*
ANDREW NESTINGEN

the cinema of RICHARD LINKLATER: *walk, don't run*
ROB STONE

the cinema of BÉLA TARR: *the circle closes*
ANDRÁS BÁLINT KOVÁCS

the cinema of STEVEN SODERBERGH: *indie sex, corporate lies, and digital videotape*
ANDREW DE WAARD & R. COLIN TATE

the cinema of TERRY GILLIAM: *it's a mad world*
JEFF BIRKENSTEIN, ANNA FROULA & KAREN RANDELL (eds)

the cinema of TAKESHI KITANO: *flowering blood*
SEAN REDMOND

the cinema of THE DARDENNE BROTHERS: *responsible realism*
PHILIP MOSLEY

the cinema of MICHAEL HANEKE: *europe utopia*
BEN MCCANN & DAVID SORFA (eds)

the cinema of SALLY POTTER: *a politics of love*
SOPHIE MAYER

the cinema of DAVID CRONENBERG: *from baron of blood to cultural hero*
ERNEST MATHIJS

the cinema of JAN SVANKMAJER: *dark alchemy*
PETER HAMES (ed.)

the cinema of LARS VON TRIER: *authenticity and artifice*
CAROLINE BAINBRIDGE

the cinema of WERNER HERZOG: *aesthetic ecstasy and truth*
BRAD PRAGER

the cinema of TERRENCE MALICK: *poetic visions of america (second edition)*
HANNAH PATTERSON (ed.)

the cinema of ANG LEE: *the other side of the screen (second edition)*
WHITNEY CROTHERS DILLEY

the cinema of STEVEN SPIELBERG: *empire of light*
NIGEL MORRIS

the cinema of TODD HAYNES: *all that heaven allows*
JAMES MORRISON (ed.)

the cinema of NANNI MORETTI: *dreams and diaries*
EWA MAZIERSKA & LAURA RASCAROLI

the cinema of DAVID LYNCH: *american dreams, nightmare visions*
ERICA SHEEN & ANNETTE DAVISON (eds)

the cinema of KRZYSZTOF KIESLOWSKI: *variations on destiny and chance*
MAREK HALTOF

the cinema of GEORGE A. ROMERO: *knight of the living dead (second edition)*
TONY WILLIAMS

the cinema of KATHRYN BIGELOW: *hollywood transgressor*
DEBORAH JERMYN & SEAN REDMOND (eds)

the cinema of
SEAN PENN

in and out of place

Deane Williams

WALLFLOWER PRESS LONDON & NEW YORK

A Wallflower Press Book
Published by
Columbia University Press
Publishers Since 1893
New York • Chichester, West Sussex
cup.columbia.edu

Copyright © 2016 Deane Williams
All rights reserved
Wallflower Press® is a registered trademark of Columbia University Press

A complete CIP record is available from the Library of Congress

ISBN 978-0-231-17624-8 (cloth : alk. paper)
ISBN 978-0-231-17625-5 (pbk. : alk. paper)
ISBN 978-0-231-85085-8 (e-book)

Series design by Rob Bowden Design

Cover image of Sean Penn courtesy of Kobal Collection

Columbia University Press books are printed on permanent
and durable acid-free paper.
This book is printed on paper with recycled content.
Printed in the United States of America

CONTENTS

Acknowledgements vii

Introduction 1

1 Politics 8
2 Penn's Performance Places 23
3 *The Indian Runner* 32
4 *The Crossing Guard* 53
5 *The Pledge* 77
6 Interlude: '*U.S.A.*' 96
7 *Into the Wild* 103

Conclusion: Places of Hope 125

Filmography 128
Bibliography 133
Index 138

For Con Verevis

ACKNOWLEDGEMENTS

This idea for this book came about, as usual, over coffee, with Constantine Verevis, when he described Todd Fields' *In the Bedroom* (2001), with all its characteristic attention to a confined and character defining sense of place, as being like a Sean Penn film. Thanks for that and ongoing support Con. Thanks to Noel King, Adrian Martin and Dana Polan for reading draft chapters of the manuscript. I have benefitted enormously from conversations with and questions from friends and colleagues at conferences where I have presented this material and in social situations. For these conversations and questions I would like to thank, in particular, Lauren Bliss, Raffaele Caputo, Ross Gibson, John Hughes, Mark Graham, Tim Groves, Selmin Kara, Richard T. Kelly, Sarinah Masukor, Raya Morag, Bill Nichols, Claire Perkins, Philip Rosen, Bill Routt, Vivien Silvey, Drake Stutesman, Amy Villarejo, and Janet Walker. Thanks to Yoram Allon, Commissioning Editor at Wallflower Press, for taking on this project and for his patience and clarity. Of course special thanks Anna, Maddie, Ella and Inka, as always, for their love and for letting me take over at least two rooms of our house with all my Sean Penn junk.

INTRODUCTION

There never was an is without a where. Both the bad things and the good that happen to human beings and other life-forms self-evidently occur when their bodies are physically located somewhere, in particular locations. […] Environment is not an 'other' to us' but 'part of our being'.

– Lawrence Buell (2001: 55)

Each of Sean Penn's directorial works, and many of the films he has acted in, are set in an immediate past where a 'stalled' time and a restricted locale contain their narratives, marking them out as films about a particular place, 'in time'. These films are concerned with the ways in which specific places and times condition individuals grounding them in specific locales in order to divine the deep cultural structures that concern each particular film. In this way these films articulate the distinct nature of each place; the Omaha, Nebraska, of *The Indian Runner* (1991), the Los Angeles of *The Crossing Guard* (1995), the Nevada of *The Pledge* (2001), the Manhattan of 'U.S.A.' (2002) and the Alaska of *Into the Wild* (2007) in order to better understand not only the cinematic places in which his narratives are set but also the close relationship between the performances and politics of these films and these places.

Place

Before considering the particular places of Penn's films it is useful to understand the ways in which place has been considered in contemporary scholarship. As Dolores Hayden, in her *The Power of Place: Urban Landscapes as Public History*, tells us:

> Place is one of the trickiest words in the English language, a suitcase so overfilled one can never shut the lid. It carries the resonance of homestead, location,

and open space in the city as well as a position in a social hierarchy. The authors of books on architecture, photography, [film], cultural geography, poetry, and travel rely on 'sense of place' as an aesthetic concept but often settle for 'the personality of a location' as a way of defining it. (1997: 15)

In his work on literature and environment Lawrence Buell, setting out the debates in human geography and place theory, concurs with Hayden's discussion of the slipperiness of the term 'place':

> Place, then, is a configuration of highly flexible subjective, social, and material dimensions, not reducible to any of these. In political geographer John Agnew's definition, 'place' can be conceived as a matter of (social) 'locale' (geographical) 'location' and 'sense of place'. It 'combines elements of nature (elemental forces), social relations (class, gender, and so on), and meaning (the mind ideas, symbols)' Placeness implies physical site, though site alone does not constitute place. It also implies affect, 'a deeply personal phenomenon founded on one's life-world and everyday practices. (2001: 60)

Yet for Buell, this 'placeness' is doubly complicated by the ways in which place is a contemplation, rendering or representation of a space emphasising that it has 'by definition both an objective and subjective face, pointing outward toward the tangible world and inward to the perceptions one brings to it' (2001: 59). This experiential aspect to place inflects any consideration of what places may be. For Buell, 'a place can be as small as a sofa – or even the particular spot on the sofa where your dog lies – or as big as a planet' or it can be 'differentiated according to the person, or culture according to nationality, racial, ethnic or gender grouping, profession, or relationship with a place. It is thus a 'configuration of highly subjective, social and material dimensions' (2001: 60). Here Buell is considering the construction of place in literary fiction drawing on Edward Casey's observation that 'places are not so much the direct objects of sight or thought or recollection as what we feel *with* and *around* and *above*, *before* and *behind* ourselves' (2001: 61) enabling him to proceed with his book about 'environmental imagination' in the works of American writers (2001: 1–2).

Place in Film

Any consideration of filmic place-making must consider the way in which realist cinema, at least, captures a pro-filmic event, making a place, while it subsequently transports that place to a host of other places (cinemas) in different locales, towns and cities, often internationally, for a variety of audiences and spectators to appreciate. In the introduction to their *Taking Place: Location and the Moving Image*, John David Rhodes and Elena Gorfinkel put this better:

> Place ... can be experienced or understood both as the ultimate, entirely natural a priori ('to be at all – to exist in any way – is to be somewhere, and to

be somewhere is to be in some kind of place') and as a fabrication – a product of human artifice, cultural construction, and ideology ('landscapes, like written texts, encode powerful social, cultural and political messages that are interpreted by their viewers'). (2011: x)

Across the history of cinema it is possible to recall a number of directors with close associations to place. John Ford's Monument Valley, Eric Rohmer's Paris, Federico Fellini's Rome, Wong Kar Wai's Hong Kong or the Dardenne Brothers' Seraing, Belgium. Whether these associations are based on the intricate rendering of a particular place in terms of location shooting, a narrative attuned to the rhythms of a life world, as in the Dardennes' extraordinary cinema, or the tracing of smaller, domestic lives lived out amongst the massive cultural and social shifts experienced due to seismic geo-political changes, as in Wong Kar Wai's cinema, or the peculiar associations made, from a distance, of a filmmaker's emblematic films, spilling out to colour a whole oeuvre, as in Ford and Fellini, few filmmakers have been as concerned with place as Sean Penn. Although his body of work is relatively brief, all his directorial works so far, and many of the films he has performed in, have at their heart, a distinct, demarcated and interiorised concern with place.

Another filmmaker who bears comparison to Penn is Michael Winterbottom. In films such as *Welcome to Sarajevo* (1997 – Sarajevo), *With or Without You* (1999 – Belfast), *Wonderland* (1999 – London), *The Claim* (2001 – the Sierra Nevadas, California), *24 Hour Party People* (2002 – Manchester) and *Genova* (2008 – Genova), Winterbottom utilises a vast range of places with which he has intertwined specific narratives. Like Penn's, Winterbottom's films are interested in what it is about these places that makes their characters what they are. As Brian McFarlane and I have argued, *24 Hour Party People* 'is a documentary-like argument about the vitality and cultural significance of Manchester' (2009: 41). At the same time the film is a personal essay film about the post-punk culture that Winterbottom and producer Andrew Eaton had grown up as a part of. In this way Winterbottom's film, like Penn's work, recalls Buell's emphasis on both the 'objective and subjective face' of place in a representational realm. While Winterbottom's films such as *24 Hour Party People* and *Wonderland* are about cultural assertion, Penn's films seek, through their fixation with place, to divine two things. First, they pursue the deep cultural struggle over identity as it stems from the places in which people live. In this way characters are subject to, seeking to understand, or in flight from the places that condition them. Second, Penn's films search for an understanding of the larger forces of modernity against which the identification with locales can be understood to be a political pursuit. In Penn's films large national and international forces are inflecting the particularity of each locale, subsequently altering, for good or not, the places that have shaped these characters. In this way Penn's rendering of place in each film, as Rhodes and Gorfinkel, following Dydia Lysner, suggest, can be seen as an ideological assertion, an argument about places and individuals. In what follows I will pay close attention to the manner in which the places of each of Penn's films are all confined temporally and spatially in various ways. All are set in an immediate past where a 'stalled' time and a restricted locale contain their narratives, marking them out as films about a particular place, 'in time'.

Intertextuality

At the same time, each of these places is rendered employing a host of figures, of actors, books, songs, photographs, myths and *mise-en-scène*, in combination with a distinct locale, forming a paradox that constitutes Penn's oeuvre. Noël Carroll in 'The Future of Allusion', proposes this strategy as a case of allusion, characteristic of New Hollywood (and Beyond):

> Allusion, specifically allusion to film history, has become a major expressive device, that is, a means that directors use to make comments on the fictional worlds of their films. *Allusion*, as I am using it, is an umbrella term covering a mixed lot of practices including quotations, the memorialization of past genres, the reworking of past genres, *homages*, and the recreation of 'classic' scenes, shots, plot motifs, lines of dialogue, themes, gestures, and so forth from film history, especially as that history was crystallized and codified in the sixties and early seventies. (1982: 52; emphasis in original).

For Carroll, allusion is 'a legacy of the American auterism' where the influence of the *Cahiers du cinéma* critics was adapted to American film culture by Andrew Sarris and others in order to venerate US directors at the same time as it produced a generation of filmmakers with what sounds like a description of Sean Penn, 'budding film-historical sensibility' (1982: 54). Carroll provides a list of these filmmakers including many directors that Penn has acted for or cited as influences: Dennis Hopper, Brian De Palma, Martin Scorsese and Terrence Malick, as well as Peter Bogdanovich, Michael Cimino, Monte Hellman, John Carpenter, Paul Schrader, Paul Bartel and others (1982: 52). In this way, for Carroll, the use of allusion involves a transition from 'organic expression for Hawks [for example] was translated into an iconographic code by a Walter Hill or a John Carpenter' (1982: 55).

In distinction from this allusionist filmmaking associated by Carroll with the New Hollywood, the cinema of Penn may be best understood as an intertextual cinema. For Carroll, New Hollywood references to figures in film history constitute vague effects. Steven Spielberg's references to the 'Night on Bald Mountain' sequence in Walt Disney's *Fantasia* (1940) in both *Close Encounters of the Third Kind* (1977) and *Raiders of the Lost Ark* (1981) are merely 'in order to swathe their supernaturals in Disneyesque wonderment' (1982: 67); or John Carpenter's *Assault on Precinct 13* (1976) alluding to Hawks' *Rio Bravo* (1959) is a matter of the gesture [having] 'the aura of the sort of mystic male bonding that cements the Hawksian brotherhood' (ibid.). While Penn uses genre, such as the social problem film or *film noir*, in an intertextual manner, it is his deliberate employment of specific quotations from earlier films that opens his films up on to the films he quotes. On the one hand this is a deliberate strategy that Penn uses; on the other this involves a deliberate strategy on my part to read Penn's films *in relation to* these earlier films.

Another distinction from Carroll's notion of allusion in relation to Penn's cinema is that *The Indian Runner*, *The Crossing Guard*, *The Pledge*, 'U.S.A.' and *Into the Wild* invariably refer to a wide array of texts, not just Hollywood cinema. Penn's use of Harry Crews in *The Indian Runner*, Charles Bukowski in *The Crossing Guard* or Henry David Thoreau in *Into the Wild* takes his cinema, and this book follows him, into a variety of cultural milieux outside the industrial entertainment systems that Carroll remains confined to.

In *The Memory of Tiresias*, Mikhail Iampolski proposes a definition of intertextuality in film that is appropriate for thinking about the cinema of Sean Penn. Drawing on the work of Ferdinand de Saussure, Julia Kristeva, Charles Sanders Peirce and others, Iampolski provides a definition: 'The quote is a fragment of the text that violates its linear development and derives the motivation that integrates it into the text from outside the text itself' (1998: 31). In this regard Penn's cinema draws on a host of quotations that are more than allusion, although they are often drawn from New Hollywood, because they provide a link not just to film history, but to a collection of other texts, as well as to the specific meaning obtained through, and because of, this link. It is the specificity of these links, the meaning generated, in a network of quotation, amongst the concerted effort to, at the same time, portray a place in a specific time, which constitutes his oeuvre.

Figures

All of Penn's films are concerned with outsider figures, either fleeing, ostracised from or mourning the loss of, families. Penn utilises these figures in order to emphasise the historical forces that shape their actions in order to divine the deep cultural structures that concern each particular film. Following the social problem film cycle of the immediate post-World War II period in the United States, Penn's outsider figures, in tandem with the actors that portray them, operate in a spectral manner, bringing to their roles, and the world of their films, an otherness derived from the intertextual relations opened up by, say, Viggo Mortensen's performance as Franky in *The Indian Runner* or Jack Nicholson's as Freddie in *The Crossing Guard*, or Harry Dean Stanton as Floyd Cage in *The Pledge*. In this regard it would be no surprise to anyone that there is quite a bit said about performance in this book. Penn is consistently described as an actor's director who trusts the actors to bring to his films what he has identified as their strengths, from their previous roles. He is also one of American cinema's most prominent contemporary actor-directors alongside Sarah Polley, Ben Affleck, Ben Stiller, Tim Robbins and Lena Dunham and in a tradition that includes Charlie Chaplin, Orson Welles, Robert Redford, Warren Beatty, John Cassavetes, Dennis Hopper, Robert Duvall and Clint Eastwood. It is probably Cassavetes, Hopper and Eastwood who bear strongest comparison, with Penn forming close friendships and working with all three.

Amongst these performances Penn utilises a panoply of intertexts, of songs, books, photographs, real-life events, televisual media, genres, myths and fairytales. In this way his oeuvre, while advancing a particular worldview – born out of the use of individual friendships, associations, personal taste and histories – and following Iampolski, seeks to divine the ways in culture works between and around as well as within texts. Of course the role of the interpreter cannot be diminished in this intertextual working. While I have avoided insisting on the veracity of the connections I have made, instead, relying on the notion of 'making available' or 'it is possible to see', I have, I'm sure, not been able to make every intertext that is obtainable in Penn's films. I am also Australian, providing a measure of distance and cultural ignorance that may prohibit the accessibility of some aspects of the discussions of both place and the intertextual workings across these places. I would hope that others will be able to see and hear some of the connections I make and others that I don't.

The first chapter will consider the public figure of Sean Penn in terms of progressive politics in distinction from the cynical approach taken to his persona by some sections of the media. Beginning with an account of Penn's parents Leo Penn and Eileen Ryan, the book will draw on the traditions of American left culture to which they belonged as it informs a reading of Penn's career and films. Eileen Ryan's career in leftist theatre and Leo Penn's television directing and acting career, including his blacklisting in the 1950s by the House Un-American Activities Committee and his performances in the social problem films of the era, provide a means to think about the Penn's continuation of a lineage that includes New Hollywood in activist terms. This chapter will also consider the emergence of Penn's activist figure in roles such as a narrator in Bill Couturié's *Dear America: Letters Home from Vietnam* (1987) and his performance in Spike Lee's *When the Levees Broke: A Requiem in Four Acts* (1996) and then on into his support for the likes of Tom Hayden, his 'An Open Letter to the President of the United States of America', his visits to Iraq, Iran, Cuba and Venezuela, his collaborations with Norman Solomon and, following the Haiti earthquake of 2001, his establishment of the J/P Haitian Relief Organization, with Sanela Diana Jenkins.

Preempting the intertextual relations that are the object of the analysis of his directorial works, chapter two examines Penn's 'Performance Places', in the films *Fast Times at Ridgemont High* (1982), *At Close Range* (1986), *Colors* (1988) and *Mystic River* (2003) as examples of the ways in which Penn's acting has consistently articulated characters, like the protagonists in the films he has directed, defined and confined by the places in which they live.

Penn's first feature film as director, *The Indian Runner*, where the director commenced his location of intertextual webs, is the focus of chapter three. The film is set in the American state of Nebraska and will be considered as an intersection of Bruce Springsteen's album *Nebraska* (1982), most specifically the song 'Highway Patrolman' and the folk traditions it draws on (such as the folk tunes, 'Night of the Johnstown Flood' and 'John Henry'), Native American relations with the land, as well as the genre of the Vietnam war movie. The appearance of cult southern gothic writer Harry Crews and Dennis Hopper, Sandy Dennis and Charles Bronson in relation to the performances by Viggo Mortensen and David Morse, are also considered.

Chapter four examines *The Crossing Guard*, Penn's Los Angeles film, drawing on a host of LA-based figures such as Nicholson, Anjelica Huston, *Chinatown* (1974) and *film noir*, Charles Bukowski, John Cassavetes and the family melodrama.

Chapter five considers Penn's adaptation of Friedrich Dürrenmatt's novel *The Pledge*, and Ladislas Vajda's *It Happened in Broad Daylight* (1958) transposed to the American state of Nevada, again utilising the figure of Jack Nicholson, as well as Harry Dean Stanton and Mickey Rourke, and European fairytales.

Penn's contribution to Alain Brigand's omnibus film *11/09/'01-September 11* (2002), the short 'U.S.A.', is the focus of chapter six, examining how that film's Manhattan emplacement allows for Penn's most intensely confined film, at the same time as it utilises the figure of Ernest Borgnine which connects the film to his performance in Delbert Mann and Paddy Chayefsky's *Marty* (1955) as well as the televisual rendering of the attacks on the Twin Towers.

Into the Wild, following Jon Krakauer's account of the life of Christopher McCandless, has Alaska as its obsession and destination. Chapter seven retraces McCandless, Krakauer and Penn in their intersubjective account of the forces, including the way that the idea of wilderness functions in the American imaginary and in the works of Jack London, Henry David Thoreau and Leo Tolstoy, and Emile Hirsch's method acting.

The book concludes with some words of speculation about Penn's place within contemporary independent American film as a reversal and combination of ways in which the American smart film has been delineated. In this distinction the cinema of Sean Penn can be understood as hopeful and communitarian, yet tragic and critical.

CHAPTER ONE

Politics

I just generically call it all responding and speaking to what I see. It's like you have a tool belt. And here's the movie-making one. Well that's not necessarily the right wrench for this bolt and nut, you know?

Sean Penn in *Iconoclasts* (2007)

For our New World I consider far less important for what it has done, or what it is, than for results to come.

– Walt Whitman (1984: 317)

In *Hollywood's New Radicalism: War, Globalisation and the Movies from Reagan to George W. Bush*, Ben Dickenson understands Sean Penn belonging to what he terms a 'new Hollywood left' or 'Hollywood's progressive talent' (2006: 144) or a 'radical actor and director' (2006: 121) alongside figures such as Tim Robbins, Susan Sarandon, Danny Glover, Michael Moore and John Sayles. This grouping is characterised in Trey Parker's *Team America: World Police* (2004) where Penn is depicted, in puppet form, as a member of Film Actors Guild (F.A.G.) alongside Alec Baldwin, Danny Glover, Tim Robbins, Susan Sarandon, Michael Moore, Helen Hunt, George Clooney, Samuel L. Jackson, Ethan Hawke, Martin Sheen, Matt Damon, Richard Gregory and Liv Tyler. Penn, as voiced by Parker, says 'Last year I went to Iraq. Before Team America showed up, it was a happy place. They had flowery meadows and rainbow skies with rivers made of chocolate where the children laughed and danced and played with gum-drop smiles.' Dickenson bases his claim mostly on an interview with Penn by *The Guardian*'s Andrew Pulver at the Edinburgh Film Festival in 2001 where Penn was promoting

The Pledge (2006: 132). This interview was conducted just after the large World Trade Organisation protests in Seattle 1999 and the G8 demonstrations that occurred in Genoa in July of that year. Pulver writes:

> Penn, in his tastefully rumpled suit and pencil moustache, is never going to take to the streets himself, but you sense that he has been waiting for this uprising all his life. Through the 1980s he acted as a one-man counter-culture, upsetting the establishment and railing against the Hollywood status quo. And he's still at it. Like the Genoa demonstrators, he really hates America – an infected culture, he calls it. [Then clearly referring to *The Indian Runner*] 'You don't get away from your past. We hustled the land. We killed a bunch of Indians to get it. And that infected one generation and it got passed on to the next. It's a culture of guilt. Every culture is, in some way – but in ours, right now, as kings of the so-called economic and military world, it's more shameful. It's like one of these superstars doing a bad picture. There's a bigger responsibility, and I think our culture isn't ready to accept any responsibility that means they have to be uncomfortable. (2001)

Dickenson also understands certain films of this period to act as metaphors for Hollywood's dissatisfaction with the then-Presidency of George W. Bush in particular and to have 'an anti-capitalist aesthetic' or 'anti-capitalist spirit' (2006: 130, 145). Included alongside Robbins' *Cradle Will Rock* (1999), Sayles' *Sunshine State* (2002), Moore's *Bowling for Columbine* (2002) and *Fahrenheit 9/11* (2004) is Alan Ball's television series *Six Feet Under* (2001–2005), Mark Joffe's *The Man Who Sued God* (2001), Lars von Trier's *Dogville* (2003), Clint Eastwood's *Mystic River* (2003) and Penn's *The Pledge* and 'USA', his contribution to *11/09/01*. In a section entitled 'Anti-capitalism in the mainstream' Dickenson writes:

> *The Pledge* is a metaphor for the demise of liberalism in the Clinton era. Here is a policeman who cannot live up to the abstract idealistic values that others place upon him. He is not a heroic special individual in the fashion I have identified to be part of the Hollywood liberal tradition, but is a failure, unable to deliver the desires and wishes of the citizens who are supposed to respect him. Black [the character played by Jack Nicholson] could even be a metaphor for Clinton's failure to deliver a progressive agenda. His speculation on the internal moral crisis that such a failure might cause. Penn's film seems to reflect the experience of Hollywood progressives who hoped Clinton would be their man but found him to be a greater friend to corporations (2006: 133).

While Dickenson's positioning of Penn and his films is, in some ways, useful, it is unsophisticated, and diminishes the familial context and the lineage of progressive culture in which it is possible to locate Penn's directorial work and the complex nature of what Access Hollywood reporter Maria Menounos has described as Penn's 'political aura' (n.d.).

Sean Penn's parents, Leo Penn and Eileen Ryan, belong to a tradition of American leftist theatre and film, providing some understanding of the familial environment that has influenced Penn's directorial and performance work. Some accounting for the ways in which the Cold War rhetoric infected Hollywood in the 1940s can also set the scene for how the careers and personal lives of Leo Penn and Eileen Ryan were affected by the anti-communist hysteria of post-World War II America. This account also provides a sketch of the kind of filmmaking community, with its friendships and associations, Eileen and Leo found themselves in.

According to Richard T. Kelly (2004), Eileen Ryan was a theatre actor having studied at the Actors Studio in New York in the late 1940s while she performed extensively in Off-Broadway and Broadway productions setting up a network of family friends from those days, including names such as Sidney Pollack, Martin Ritt, Peter Falk, Ed Asner and Art Wolff. Later, possibly with the agency of her husband, she acted in programmes he also directed such as *Ben Casey* (1961–66), *Bonanza* (1959–1973) and *Marcus Welby, M.D.* (1969–1976). She has appeared alongside Sean in James Foley's *At Close Range* (1986; also featuring Chris Penn), Leo Penn's *Judgement in Berlin* (1988), Jessie Nelson's *I am Sam* (2001) and Niels Mueller's *The Assassination of Richard Nixon* (2004) as well as her son's *The Indian Runner*, *The Crossing Guard* and *The Pledge*.

Leo Penn emerged from the University of California, where he studied drama, to commence an acting career after his war service. In 1945, Diane Haithman in 'Their Son, the Producer' tells us, Paramount refused to renew his contract after he was blacklisted for 'attending meetings of actors sympathetic to Hollywood Trade Union members' (1997) and supporting the screenwriters, producers and directors known as the Hollywood 10, who refused to answer questions before the House Un-American Activities Committee (HUAC).

The events Haithman refers to here are what are often known as the Hollywood Strikes of 1945 and 1946. Reynold Humphries, in *Hollywood's Blacklists: A Political and Cultural History*, states that the strikes initially 'involved back-lot workers and not actors, writers and directors, although these became involved, voluntarily or not' (2008: 65). While the cause of the strike was somewhat incidental – a dispute between painters and set decorators – it nevertheless led to the involvement of rival unions and impacted on members' livelihoods and the finances of those unions and to the break-up of the Conference of Studio Unions (CSU) and of HUAC establishing itself in Hollywood due to the concomitant furore. It is important to understand that this period in Hollywood history was the response of one of the unions, the CSU, in it's battles with the International Alliance of Theatrical Stage Employees (IATSE) who received support from the studios, while apparently orchestrated by the studios. These strikes were violent (the IATSE was said to have its roots in the gangsterism of the 1930s), due to the presence of 'goons' and local police, provoking violence on both sides of the pickets and involved over 10,000 workers. Inevitably the perceived cause of the strike shifted from one of jurisdiction to that of the communist infiltration of the unions.

Richard T. Kelly states that Leo was also a member of the 'socially conscientious' Actors Laboratory Theatre of Los Angeles, founded in 1941 and which essentially performed for returned servicemen but was also loosely aligned with the unions and industrial protest (2004: 16). Penn is listed in Delia Nora Salvi's 'The History of the Actor's Laboratory 1941–1950' in a theatre production of Arthur Laurents' *Home of the Brave* on 13 August 1946, directed by Phil Brown starring Robert Karnes and Kenneth Patterson and a 22 December 1946 production of *The Wizard of Oz* adapted by Elizabeth Fuller Goodspeed, directed by Jacobina Caro starring Pat Alphand and Howard Chamberlain. The film version of *Home of the Brave* (1949) was later directed by Mark Robson and produced by Stanley Kramer.

In *Actors on Red Alert: Career Interviews with Five Actors and Actresses Affected by the Blacklist*, Anthony Slide states that the Actors Laboratory Theatre was established in May 1941 as a West Coast extension of New York's Group Theatre and New Deal Works Progress Administration Federal Theatre Project and a 'successor to the Hollywood Theatre Alliance' (1999: 6). The Alliance, according to Michael Denning in *The Cultural Front: The Laboring of American Culture in the Twentieth Century*, included such left-wing figures as Dashiell Hammett, Lillian Hellman, Langston Hughes and Ira Gershwin (1997: 311). The Actors Laboratory, according to *The Hollywood Reporter* of 1945, as quoted by Kelly, was understood by the Hollywood right, to be 'as red as a burlesque queen's garters'. Slide tells us that Myron C. Fagan, a virulent anti-communist and author of publications such as *Red Channels*, named 150 actors that purported to identify as 'communists' or 'communist sympathisers' including Lee J. Cobb, John Garfield, Burgess Meredith, Edward G. Robinson, Lionel Stander and Orson Welles (1999: 6).

Leo Penn's blacklisting, Kathrun Shattuck states in her obituary, saw him return to theatre, including a New York production of *Cat on a Hot Tin Roof* directed by Elia Kazan. Later, in the 1950s, Penn emerged to appear uncredited in William Wyler's *The Best Years of Our Lives* (1946), as Steve Ryan alongside Ida Lupino in her *Not Wanted* (1949) as Tom Cochran (under the name 'Clifford Penn') in Reginald Le Borg's *Fall Guy* (1947), as Sydney Gordon in Joseph H. Lewis's *The Undercover Man* (1949) and as Morrie Gertz alongside Rita Hayworth and Gig Young in Clifford Odets' *The Story on Page One* (1959). Amongst these productions Leo Penn acted in numerous television series such as *Danger* (1950–55), *The Untouchables* (1959–63), *Ripcord* (1961–63) and *Ben Casey*. It was on the set of *Ben Casey* that he shifted into television directing, helming series such as *Dr. Kildare* (1961–66), *Run For Your Life* (1965–68), *Bonanza*, *Marcus Welby, M.D.*, *Starsky and Hutch* (1975–79), *Hart to Hart* (1979–84), *In the Heat of the Night* (1988–95) and *Matlock* (1986–95). Penn also directed Sammy Davis Jr., Cicely Tyson, Ossie Davis and Louis Armstrong in *A Man Called Adam* (1966), a feature about a jazz musician's struggle with racism. In 1988 Penn directed his son Sean and Martin Sheen in the feature film *Judgement in Berlin* and appeared in *The Crossing Guard*.

Leo Penn's appearances in the films *The Best Years of Our Lives*, *Not Wanted*, *The Undercover Man* and *Fall Guy* provide some context to the kind of acting/performance world he moved in. It is possible to understand these films as part of a particular kind of post-war cinema, what Pam Cook – discussing Wyler's film, yet what could be a description of Sean's own directorial work, in particular *The Indian Runner* – claims

Leo Penn as Steve Ryan in Ida Lupino's *Not Wanted* (1949)

is centrally concerned with the war-damaged psyches of soldiers returning home to a materialistic and uncaring society, and with the pivotal role of women in providing a nurturing environment in which the men can pick up the pieces of their lives. (1995: 60)

Not Wanted is similar in this regard, although with a female protagonist at the mercy of a society unwilling to cater for an unwed mother. Sally Kelton (Sally Kellerman) falls in love with bar-room piano player Steve Ryan (Penn) with whom she becomes pregnant. After Sally follows him to another city, Ryan continues on his itinerant lifestyle, unwilling to continue the relationship. Sally becomes involved with a gas station manager, Drew (Keefe Brasselle), but she is unable to return his love. Sally is eventually taken in by a women's refuge to have the child and through their agency and with Drew's help, it seems, is saved from conviction for kidnapping and put on a path to recovery and support. While it is possible to see this film as another narrative where the female protagonist is at the mercy of patriarchal society, for this discussion it is useful to recall the 'progressive' factors in the production. The script was written by Ida Lupino and by later Hollywood 10 member Paul Jarrico, who later collaborated on the left-wing cause célèbre *Salt of the Earth* (1954). *Not Wanted* was the initial production of Lupino's Emerald Productions, later The Filmmakers, and a film she co-wrote, produced and, despite Elmer Clifton being credited, probably directed. The Filmmakers productions, as Pam Cook states, were 'a string of low-budget, black and white films about contemporary issues, featuring lesser known actors and often based on real events' (1995: 58).

Social Problem Films

Amongst the post-World War II cycle of social problems films that Leo Penn acted in were the likes of Edward Dmytryk's *Till the End of Time* (1946) and *Crossfire* (1947),

John Berry's *From This Day Forward* (1946), Charlie Chaplin's *Monsieur Verdoux* (1947), Elia Kazan's *Gentlemen's Agreement* (1947) and *Pinky* (1949), Abraham Polonsky's *Force of Evil* (1949), Fred Zinneman's *The Men* (1950) and Mark Robson's *Bright Victory* (1951). It is possible to understand these films emerging from a direct connection between the problems faced by individuals and the societal conditions in which they find themselves, something that Peter Roffman and Jim Purdy in *The Hollywood Social Problem Film*, argue is a result of a particular era's 'socially conscious sentiments' writing, 'from the advent of the Depression to the rise of McCarthyism, a strong sensibility of social concern was given play in America' (1981: ix). For Roffman and Purdy the government of Franklin D. Roosevelt and the New Deal provided a stimulation not just of economic systems but also the arts, including photography, theatre and literature, while the rise of Fascism in Europe and the commencement of World War II 'fostered a concern with social conditions, an impulse towards political change' (ibid.). Art that may have been socially conscious or marginal became popular, such as the folk music of Woody Guthrie, or the plays of Clifford Odets, while already popular art forms including Hollywood studio movies were, in turn, influenced by the broader cultural shifts adopting the didacticism of other art forms combined effortlessly with the conventions of the studio system.

The focus of the genre was very specific: the central dramatic conflict revolves around the interaction of the individual with social institutions (such as government, business, political movements, etc.) While the genre places great importance on the surface mechanisms of society, there is only an indirect concern with broader social values (those of the family, sexuality, religion, etc.), the values that function behind the mechanisms. As such the genre often seemed glib in its social analysis, viewing America as a series of social agencies that from time to time experience 'problems which must be corrected. For the most part, the films attacked such problems in order to inspire limited social change or reinforce the status quo' (Roffman and Purdy 1981: viii).

The lineage of social problem films that Leo Penn worked in provides some background to an understanding of the progressive politics of his son's features as a director. As Gaylyn Studlar points out, *The Best Years of Our Lives* 'shows the inscription of *noir* masculinity in its depiction of Fred Derry (Dana Andrews)' whose return from service as a decorated pilot descends into a dull existence with his old job as a Soda Jerk and an unloving wife; Studlar suggests that 'with a slight twist of the plot – the death of his wife – Fred Derry could easily become a *noir* protagonist' (2013: 375). This overlapping with *noir* can be observed in many of the social problems films, particularly in their portrayal and ultimately, critique, of masculinity.

It is possible to see Leo Penn's involvement in both the social problem cinema of the 1940s and 1950s and Repertory Theatre mirrored in his son's adolescent fervour for the New Hollywood of the 1970s and his own beginnings with Peggy Feury and the Actors Repertory Theatre of Los Angeles around the same time. Penn has consistently cited three films as major influences; Hal Ashby's *Harold and Maude* (1971), Martin Scorsese's *Mean Streets* (1973) and Jerry Schatzberg's *Scarecrow* (1973). According to Richard T. Kelly, watching these as well as William Friedkin's *The French Connection* (1971), Terrence Malick's *Badlands* (1973), Bob Fosse's *Lenny* (1974) and Scorsese's

Taxi Driver (1976) at repertory cinemas in Los Angeles, was significant in his early awakening to auteur cinema of the period (2004: 51–2). These films, and others of the New Hollywood, were crucial to the counter-culture of the period when, as David Thomson in 'The Decade When Movies Mattered' puts it, 'it was a time of travail and upheaval when the world took it for granted that grownups were born to take notice. We had movies then that you had to watch' (2004: 73). Thomson's understanding of the cinema of the 1970s is a reiteration of Roffman and Purdy's positioning of the Social Problem Film, as a result of that particular era's 'socially conscious sentiments':

> In films of the 1970s, the curtain called 'happy ending' was ripped away by the life force of the people, and by the actual conditions of America. So many kinds of dismay and disenchantment made for the short-lived but still beguiling honesty of the 1970s. There was a recognition of what violence meant in the age of assassinations. No matter the enactment of so much civil rights legislation, and the determination to enforce it, we began to see how much harder it would be to dislodge racism from our imaginations. Vietnam exposed the limits of American power, the brittleness of its morale, and the helplessness of its leadership. The disasters of war were a focus for intergenerational antagonisms that flared out in Chicago at the 1968 Democratic Convention, at Kent State, and in so many other smaller communities. Americans were beginning to see how thoroughly and intelligently they were despised in other parts of the world. (2004: 75)

As we will see, Penn's rendering of Nebraska of 1968 with the riots in Chicago as its backdrop, in *The Indian Runner*, with all its recalling of the New Hollywood, and the theme of colonialism at its heart, rhymes well with Thomson's recollection.

One of the earliest of Penn's associations with an activist persona, amongst his Hollywood colleagues, as well as one of his earliest narrations, was for Bill Couturié's *Dear America: Letters Home from Vietnam* (1987). Here Penn reads one of the real letters from US soldiers serving in Vietnam that forms the narration of the film alongside a host of other readers, including Robert De Niro, Michael J. Fox, Willem Dafoe, Tom Berenger, Harvey Keitel, Martin Sheen, Matt Dillon, Kevin Dillon, Robert Downey Jr., Judd Nelson and others. Penn's narration, like the others in *Dear America*, is performative, affected and fictive, attempting to give some life, some passion to the letter. Penn's inclusion in *Dear America* invokes the lineage of Hollywood Vietnam War films in which these actors providing the narration figure – *Taxi Driver*, *The Deer Hunter* (1978), *Apocalypse Now* (1979), *Platoon* (1986), and subsequently Brian De Palma's *Casualties of War* (1989) which also featured Penn. It also provides a kind of requiem for Vietnam, a tragic anti-war document prior to his own *The Indian Runner* four years later.

Despite the contemporary familiarity of Penn as an activist figure in American public life, it was not until around the beginning 1991, according to Kelly, that, following the birth of his daughter Dylan and around the time of the LA riots of the following year, Penn is said to have commenced a more active political role. Sparked by the video of the police beating of Rodney King and the subsequent trial and exoneration of the police officers, Penn 'started sponsoring some political lectures in Los Angeles, and one of the guys I ended up with was Craig Hulet' (2004: 265). Hulet is a speaker and one time advisor to American Republican politician Jack Metcalf and author of the self-published *Hussein's Mythical Nukes and Iraq's Military Power* (1990) and *The Hydra of Carnage: Bush's Imperial War-Making and the Rule of Law* (2002).

In 1997 Penn publicly supported Democrat Senator Tom Hayden's campaign for the Mayor of Los Angeles, formally endorsing the former husband of Jane Fonda and fellow visitor to Vietnam, and member of the Chicago Seven, counter-cultural activists who targeted the 1968 Chicago Democratic Convention. But it was the 9/11 attacks on the World Trade Center and the Pentagon and their aftermath that saw Penn's activism push him to the forefront of criticisms of the Bush Administration.

On 28 October 2002 Penn paid $US56,000 for 'An Open Letter to the President of the United States of America', taking up a full page in the *Washington Post*. Penn directly addresses the letter to 'Mr Bush' and begins: 'Good morning, sir. Like you, I am a father and an American. Like you, I consider myself a patriot. Like you, I was horrified by the events of this past year, concerned for my family and my country.' Penn then goes on to invoke the Constitution, the Bill of Rights and his father's memory – 'My father, like yours, was decorated for service in World War II' – before questioning the Bush Administration's economic management ('an enormous economic surplus has been squandered'), and environmental record ('dismissed the most fundamental environmental concerns') before calling on a combination of national figures and humanist values to rethink the decision to go to war in Iraq: 'I beg you Mr. President, listen to Gershwin, read chapters of [Wallace] Stegner, of [William] Saroyan, the speeches of Martin Luther King. Remind yourself of America. Remember the Iraqi children, our children, and your own.' Penn then concedes that the difficulty of dealing with national security while 'avoiding war … is no simple task', but points to the 'restraint' displayed by President Kennedy '(and that of the nuclear submarine captain, Arkhipov)' during the Cuban missile crisis. In the concluding paragraph Penn invokes his children 'who will live their lives in the world as it will be affected by critical choices today' understanding that Americans are 'frightened and angry' calling on the President to avoid attacking Iraq:

> … sacrificing American soldiers or innocent civilians in an unprecedented preemptive attack on a separate sovereign nation, may well prove itself a most temporary medicine. On the other hand, should you mine and have faith in the best of this country to support your leadership in representing a strong, thoughtful, and educated United States, you may well triumph for the long haul. Lead us there, Mr. President, and we will stand with you. (2002)

Penn's criticisms here invoke the traditions of American democracy as it is aligned with a nationalist rhetoric. In the context of the immediate post-9/11 milieu this criticism ran against prevailing nationalist rhetoric emanating from mainstream media and politics. It also further elevated Penn into the highest echelons of the kind of celebrity activism we have seen from the actors mentioned earlier in this chapter.

In December 2002 Penn compounded his 'Open Letter to the President of the United States', in a reflection of Jane Fonda and Tom Hayden's visit to Vietnam during that war, by visiting Iraq in the weeks prior to the United States bombing campaign. Sponsored by the Institute for Public Accuracy, an organisation founded by Norman Solomon, which, according to its website, 'increases the reach and capacity of progressive and grassroots organizations (at no cost to them) to address public policy by getting them and their ideas into the mainstream media' and in association with the United Nations Children's Fund (UNICEF), Penn accompanied Solomon to Iraq, met with Iraqi Deputy Prime Minister Tariq Aziz, visited the Al-Mansour Children's Hospital, schools and UNICEF's Iraq offices. On 15 December 2002 Penn read a prepared statement to a news conference in Baghdad, which, according to the Institute for Public Accuracy website read, in part:

> I am privileged in particular to raise my children in a country of high standards in health, welfare, and safety. I am also privileged to have lived a life under our Constitution that has allowed me to dream and prosper. In response to these privileges I feel, both as an American and as a human being, the obligation to accept some level of personal accountability for the policies of my government, both those I support and any that I may not. Simply put, if there is a war or continued sanctions against Iraq, the blood of Americans and Iraqis alike will be on our hands. (http://www.accuracy.org)

Penn's actions were part of a larger groundswell amongst Hollywood actors. Initiated by Mike Farrell, best known as Captain B. J. Honeycutt from the television series *M*A*S*H* (1972–1983) and Robert Greenwald, director of documentaries such as *Uncovered: The War on Iraq* (2004) and *Outfoxed: Rupert Murdoch's War on Journalism* (2004), Artists Say Win Without War was a campaign as part of a larger coalition called 'Win Without War' organised by Tom Andrews, which, according to its website, 'formed in 2002 to lead the first national campaign against the war in Iraq and the disastrous policies of the Bush/Cheney Administration, our coalition reflects the diversity of the progressive movement' (http://winwithoutwar.org/about/). In a petition to President Bush, writers, directors, producers, actors and former ambassadors and armed services personnel, proclaimed their support for weapons inspectors in Iraq:

> The valid US and UN objective of disarming Saddam Hussein can be achieved through legal diplomatic means. There is no need for war. Let us instead devote our resources to improving the security and well being of people here at home and around the world. (http://civic.moveon.org/artistswinwithoutwar)

In 2006 Penn's appearance in Spike Lee's *When the Levees Broke: A Requiem in Four Acts* brought about the first melding of his celebrity and activist figures on film. Penn appears in interview and in news footage in Act I carrying an elderly man from a boat to safety from the floodwaters following the lead of Noah's Ark Church Pastor Willie Walker Jr. whose congregation had been affected by the waters.

Penn's appearance in Lee's film was responded to by many media outlets as another photo opportunity from a celebrity yet the film tapped into and helped propel the groundswell of dissatisfaction with the Bush administration's handling of the crisis that emerged from the devastation wreaked by Hurricane Katrina on New Orleans in 2005. While New Orleans and its surrounds were largely destroyed, it was the failure of the city's flood walls, subsequent delays in rescuing people, lack of leadership and support from local and State government, the inability of the Federal Emergency Management Agency to provide logistical support, ranging from rescue and medical services to provisional housing, that received enormous criticism from locals and a broad section of the American population.

In 2007 Penn continued his association with Norman Solomon by narrating Loretta Alder and Jeremy Earp's *War Made Easy: How Presidents & Pundits Keep Spinning Us to Death* (2007), a film that firmly has Penn in the activist role. *War Made Easy* is in effect an illustrated interview with author, activist and politician Solomon based on his book of the same name. Penn is also credited as Executive Producer. Penn's narration relies on a deep, thicker register of Penn's voicing, the voice he uses in all voice-overs and in live speeches such as awards ceremonies, lectures and interviews – a voice in contrast to his thinner, reedy, emotional voice of anger or hysteria (we could think of his voice in the well-known scene from *Mystic River* where he is restrained by the police after his murdered daughter is found). It is possible to understand this film as a bringing together of the Vietnam Penn and activist Penn, as *War Made Easy* recalls *Dear America* in its compilation film mode. *War Made Easy* uses the Vietnam War and its footage as a launching pad for Norman Solomon's theories on media participation in the contemporary war mode, in particular the first Iraq War and on into Afghanistan and the Second Iraq War. In 2003 Penn contributed an Afterword to Norman Solomon, Reese Erlich and Howard Zinn's book *Target Iraq: What the News Media Didn't Tell You*.

Penn's 2002 visit to Iraq was reprised in June 2005 when the actor, on assignment for the *San Francisco Chronicle,* returned to that country and reported on post-invasion Iraq. The tenor of one of the articles is dramatic and incisive:

> This is an occupied country. A country at war. Many Iraqis I speak to tell me there is no freedom in occupation, nor trust in unilateral intervention. People from all sides of the debate acknowledge that the insurgency movement builds every day in manpower and organizational strength. The insurgents are made up of Saddam loyalists, displaced Sunni elite, resentful victims of U.S. raids, the Fedayeen, foreign terrorist cells and of course many of Hussein's soldiers, who, as participants in the Baathist regime, were sent home with their weapons and told, 'You'll never work in this town again.' The Iraqis I speak to say that the U.S. policy of de-Baathification is devoid of consideration of long-term goals, human nature and Arab culture and thus could ignite a powder keg. (2004)

Penn's performance as a reporter can be understood as an attempt to both raise the profile of the report from Iraq for the *Chronicle* at the same time as give some credence to Penn's activist mode – one inevitably teased in a wonderful commingling of film studies rhetoric and slander by the right-wing *FrontPageMag* website in the article 'Penn's Pontifications' as 'Method Acting Foreign Policy'.

In June 2005 Penn, travelling with Norman Solomon and his co-author Reese Erlich, again on the payroll of the *San Francisco Chronicle*, visited Iran and filed five reports to the newspaper. On 15 December 2008 Penn reported in *The Nation* on his visit to Venezuela and Cuba to interview presidents Hugo Chávez and Raul Castro respectively. These conversations are couched in terms of Penn's reaction to mainstream media in the US, writing, 'in hopes of demythologizing this "dictator," I decided to pay him another visit. By this time I had come to say to friends in private, "'It's true, Chávez may not be a good man. But he may well be a great one"' (2008).

Penn's activist figure reached its apotheosis with his co-founding, with Sanela Diana Jenkins, of the J/P Haitian Relief Organisation, following the earthquake in that country in 2010. J/P, according to its website, 'employs nearly 350 staff' in its mission to 'save lives and build sustainable programs with the Haitian people quickly and effectively'.

More recently in July 2013, Penn, David Lynch, Susan Sarandon, Ben Kingsley, James Fox and others including barristers, sculptors and novelists took out a paid advertisement in the UK's *Times* newspaper to publish an 'Open Letter to Turkey's Prime Minister Tayyip Erdogan' to 'vigorously condemn the heavy-handed clamp down of your police forces on the peaceful protesters'; following the 'peaceful protests in Taksim Square and Gezi Park relying on untold brutal force, you held a meeting in Istanbul reminiscent of the Nuremburg Rally with total disregard for the five dead whose only crime was to oppose your dictatorial rule' (https://syrianfreepress.files.wordpress.com/2013/07/the-times-24-july-ad-letter-to-the-prime-minister-of-turkey1.jpg).

In recent years it is possible to divine a shift in the utilisation of Penn's celebrity activist persona in more playful and self-referential ways. *Americans* (2012), a short film Penn acted in with Kid Rock, directed by Jameson Stafford, is a product of Strand Studios, which has made television commercials and music videos for Kid Rock. *Americans* features Penn representing the Democrat 'blue' states and Kid Rock representing the Republican 'red' states. In this regard Penn manages to harness his activist interests. Penn enters a bar and asks the bartender (Shanna Colins) to change the channel of the television that is playing a speech by Republican Presidential nominee Mitt Romney and his introduction of Rap-Rocker/Country artist Kid Rock singing what became Romney's campaign theme song 'Born Free'. As the bartender changes the television channel, we hear a reiteration of the chorus line 'we are born free' coming from within the bar. When Penn looks over he sees Kid Rock entertaining the bar crowd singing into a beer bottle. The scene cuts back to the television where we witness President Barack Obama dancing with Ellen Degeneres on her daytime talkshow, *Ellen*. Rock looks over to Penn and approaches him at the bar. Penn and Rock then enter into an argument based on their respective personas. This scene escalates into Rock telling

Kid Rock and Sean Penn in Jameson Stafford's *Americans* (2012)

Penn to 'fuckin' suck it, commie' to which Penn responds with the rant, 'Commie? At least I'm not a seal-clubbing, confederate flag-waving, oil-whoring, chick-flaying, water-boarding, Nascar-loving, Cayman Island bank-account-having, endangered species-hunting, war-mongering, redneck, toothless, Wall Street troglodyte.' Rock's response is in-kind: 'Yeah, I guess not. That's because you're basically a tofu-munching, welfare-loving, Prius-driving, Obama-sucking, tree-hugging, whale-saving, gay-marriage-fantasising, big government-voting, PETA-chasing, Oprah Winfrey-masturbating, flag-burning, socialist, ACLU, whiney-arsed, granola-crat.' By the end of the film, Penn and Rock are, of course, best friends with Penn wearing a NASCAR t-shirt and Rock wearing a PETA shirt, making a sandcastle sculpture of the American Stars and stripes flag, with the words DON'T LET POLITICS DIVIDE US, THINKING DIFFERENTLY ... IS WHAT MADE THIS COUNTRY GREAT, AMERICANS, FUCK YEAH emblazoned across the screen.

In '"Politics Is Theater": Performance, Sexuality, and *Milk*', Donna Peberdy, utilising a line from Penn's performance as Harvey Milk for her title, points to the manner in which the fictional Harvey Milk, created by Penn and Gus Van Sant, spills over into the Harvey Milk of the historical world, and Rob Epstein and Richard Schmiechen's documentary *The Times of Harvey Milk* (1984). In his Academy Award acceptance speech, as Peberdy points out, Penn adopts the role once performed by Milk, one that the actor had reperformed for the film, addressing the anti-gay protesters picketing the awards:

> I think that it is a good time for those who voted for the ban against gay marriage to sit and reflect and anticipate their great shame and the shame in their grandchildren's eyes if they continue that way of support ... We've got to have equal rights for everyone. (2012: 52)

Peberdy also points out that at the 2009 Academy Awards, 'the Best Actor, Best Actress, and Best Supporting Actor awards were presented by five former winners in each category who introduced each of the nominees'. Robert De Niro's introduction for Penn winning the Best Actor in a Leading Role Oscar at the 2009 Academy Awards went like this:

> How did he do it? How for so many years did Sean Penn get all those jobs playing straight men? Being a movie star can get in the way of acting, but not for Sean. Sean Penn the actor loses himself in every role so we can discover men named Sam, *Mystic River*'s Jimmy Markham, the superdude Spiccoli, a dead man walking, and Harvey Milk. Sean brings the same commitment to his off-screen life. You see it when he campaigns for human rights, respectfully advises world leaders, and gently, gently reasons with the paparazzi. Tonight it's important to be a great actor; in life it's more important to be a great human. (2012: 53)

As Peberdy argues, there is a greater emphasis on 'Penn as a political figure, one who campaigns and advises world leaders' than there is to his performance work, whose political activism is now seen alongside his acting; or even more pointedly 'his offscreen persona is inseparable from and even overwhelms his onscreen performances' (ibid.). For Peberdy, these two speeches, in the context of a globally broadcast television event celebrating Hollywood, suggested that Penn, in receiving an award for playing Harvey Milk, was taking up the role of politics as performance, an actor who inhabits the character, eventuating in a scenario where 'the performance then becomes political in Penn's engagement with contemporary discourses around same-sex marriage and equal rights' (ibid.). As de Niro suggests, it is possible to extend this attention to *Milk* to his other performances in films such as Harold Becker's *Taps* (1981), John Schlesinger's *The Falcon and the Snowman* (1985), *Judgment in Berlin*, *Casualities of War*, Tim Robbins' *Dead Man Walking* (1995), Terrence Malick's *The Thin Red Line* (1998), *I Am Sam*, *The Assassination of Richard Nixon* or Doug Liman's *Fair Game* (2010). These 'serious' roles are easier to align with a general understanding of politics, of power relations in formalised settings, while it is more difficult to account for Penn's performances in Neil Jordan's *We're No Angels* (1989), Brian De Palma's *Carlito's Way* (1993), Woody Allen's *Sweet and Lowdown* (1999) or Paolo Sorrentino's *This Must Be The Place* (2011) in this regard. However, as Peberdy points out, it is the extra-textual activist persona of Penn that influences the reading of any film he is associated with. While a host of these 'serious' roles add weight to public perceptions, in his directorial work, with its melodramatic overtones and earnest subject matter and social problem alignment, it is possible to see a certain slippage between Penn's filmic performances, directorial work, journalistic reporting, documentary narration, executive production and interviewing of America's political adversaries.

Hope and the Cultural Left

In distinction from a generally dismissive characterisation of Penn as a part of the new Hollywood left, one way to reconsider Penn's activism, as well as his acting and performance work, is in relation to Richard Rorty's recuperation of pragmatism for the left following John Dewey and Walt Whitman. This is not to suggest that Penn is a Rortian, a Deweyan or Whitmanesque; but, rather, a means to seek an understanding of the figure of Sean Penn in his various roles and guises.

In his series of lectures collected in the volume *Achieving Our Country: Leftist Thought in Twentieth-Century America*, Richard Rorty proposes a way of thinking about what he understands to be a particular decline of the intellectual left in the United States in the post-Vietnam War period, delineating a pre-1960s left and the rise since that period of what he terms, in the title of one of his lectures, 'A Cultural Left' (1998b). For Rorty what he terms 'the Reformist left of the first two-thirds of the twentieth century' (1998b: 75) was promulgated on the notions of 'liberty' and 'humanism', words that are in the present context are markers of 'naiveté' (1998b: 95–6). Rorty is particularly critical of what he understands to be a lineage in post-structural thought, 'philosophers most often cited by cultural leftists' including Nietzsche, Heidegger, Foucault and Derrida, marking the shift from the old left to the cultural left with a blunt example:

> The difference between this residual left and the academic left is the difference between the people who read books like George Geoghegan's *Which Side Are You On?* [1991] – a brilliant explanation of how unions get busted – and people who read Fredric Jameson's *Postmodernism, or The Cultural Logic of Late Capitalism* [1991]. The latter is an equally brilliant book but it operates on a level of abstraction too high to encourage any particular political initiative. After reading Geoghegan, you have views on some of the things which need to be done. After reading Jameson, you have views on practically everything except what needs to be done. (1998b: 78)

This principle of practice of 'what needs to be done', echoing Lenin, lies at the heart of Rorty's criticism. While he discerns some continuity of the activity of the old left in the work of 'labor lawyers and labor organisers, congressional staffers, low-level bureaucrats hoping to rescue the welfare state from the Republicans, journalists, social workers, and people who work for foundations' (1998b: 77) at the same time, the post-1960s break has seen the emergence of a left 'unable to engage in national politics' (1998b: 91). Hamstrung by a specialisation in the '"politics of difference," or of "identity" or "of recognition"', this cultural left thinks more about stigma than about money, more about deep and hidden psychosexual motivations than about shallow and evident greed' (1998b: 77). For Rorty, the rise of French philosophy in the estimations of the academic left is partly to blame, particularly notions of 'power' emanating from the work of Michel Foucault, where the term 'denotes an agency which has left an indelible stain on every word in our language and on very institution in our society' meaning that 'one cannot block off power in the Foucauldian sense. Power is as much inside one as outside one' (1998b: 94). Like the unassailable concept of 'sin' in Rorty's estimation, stories of the webs of power and the insidious influence of a hegemonic ideology, are paralysing for the contemporary left.

In response to this paralysis within a cultural left, Rory returns to John Dewey and Walt Whitman to propose a pragmatist, nationalist sense of hope in democracy in 'a rhetoric of commonality' that reverberates through Penn's activism, performances and directorial oeuvre.

> We were supposed to love our country because it showed promise of being kinder and more generous than other countries. As the blacks and the gays, among others, were well aware, this was a counsel of perfection rather than description of fact. But you cannot urge national political renewal on the basis of descriptions of act. You have to describe the country in terms of what you passionately hope it will become, as well as in terms of what you know it ought to be now. You have to be loyal to a dream country rather than to one to which you wake up every morning. Unless such loyalty exists, the ideal has no chance of becoming actual. (Rorty 1998b: 101)

Rorty's words, coloured with a romantic and nostalgic hue, sit well with Penn's' worldview which is at once radical and old-fashioned, a kind of neo-traditional radicalism in that there is some accord with nineteenth-century American thinkers from whom the notion of hope sits at the inception of the United States, is its motivating force. In this way, as we will see, the characters in Penn's 'social problem films' – returning Vietnam vets, drunk hit-and-run drivers, obsessive detectives driven to insanity, or the single-minded Christopher McCandless starving to death in the wilds of Alaska – can be understood in relation to their surroundings, embraced and activated. For Dewey and Whitman, it is the activity of social hope for what might become real that is at the heart of democracy, in particular, American democracy. As Whitman wrote, 'Democracy is a great word, whose history ... remains unwritten, because that history has yet to be enacted' (quoted in Rorty 1998a: 19). In this schema, Penn's body of directorial work, commencing with *The Indian Runner*, set in 1968, rhymes with Rorty's delineation between a Deweyan, participatory left prior to the Vietnam War and a spectatorial left which has taken its place. This participatory left, the realm of active citizenship, is in contrast with the characterisation of Penn quoted from Ben Dickinson earlier in this chapter. Following Rorty, Penn's films are, at once, interiorised and individualised, ultimately giving way to the unknown. Each of his films in this way opens toward the future, a turn towards hope. In understanding Penn's films in relation to his activism, but also back to his critical accounting for the 'ancestral sins' that Penn saw at the heart of *The Indian Runner*, it is possible to see the trace of pragmatism emerging.

CHAPTER TWO

Penn's Performance Places

In more than fifty feature films, television shows and in his narrations and appearances in documentaries, Sean Penn has developed an ongoing association with the rendering of stories as they emerge from the places in which they are located. It would be impractical to examine all of Penn's performances here but it is possible to divine a set of relations between films that Penn has performed in as an indicative model of the quite different ways in which place and performance are closely aligned in films Penn has acted in. His various roles across a broad timeframe have seen him, again and again, portray figures characterised by their environments. From Jeff Spicoli, Danny McGavin and Jimmy Markham, to real-life historical figures in Brad Whitewood Jr. and Harvey Milk, Penn has performed the places in which his characters are located.

Fast Times at Ridgemont High (1982)

One of Penn's earliest performances was as the stoned surfer Jeff Spicoli as part of an ensemble cast in Amy Heckerling's *Fast Times at Ridgemont High* (1982). Heckerling's film was based on Cameron Crowe's ethnographic research and book *Fast Times at Ridgemont High: A True Story* (1981). In 1979 Crowe embedded himself as a student for a full year at a San Diego High School, California to record his observations about the various sub-cultures that exist in teen life. In 'Cameron Crow, Rock Journalist', Noel Murray tells us,

> ... in *Fast Times*, Crowe doesn't exoticise, chasten, or mock teenagers. Again, as was his habit, he just listens, with genuine fascination, as these high-school students share advice about sex, explain the hierarchy of fast-food jobs, and spread rumours that grow into legends. That element of self-mythologizing

is missing from Amy Heckerling's movie version of *Fast Times*, which is more matter-of-fact, but otherwise, Heckerling too is on the side of 'the kids', watching with no small amount of empathy at their awkward lurches toward adulthood. (2003)

In a reflection of the intimacy of Crowe's book, Heckerling's film utilises mainly familiar, interior spaces; bedrooms, classrooms, the mall, car interiors and work places, such as Penny's Pizza where Stacy Hamilton (Jennifer Jason Leigh) and Linda Barrett (Phoebe Cates) work, or All American Burger where Brad Hamilton (Judge Reinhold) flips burgers. Even Stacy's first sexual experience with Ron Jonson (D.W. Brown) occurs in an enclosed dug-out at a deserted baseball pitch.

This sense of intimacy and familiarity is conveyed in the film's opening montage sequence. Accompanied by the Go-Go Girls' 'We Got the Beat', Heckerling includes shots of teenagers fooling with a woman on an escalator, Rat (Brian Backer) dispensing movie tickets, pizzas being made, a record store, a video arcade, fast food being prepared, and two women fighting over clothing. In all these shots teenagers are shown at home and relaxing in public spaces. Even the most awkward of encounters between characters, such as the sex scene between Stacy and Mike Damone (Robert Romanus) in the Hamilton family's pool house, is expected and moved on from, particularly by the girls, as they simply form the rituals of teenage life.

Penn's Jeff Spicoli moves through these spaces with ease. His blasé attitude to the norms and conventions of the restaurant at All American Burgers, where he and his Stoner Buds (Eric Stoltz and Anthony Edwards) remove their shirts, or the understood rules of the History classroom of Mr Hand (Ray Walston), where Spicoli orders in pizza, or the privacy of his own bedroom, when Mr Hand appears to recoup the eight hours of study time Spicoli had wasted in the classroom. Penn's Spicoli embodies the language and intonation which came to be associated with a particular 'slacker' type of the 1980s, mostly promulgated by Penn's defining performance. As Scott F. Kiesling tells us, the term 'Dude' is redolent of this masculine character type, and a 'cool solidarity and in-group meaning' that recurs in films such as *Bill and Ted's Excellent Adventure* (1989), *Clerks* (1994) and *Dude, Where's My Car?* (2000) (2004: 288). These films are all set in suburban California and, although concerned with dialogue, utilise the same intimate spaces that recur in *Fast Times at Ridgemont High*.

Another film that further informs this discussion of Penn's performance in Heckerling's film is Stacy Peralta's *Dogtown and Z-Boys* from 2001, a largely promotional documentary about the 1970s Santa Monica, California skate sub-culture, in particular the rise of the Zephyr skateboarding team including skaters Stacy Peralta, Tony Alva, Jay Adams and Peggy Oki. Penn reads what is an overwrought, wordy voice-over in a largely monotone voice.

Penn was approached by the filmmakers to do the narration, according to Peralta in an interview with Robert Blackwelder, because 'he just seemed like the logical choice, culturally and personally. He grew up thirty minutes north of us. He went to the same high school that Tony and Jay went to. He is a surfer, he was a skateboarder, and we just figured he was the right person.' Blackwelder replies: 'And he had that whole Spicoli thing going for him.' Peralta: 'Well ... it was beyond that. Sean grew up on our culture' (Blackwelder n.d.). It does seem to be 'beyond that' in that Penn's Spicoli has been modelled on the Dogtown surfers and skaters, in particular Peralta himself, whom Penn would have been intimately familiar with. In a culmination of the intimate and familiar, Penn's Spicolo looks uncannily like the young Peralta with long blond hair often tucked behind his ears, fine features and freckled face.

At Close Range (1986)

Prior to *The Indian Runner*, Penn collaborated with director James Foley, including casting and location scouting for *At Close Range*, a film which bears fruitful comparison with Penn's directorial debut.

Penn plays Brad Whitewood Jr. who lives with his mother (Millie Perkins), grandmother (Eileen Ryan) and brother Tommy Whitewood (Chris Penn) in a semi-rural township. Brad's father, Brad Whitewood Sr. (Christopher Walken) is the local leader of a burglary gang that includes Tony Pine (David Strathairn), Patch (Tracey Walter) and Dickie (R. D. Call), which provides a means for Brad Jr. to make a name for himself and a way out of his poverty and teen *ennui*.

Like *The Indian Runner*'s use of the real-life story of Charles Starkweather and Caril Ann Fugate's murder spree across Nebraska as its inspiration, *At Close Range* is based on the real-life story of a criminal gang and follows the events that lead to the downfall of the gang. It was filmed on location in the cities of Franklin and Spring Hill in Williamson County, Tennessee, while the incidents occurred in Chester County and Lancaster County, both south-eastern counties in Pennsylvania. Lewis Beale (1985) tells us that Bruce Johnston Sr. ran a criminal gang which operated during the 1960s and 1970s in rural Pennsylvania. Johnston enlisted a 'kiddie gang' including his son, Bruce Jr. and his friends. Bruce Jr. was falling in love with Robin Miller; following his arrest on a minor charge, Miller accused the father of getting her drunk and raping her, leading to Bruce Jr. agreeing to cooperate with the authorities providing information about this father's activities (ibid.). Having heard about his son's deceit, Johnston Sr. contracted the killing of the 'kiddie gang' including his son, and his stepson. In the attempt to murder Johnston Jr., Miller was accidentally killed and Johnston Jr. was only injured.

While *At Close Range* is set in an indistinct, rural location, with its smalltown production design – an Amish family in a horse and buggy, pickup trucks, verdant woodlands and roadsides, corn-fields – it recalls similar locations in Penn's directorial debut.

In a scene early in *At Close Range*, Brad Jr. and his gang of teenage associates including Tommy, Tim (Keifer Sutherland) and Lucas (Crispin Glover) are setting out to prove their criminal worth to Brad Sr. by stealing a tractor at night, when the farmer (Bob McDivitt) discovers them and fires on them with a shotgun. The boys flee into a cornfield on foot and there follows a succession of shots, including panning and point-of-view from eye-level in amongst the corn, with overhead lighting and diegetic sound of the corn rustling as the boys run through it. Similar shots recur in *The Indian*

Runner when Joe and Franky are chasing each other in the cornfield at the farm that Joe worked before he became a highway patrolman.

Later in *At Close Range* another precursor to *The Indian Runner* occurs when Brad Jr. visits his prospective girlfriend, Terry (Mary Stuart Masterson), at her parents' farm. After hitching a ride to the farm, Brad Jr. leaves the bitumen to walk along a dirt track snaking into the distance, left of frame. As he continues to walk down the track, the previously eye-level shot begins to rise above the expansive cornfield, filling the frame as a double-story columned-fronted homestead emerges in the far top right of the frame. As the camera rises, Brad Jr. diminishes and the immense field marks the commencement of the narrative arc of what is principally that of a teen film; Brad's relationship with Terry, a girl from a wealthy pastoral family. Like the scene following the tractor theft mentioned above, this scene recalls the images of the house that recur in *The Indian Runner*.

Colors (1988)

In Dennis Hopper's film Penn plays Danny McGavin, a policeman who has recently joined the Flying CRASH (Community Resources Against Street Hoodlums) squad policing Watts and South Central, Los Angeles, and a naïve outsider. Although he is a 'hotshot' rookie policeman, a representative of law and order, McGavin is depicted as lacking the street smarts that characterise the senior, experienced jovial Bob Hodges (Robert Duvall), whose neighbourhood community approach to his work yields better results than the aggressive and adversarial one initially taken by McGavin, who earns the nickname 'Pacman'. In the title montage sequence McGavin and Hodges drive around in their police car and we witness a mixture of iconic Los Angeles locations such as the LA River, the Los Angeles Library and the city's freeways.

Interspersed between these icons are sidewalks and streetscapes of the downtown area including suburban houses, cinemas, restaurants, department stores and office buildings all shot as if from the moving vehicle. Later in this sequence, beneath the producer (Robert H. Solo) and director credits, we see the obligatory night-time cityscape in its blues and reds. As the title song 'One Time, One Night' by Los Lobos fades on the soundtrack, the sound of police sirens increases in volume and gives way to a hardcore hip hop beat. This sequence follows the introduction of McGavin as a wise-

Bob Hodges (Robert Duvall and Danny McGavin (Sean Penn) take us on a tour of Los Angeles in Denis Hopper's *Colors* (1988)

cracking self-centred individual, concerned with his hair style, compared to Hodges' calm, relaxed demeanour (and balding pate). These opening images recall director Hopper's photography, in particular his interest in signs, facades and symbols. In 'Making the Invisible Visible', Pierre Evil provides a correlation between this opening sequence and Hopper's directorial debut:

> *Colors* ... starts with an in-car travelling shot in which one sees once again darting over the screen buildings, posters, the frontage of a cinema, in a succession of shots that seem lifted straight from *Easy Rider*. Except that *Colors* is no road movie, but a street movie. A film inside the city. A film of walls. (2009: 159).

Later in the film the travelling shots from the title sequence are repeated as Hodges and McGavin approach Cripps gang members Leon (Leon Robinson), Rocket (Don Cheadle) and T-Bone (Damon Wayans) on a sidewalk outside a store. Hodges, in the passenger seat, addresses the gang members with familiarity, as 'homes', knowing them as they know his name and he smiles at their responses. In the following scene, McGavin apprehends High Top (Glenn Plummer) and locates some concealed drugs but is released by Hodges who tells High Top 'You owe me one'. McGavin is upset and berates Hodges for letting High Top go. Hodges explains that McGavin would be better off getting to know the neighbourhood than booking someone for a piece of rock and doing hours of paperwork. Much of the first third of the film involves Hodges counselling McGavin on the history and mores of gang life in the city as the pair visit the elder gang members such as Frog (Trinidad Silva) and Larry 'Looney Toons' Sylvester (Grand Bush) on their rounds. Later McGavin and Hodges are involved in a major drug bust at the San Pedro docks, which also feature in *The Crossing Guard*.

McGavin falls for 'homegirl' Louisa Gomez (Maria Conchita Alonso) and after he inadvertently sprays the face of Maria's cousin with spray-paint and she doesn't want to see him, he is placed in conflict between his feelings for Maria and his identity as a policeman. After a falling out with Hodges, McGavin begins to adopt his elder partner's ways of policing. When Hodges is shot and killed in a raid on Frog's gang on the hills overlooking the city, in a scene recalling one from Kent MacKenzie's *The Exiles* (1961), Hopper utilises an overhead shot with the dead Hodges being accompanied by McGavin, bathed in the helicopter light, ascending higher and higher. Following this scene *Colors* has McGavin school a rookie cop partnering him in the ways of the street he gleaned from Hodges, including a retelling of Hodges' tale about the two bulls who perched on a 'grassy knoll' above a herd of cows: '"[the young bull says] let's go down and fuck one of those cows." The Papa bull says, "no son, let's walk down and fuck 'em all".'

In their interview Hopper tells Matthieu Orléan how on the set of *Rumble Fish* (1983) Chris Penn introduced him to his brother Sean who 'brought me the project. It was about a white cop and a black cop in Chicago and a white guy who has these black kids dealing medicine that was heavily addictive ... the script was really bad but Sean wanted to make something out of it and he convinced Robert Solo that I should come on board' (2009: 139). Penn's approach to Hopper and the subsequent shift in the location of the film may have been due to Hopper's intimate knowledge of the imagery of Los Angeles gangs divined in his retracing of his 1960s sojourns across LA for his photographs of the metropolis. In this regard Hopper is a photographer who Pierre Evil describes as having 'crisscrossed Los Angeles taking photos of gang graffiti with the same passion with which twenty years earlier … he had immortalised those melancholic, sublime, and unconscionably elegant bikers' (2009: 159). Penn's performance in tandem with Hopper's 'street knowledge' works towards not only a narrative about the importance of local knowledge but also a documentary fiction that 'makes the invisible visible'.

Mystic River (2003)

One of Penn's most celebrated roles is his performance as Jimmy Markum, an outsider unable to escape from his criminal past as it belongs to the South Boston setting of Clint Eastwood's *Mystic River*, based on a 2001 novel by Dennis Lehane. His early novels include *A Drink Before the War* (1994), *Darkness, Take My Hand* (1996), *Sacred* (1997), *Gone, Baby, Gone* (1998) and *Prayers for Rain* (1999), which feature Patrick Kenzie and Angela Gennaro, a couple of seasoned private detectives who work the streets of Dorchester, a large historically real South Boston, Massachusetts, neighbourhood where Lehane was born and raised. Like Lawrence Block's New York, George Pelecanos's Washington D.C. or even David Simon's Baltimore, Lehane's Dorchester, including the fictitious East Buckingham, has been a location and specific 'life world' that he has continually worked over, bringing to the committed reader an intrigue with an at once unknowable yet familiar set of characters and the places that they inhabit. Another Massachusetts native, Ben Affleck, directed an adaptation of *Gone, Baby, Gone* (2007), and Lehane wrote the teleplay for three episodes of Simon's *The Wire* (2002–08) and, more recently, the screenplay for Michaël R. Roskam's Brooklyn-set *The Drop* (2014) based on Lehane's own 1999 short story 'Animal Rescue'. In all these works Lehane has become associated with a forensic attention to locale, including street names and neighbourhood personalities, as well as the mores that condition acceptable behaviour. Lehane's *Mystic River* is similarly focused:

> They all lived in East Buckingham, just west of downtown, a neighbourhood of cramped corner stores, small playgrounds, and butcher shops where meat, still pink with blood, hung in the windows. The bars had Irish names and Dodge Darts by the curbs. Women wore handkerchiefs tied off at the backs of their skulls and carried mock leather snap purses for their cigarettes. Until a couple of years ago, older boys had been plucked from the streets, as if by spaceships, and sent to war. They came back hollow and sullen a year or so later, or they didn't come back at all. Days, the mothers searched the papers for coupons. Nights the fathers went to the bars. You knew everyone; nobody except those older boys ever left. (2001: 4)

The interiority of the Flats where Jimmy Markum (Marcus in the novel) and Dave Boyle (Tim Robbins) hail from is in distinction from the Point where Detective Sean

Devine (Kevin Bacon) grew up, and the outside world, alongside an exterior viewpoint that Devine's colleague Whitey Powers (Laurence Fishburne) brings to the investigation of the murder of Jimmy's daughter, Katie (Emmy Rossum). In fact, much of the interplay between the two detectives is founded on Powers quizzing Devine about the history and nuances of the 'East Bucky' neighbourhood. Eastwood, or his screenwriter Brian Helgeland, omits nearly a whole chapter from Lehane's novel focusing on a scene where Dave Boyle returns to the neighbourhood after being abducted and assaulted (which nonetheless remains a key event in the film's narrative). This scene functions to further characterise the young Jimmy Marcus through the close-knit community culminating in a street party:

> *This* was what he loved about growing up here. It was the way people could suddenly throw off a year of aches and complaints and split lips and job worries and old grudges and just let loose, like nothing bad had ever happened in their lives. On St. Pat's or Buckingham Day, sometimes on the Fourth of July, or when the Sox were playing well in September, or, like now, when something collectively lost had been found – especially then – this neighbourhood could erupt into a kind of furious delirium. (2001: 22)

Lehane's Jimmy Marcus holds to this nostalgic view of his surroundings, ignoring the changes that Dave Boyle, for instance, observes, or that Sean Devine embodies. As Nicolette Rowe argues, 'Jimmy clings to a romanticized definition of a perfect Irish Catholic family' (2008: 83) despite his horrific crimes.

Eastwood's film takes up this use of location with Penn's Jimmy defined by his immediate surroundings, embodying his Catholic heritage with a large Celtic cross tattooed on his back, his ongoing reliance on his childhood friends, the neighbourhood gangsters the Savage brothers, Nick and Kevin (Adam Nelson and Adam Wahlberg), and his proprietorship of the small, local store, the Cottage Market, replete with Budweiser sign, Red Sox symbol and American flag (see Rowe 2008: 85). And in many scenes, such as those in the store, the church, in domestic settings and in the famous scene where he is restrained by policemen when he attempts to get to Katie's body, Penn is tightly hemmed in. In a style recalling Hodges' death in *Colors*, the overhead shot ascends until the image fades to an overhead shot of the empty bear pen which then tilts 180° to a shot of the open sky frames by trees.

Jimmy Markham (Sean Penn) hemmed in by his surroundings in Clint Eastwood's *Mystic River* (2003)

In these scenes Jimmy is both comforted and suffocated, unable to move on from the historical binds that contain him. In *Mystic River* the other characters are depicted in a crowded *mise-en-scène* with every frame filled with the peculiar three-story apartments and houses of the location-shot Dorchester area, the streets and people of the neighbourhood mostly shot at chest height with little depth of field. In interiors such as cars, bars and houses, people are framed tightly.

Eastwood contrasts these images of the Flats with overhead helicopter shots such as those of the Tobin Bridge over the 'mystic river' where we first encounter Sean and Whitey attending a traffic incident and Sean is looking out over 'the old neighbourhood' with the Boston skyline in the background; or when the helicopters hover over the neighbourhood moving towards the scene of Katie's murder. These overhead shots serve to further emphasise the confined particularity of the neighbourhood scenes, which have created and defined their inhabitants.

Milk (2008)

In 2008 Penn took on the role of Harvey Milk in Gus Van Sant's feature narrative, an echo and incorporation of Rob Epstein and Richard Schmiechen's documentary *The Times of Harvey Milk*. Van Sant went to extraordinary lengths to capture what Armistead Maupin, in an interview with Van Sant, called 'that gritty street thing that you did in *Drugstore Cowboy* [1989]'. Van Sant replies: 'Well, that's what I'm always trying for, but I never know whether it actually happens. There are all kinds of ways that people present their films, but that's kind of a good feeling, if you can make it seem like the characters are really there' (Maupin n.d.). Van Sant tells Maupin about transforming 'a rather stylish home-furnishing shop into his funky, old digs' that was the exact place where Harvey Milk's Castro Street camera store was. Van Sant: 'Yeah, we worked from a lot of pictures. There were scenes that took place at the camera shop during all these different periods of time, so we had the early-70s look and then the more developed, mid-70s look' (ibid.).

Van Sant's film also employs moving image footage from the era including from *The Times of Harvey Milk* interspersed throughout his own film but also by including historical figures from the gay rights movement surrounding Milk in Castro Street. Figures such as activist and friend of Harvey Milk, Cleve Jones, played by Emile Hirsch in Van Sant's film, current member of San Francisco Supervisors board, Tom

Harvey Milk (Sean Penn) outside the historical camera store on Castro Street in Gus Van Sant's *Milk* (2008)

Ammiano, a photographer who worked in Milk's camera shop, Daniel Nicoletta, Teamster Leader and Coors Boycott Director Allan Baird appear as themselves, and the co-sponsor of the Gay Rights Bill with Harvey Milk, Carol Ruth Silver appear as an extra amongst the actors in the film while historical figures such as Cleve Jones and Anne Kronenberg were historical advisors on the film. In an interview on the DVD extras of *Milk*, producer Bruce Cohen comments that the mix of historical figures and actors on the set led to an interplay between the people who had experienced these events and who directly were able to convey how they experienced, and responded, emotionally, to the times and places in which they found themselves. Also on the DVD extras, Alison Pill, who plays Anne Kronenberg, extends the idea of representing historical figures in performance by remarking about the method of the lead actor in *Milk*: '…just watching the physicality of [Penn] change. You can watch Sean walk down the hall and then see Harvey walk down the hall the next moment. It's pretty incredible.' For B. Ruby Rich, in 'Ghosts of a Vanished World', *Milk* brings together ideas of performance and place:

> In a flash, *Milk* was on. And it would be shot on the very streets of San Francisco where the original events transpired. 'If it's something specific, my thing is always to go to the real place,' says Van Sant, while admitting he 'never would have been able to insist on it' given the budget pressures to shoot in a cheaper location. 'It was all Sean.' Sean Penn agreed to play Harvey Milk on the condition that the film would be shot in San Francisco.
>
> It's thanks to Penn, then, that I could stroll down Castro Street last February and find myself mesmerised by a 1970s version of my own city. Real estate offices advertised houses for sale for $40,000. Gas prices were laughable. An Aquarius Record Store packed its windows with vinyl records and acid-rock posters. The Castro cinema marquee, restored to full-colour brilliance, touted *The Poseidon Adventure*. And Harvey Milk's fabled Castro Camera shop was there again, popping up in the middle of the block like an apparition. … Then, the film started and silence descended, as the audience began to realise what a house of mirrors we had entered. As Sean Penn brilliantly disappeared into the body, voice and mannerisms of Harvey Milk, it got harder and harder to separate the world on the screen from the one we lived in. And when the film ended and the credits rolled, there could be no exit: we left the theatre only to enter the same streets we'd been watching inside, just moments ago. (2009)

Again, the idea of Penn 'disappearing into the body of his character[s]', in relation to the places in which they belong. In places such as Ridgemont, the south-east counties of Pennsylvania, the lifeways of South Boston, as an outsider learning the ropes in the streets and alleyways of Los Angeles, or in the Castro in 1970s San Francisco, Penn's characters have been formed, sometimes at ease, often suffocated, in the imbrication of performance and place. In the next chapter, focusing on *The Indian Runner*, we will explore this rendering of place, Nebraska in 1968, as an intersection of a host of intertextual relations further articulating a personal worldview.

CHAPTER THREE

The Indian Runner

> And there's something about growing up in the Midwest. There's no check on you. People imagine it's the kind of place where your behaviour is under constant observation, where you really have to toe the line. They got that idea from Sinclair Lewis. But people can really get ignored there and fall into bad soil. Kit did, and he grew up like a big poisonous weed.
> — Terrence Malick (1975: 83)

The Indian Runner (1991), like the rest of Penn's oeuvre, can be seen to assemble a host of figures – Bruce Springsteen, Harry Crews, the Johnstown Flood, Peter Nabokov's *Indian Running*, Dennis Hopper, Charles Bronson, Robert Frank, Diane Arbus, the Method – to facilitate a narrative concerned with the ways in which places and times condition individuals. Penn's rendering of distinct locations – the Los Angeles of *The Crossing Guard*, his Nevada of *The Pledge*, the New York of 'U.S.A.' and the Alaska of *Into the Wild* – is also at the mercy of the paradox: while the stories are contained, it is also possible to ascertain a host of intertexts resulting in what Mikhail Iampolski terms 'the presence of cultural history' (1998: 9) endlessly spinning out of these places. This paradox is at the heart of Penn's cinema.

The Indian Runner is principally concerned with two brothers, Franky (Viggo Mortensen) and Joe (David Morse), one a tearaway, a hell raiser, the other, custodian of the family farm lost in an economic downturn and now a highway patrolman. The loss of the family farm and Franky heading off to the Vietnam War are just some of the forces of modernity, the unsettling of the familiar, localised community.

The place of *The Indian Runner* is evoked following the initial images illustrating David Morse's narration – the images of the deer being killed and the title sequence with stilled images accompanied only by the sound of wind whistling on the soundtrack. The opening car chase of the film is intercut with lengthy, landscape images of snow-covered grasses moving in the wind, a desolate dirt road, a frost-covered strand of barbed wire, a bitumen road in a snow-bound landscape, a windmill, a bird alone on a branch, cattle in a field, a church in the distance, a field with a 'No Hunting' sign written on a tyre, farm sheds at the end of a field, another church with a high steeple on a hill, a factory chimney bellowing steam into the air, and finally, a traffic light at an intersection blinking an amber warning.

These images, following the opening narration, titles and the use of Traffic's 'Feeling Alright?' and the location sounds of the patrolman's siren, the squelching of tyres of snow and bitumen and engines revving recede to immobility and quiet, a pastoral land frozen in time. These images contrast with the ensuing car chase, setting a limit to the place of this story, further emphasised by the appearance out of this landscape of a sign reading 'State Line 5' by the side of the road.

These images situate Penn's film in an unspecified mid-west America, but one that is prefigured by the titles which tell us that it was 'inspired by the song Highway Patrolman by Bruce Springsteen'. The mention of Springsteen's song provides an immediate intertext with the 1982 album *Nebraska*, locating the film in this mid-west region.[1] The album, in particular the title song, invokes the 'badlands' mythology that is most familiar in the story of 1950s serial killer Charlie Starkweather and that historical figure's ranging across mid-west America. Any mention of Starkweather gestures further to Terrence Malick's *Badlands* (1973). The film is set in 1968 and includes the Vietnam War as its historical setting and backstory and utilises performances from Dennis Hopper, Charles Bronson and Sandy Dennis to get at the resonances of their personas, in relation to those of Viggo Mortensen, to articulate the debilitating violence at the heart of American culture that inspired, and is the echo of, that war. These performers further signal Penn's belonging to the tradition of filmmaking that emerges from the 1970s New Hollywood of which Hopper, Bronson and Dennis are significant figures. Coupled with Hopper and Bronson is the figure of Harry Crews and his performance of the folk song 'John Henry' as it represents the peculiarity of US class relations in relation to Crews's oeuvre of Southern identity and locale.

In Country

The Indian Runner, the film's titles tell us, is 'inspired' by Springsteen's song 'Highway Patrolman'. Sung in the first person, by a character, Joe Roberts, about himself and his brother Franky, it is about how,

> Franky went in the army back in 1965
> I got a farm deferment, settled down, took Maria for my wife
> But them wheat prices kept on droppin' till it was like we were gettin' robbed
> Franky came home in '68 and me I took this job

Franky is a troublemaker and Joe has to look out for him because 'Man turns his back on his family, he just ain't no good'. As the chorus says:

Me and Franky laughin' and drinkin'
nothin' feels better than blood on blood
Takin' turns dancin' with Maria
as the band plays 'Night of the Johnstown Flood'

Nebraska is often described as a watershed in Springsteen's work. Following the enormous commercial and critical success of the larger, anthemic albums *Born to Run*, *Darkness on the Edge of Town* and *The River*, *Nebraska* is a stripped back set of songs recorded on a four-track tape player at Springsteen's house as a demo tape for his band. But because it had qualities that couldn't be replicated with a full band, the demo tapes essentially became the album. Geoffrey Hines tells us that Springsteen, around this time, was reading Flannery O'Connor's collection of short stories, *A Good Man is Hard to Find* after seeing John Huston's film *Wise Blood* (1979), as well as Joe Klein's biography, *Woody Guthrie: A Life*, a couple of books that resulted in songs such as 'A Good Man is Hard to Find' and 'The River' and a shift to an interest in folk music such as Guthrie's (2007: 69). It also marked a shift into first-person storytelling – as in 'Highway Patrolman' – as well as away from a focus on New Jersey and the world Springsteen knew to an interest in different locales such as Nebraska, Texas and Florida. *Nebraska*, Springsteen told Kurt Loder, is

> about that American isolation: what happens to people when they're alienated from their friends and their community and their government and their job. Because those are the things that keep you sane, that give meaning to life in some fashion. And if they slip away, and you start to exist in some void where the basic constraints of society are a joke, then life becomes kind of a joke. And anything can happen. (Loder n.d.)

For some time Springsteen had been giving songs titles taken from some of his favourite films. These included Malick's *Badlands* and Arthur Ripley's *Thunder Road* (1958), starring Robert Mitchum; and although not represented in song titles he mined films such as Richard Brooks's *In Cold Blood* (1967) and John Ford's *The Grapes of Wrath* (1940). The title song 'Nebraska' is a reworking of the Charlie Starkweather story that also informed Malick's film. In all, Springsteen moved into a mode of working, of reworking stories, songs and films and utilising a host of characters through which the world is experienced, in the manner of a folk singer. In this way we might be able to see the Springsteen persona evolving from a songwriter into a storyteller involving individuals whose identity, and possibly its loss, is closely linked to an affinity with a particular locale, mirroring Penn's directorial oeuvre.[2] Later, Springsteen was to sing a version of Woody Guthrie's 'Tom Joad', a song Guthrie was asked to write by his record company after the success of Ford's adaptation of Steinbeck's novel. Springsteen, a huge fan of the film, explicitly explored and referenced this terrain on his 1995 album, *The Ghost of Tom Joad*.

As Geoffrey Hines states in *Born in the U.S.A.*, around this time Springsteen developed an interest in the cause of Vietnam Veterans as he worked on six songs between 1981 and 1983 including 'Born in the USA', 'Brothers Under the Bridge' and 'Highway Patrolman' (2007: 14). All of these songs dealt with an interest in the life of Veterans after they had returned to their everyday lives and dealing with the post-traumatic stress, alienation and ghost-like existence in a country that up until relatively recently wanted to ignore them.

One of the best accounts of these issues is Bobbie Anne Mason's *In Country* (1985) which features Springsteen's 'Born in the USA' as a kind of coda to the narrative. The phrase 'in country' is a euphemism for Vietnam as experienced by soldiers and relates to the feelings of helplessness, anger and dislocation felt by servicemen. Mason translates those feelings to home soil, and utilises a journey structure to encompass the United States. Like *The Indian Runner*, *In Country*, is a story contained, for the most part, within a fictional town, Hopewell, Kentucky, where the protagonists are subjected to an insular, workaday series of events, impacted by the return of Vietnam Veterans, in particular the depressed Agent Orange-affected character, Emmett Smith. The novel concludes with a road trip Emmett, his brother Sam and his Mama take to the Vietnam Veterans Memorial in Washington. Like *The Indian Runner*, *In Country*'s portrait of Middle America is stultifying, even more so in relation to the driving force of confrontation with the past in the form of the Vietnam War brought about in its dénouement.

Another thread, marking Penn's articulation of Springsteen's interest in Vietnam Veterans conjoined with issues of place and identity, is the research of Berkeley Anthropology Professor Peter Nabokov, whose *Indian Running: Native American History and Tradition* lends itself to Joe Roberts' narration. In an interview with Gavin Smith, Penn says:

> I came across this book ... called *Indian Running*. Nabokov went back into the history of Indian running as a spiritual, as well as practical tool. It stuck in my head, and during the writing process I started thinking about how it represented certain themes I was interested in. So I got in touch with Nabokov; he's a professor at Berkeley. So I flew up to meet him and he gave me a one-day crash-course – slide show, lecture, the whole bit. And I found out so many things this day we spent together, things that really hit home. It was like going on an adventure through my own intentions in what I was writing. (1991: 66).

The book is a chronicle of 'Indian Running', a sophisticated system in native American tribes whose running prowess facilitated everything from trade, message delivery, cultural communication, hunting and competitive games. For Penn, it is colonialism that is at the heart of the movie. In an interview with Richard T. Kelly, Penn says:

> I've been asked many times, 'Where did Frank's anger come from?' Springsteen wanted to know that too. And I referred him to his own lyrics from another song on *Nebraska* [the song 'Nebraska']: 'Sir, I guess there's just a meanness in this world.' That was answer enough for me, because I don't always think there's

an explanation for these things. But there are our ancestral sins: the criminal past of the settlers in the United States, this hustled land. It inhabits some part of our consciousness, because it got passed on by our fathers, and their fathers, and those before. I viewed that as a sort of shared disease in the culture, and – it's a leap – but I wanted to see if that had anything to do, if not literally then politically, with the damaged spirit of people like Frank. (2004: 242)

The Indian Runner contains, at its heart, a reflection of the folk traditions of Native American culture only to throw light on the notion of original sin which functions as the loosest kind of explanation for the actions of Franky. Of course, part of the culture of Indian running is about knowing your place and community so well that you can move through it silently, carefully, swiftly and with knowledge. This conception of knowledge is spectral, fractured and radical in Penn's film. Franky is at once both the message and the messenger, the Indian runner of the film's title, haunted by the ghost-like American Indian figure (Kenny Stabler) that drifts pass him at several intervals in the film. But this isn't so much a message of hope and guidance, as a message of inequality, isolation and violence that motivates the drama of the film.

The Johnstown Flood

As we have seen, the song 'Highway Patrolman' contains the lines 'and the band played "The Night of the Johnstown Flood"'. Apparently there is no such song, but it may not matter. Springsteen has taken a famous tragedy in American folklore and reworked it into the spectre of a song within a song. The story goes that some of the wealthiest men in the United States, members of South Fork Fishing and Hunting Club, such as Andrew Carnegie, rebuilt an old earthen dam to create a lake high above the booming coal and steel town of Johnstown, Pennsylvania (a town, incidentally, where a young Springsteen worked in steel manufacturing). The lake was a centrepiece of an exclusive summer resort for these men and their families who had benefited from the industry that lay below in the Johnstown valley. According to David McCullough, in *The Johnstown Flood*, despite repeated warnings about the need for maintenance work, none were undertaken; on 31 May 1889 the dam broke and water hurtled down the valley demolishing Johnstown and killing more than 2,000 people. The Johnstown Flood became a national scandal. Like the song 'John Henry', the flood almost immediately became a legend of working class or blue-collar people pitted against the might and wealth of America particularly when the victims were unsuccessful in suing the members of the South Fork Fishing and Hunting Club for damages. The court ruled that the flood was an act of God. In Springsteen's 'Highway Patrolman' and Penn's *The Indian Runner*, the Johnstown tale operates as a touchstone for the injustice of the capitalist system, how working people, the people who rebuilt Johnstown (and Joe Roberts, who lost his farm), so that manufacturing could supply the US with the steel it needed to build the country, would carry on with their workaday lives. This sentiment about working people is the mainstay of Guthrie's ballads, Springsteen's *Nebraska* album and Penn's first film.

Penn's adaptation of Robert Frank's 'US 285 New Mexico' in *The Indian Runner* (1991)

Robert Frank

The Indian Runner opens with a stilled image of a road into which the police chase plunges, or is motivated, given action, brought to life. This image also resembles the cover of Springsteen's album *Nebraska*. Photographer David Michael Kennedy, David Burke in *Heart of Darkness: Bruce Springsteen's Nebraska* states, was commissioned by Springsteen to mimic Robert Frank's famous image from his series *The Americans*, entitled 'US 285 New Mexico' from 1956 (2011: 65–6).

Facilitated by Walker Evans, the famous New Deal photographer and contributor to the photo essay *Let Us Now Praise Famous Men*, Frank's *The Americans* received much criticism upon release attended by the famous line from *Popular Photography* in 1959, that they were characterised by 'meaningless blur, grain, muddy exposures, drunken horizons and general sloppiness'. The photographs featured unusual angles, cropping and focus. But when Frank teamed up with Jack Kerouac, who wrote an introduction to the book and became subsequent friends with the Beats, Allen Ginsberg and Gregory Corso, Frank also became a kind of official photographer for the Beat movement. This association meant that Frank's images of loneliness, desolation, of race and class divisions, were, despite the prevailing optimism of the 1950s, understood as documents of the heartland of the country. 'US 285 New Mexico' is also a take on Dorothea Lange's 'Road to the West' from 1938. Lange was a contemporary of Walker Evans and an official photographer during the New Deal documenting of Depression-era United States. Both Frank's and Lange's images have achieved legendary status as representations of the 'real America'. Frank's photo includes a car in the image and is not so much connected to the New Deal era of Roosevelt and the whole *Grapes of Wrath* ethos which narrrativised, once again, the movement of mid-West Americans ('the Okies') West to California, but expressed the kind of desolation, loneliness and movement the Beats saw at the heart of American culture. We can also see Frank's influence on Michael Haller's production design for *The Indian Runner*. Haller was also Hal Ashby's production designer on *Harold and Maude*, *The Last Detail* (1973), *Bound for Glory* (1976 – about Woody Guthrie), *Coming Home* (1978) and *Being There* (1979) as well as Penn's second film *The Crossing Guard*. *The Indian Runner* is also co-dedicated to Hal Ashby (as well as Frank Bianco and John Cassavetes).

The lineage of photography that includes Walker Evans and Robert Frank, in distinction from the 'good news' photographers of *Life* and *Look* magazines, could also include Diane Arbus and William Klein. According to James Guimond in *American Photography and the American Dream,* these magazines 'were filled, cover to cover, with nothing but good news about the nation's economy and prosperity – all illustrated with pictures of the satisfied consumers, happy families, grinning young people, and smiling workers who inhabited what *Life*'s editors called, in 1947, "This Pleasant Land"' (1991: 207). For Guimond, Frank, Arbus and Klein 'transfigured photography itself in to a far more personal and daring medium, and in the process they also changed and helped re-establish documentary as an important form of photography' (1991: 208).

Diane Arbus's gallery of freaks and eccentrics can be seen as a direct contrast to the prevailing mythology of the American Dream. Portraits of carnival freaks, of midgets, dwarfs transvestites, heavily tattooed men, giants, triplets, nudists, etc. were incorporated into a vision of alienation that encompassed the whole of 1960s America. In her accounting for Arbus's work, Susan Sontag, in 'America, Seen Through Photographs, Darkly', writes:

> For Arbus, both freaks and Middle America were equally exotic: a boy marching in a pro-war parade and a Levittown housewife were as alien as a dwarf or a transvestite; lower-middle-class suburbia was as remote as Times Square, lunatic asylums, and gay bars. Arbus's work expressed her turn against what was public (as she experienced it), conventional, safe, reassuring – and boring – in favor of what was private, hidden, ugly, dangerous, and fascinating. (1984: 45)

Sontag also points out that the 1960s was 'the decade of Arbus's serious work', when 'the inhabitants of deviant underworlds are evicted from their restricted territories', entering public consciousness in an unprecedented way (1984: 43–4).

A key sequence of *The Indian Runner* provides two distinct filmic mirrors; first, to Frank's *The Americans* and, second, Arbus's world of eccentrics. Hearing that his brother is about to be released from jail for time served for assaulting his girlfriend Dorothy (Patricia Arquette), Joe Roberts travels to Columbus, Ohio, to meet him. In a scene in the waiting area full of location sound including muffled conversation and movement amplified by the linoleum floor, Joe observes Dorothy and a collection of people all waiting for their men to be released from prison. Utilising a series of fluid pans, we witness, as Joe does, transient portraits of children, girlfriends, mothers, families, a close-up of a hand holding a Coca-Cola bottle, a children's teddy-bear sitting up on the floor as his owner hop-scotches, men sharing a light for their cigarettes, and a teenage girl reading *1001 Ways to Beat the Draft*.[3] Christopher Connelly in his report from *The Indian Runner* shoot, 'Sean Penn Bites back', describes Penn's documentary method in capturing these images.:

> Penn's camera is mounted above the action in the far corner of the large room, and as he surveys the situation, he looks out on a Sargasso sea of extras who are providing the smoky atmosphere in which the wordless scene plays itself

Franky (Viggo Mortensen) and Dorothy (Patricia Arquette) return to America in *The Indian Runner*

out ... Penn shoots until he seems satisfied, then announces to the extras that he'll be changing lenses. 'Thanks for your patience,' he tells the locals. 'I'll just be a few minutes.' But he's lying. As the extras lapse into normal behavior – talking, laughing, their kids playing hopscotch on the floor – Penn whispers terse instructions to his camera operator: 'Black guy ... the guard.' He is grabbing shots of oblivious individuals. The idea he tells his operator, 'is to catch people unawares.' (1991: 62)

These images recall Robert Frank's cluttered, noisy, incomplete images of everyday mid-west America, of everyday people going about their lives.

Upon seeing Dorothy also waiting to meet Franky, Joe, decides to keep his distance, instead following Franky and Dorothy as they take a seedy hotel room. In the transition between the jail and the hotel room we also see Dorothy and Franky's car, followed by Joe's, foregrounded with a large American flag billowing across the screen into which they both plunge, emphasising the connection to Robert Frank as well as Franky's re-entry into the USA.

In the following scene, Dorothy and Franky take up residence at the Delmar Hotel, in a downtown area, to which Joe follows them. The Delmar is a noisy, thin-walled hotel with the sound of coughing, conversation and a resident, Clyde (Phil Gould), hanging out in the hallway. Franky is revealed to be heavily tattooed, at home at the Delmar. Later when Franky, Dorothy and Joe are returning from a meal, Dorothy notices a bearded lady (Elaine Shoonover) and a circus dwarf (Neal Stark) out on the street while what looks like a circus strong man fixes a caravan. Later in the film, the Delmar manager (Annie Pearson), a large, sweaty, unkempt woman in an Elvis t-shirt, delivers the message about 'a family emergency', the death of Franky's father, Franky pulls her t-shirt over her head much to the amusement of Clyde, permanently, it seems camped in the hallway, whose drawing on a cigarette rhymes with Franky's. These characters recall the subjects of Arbus's late 1960s work.

The world of the Delmar Hotel and Joe's hometown is linked by a scene where Joe is washing his patrol car while he talks with a lady at the carwash (Kathy Jensen). This woman is dressed in an outlandish pink dress and matching hat with pearl earrings, scarf, brooch, white handbag, short hair, an upturned nose and arched eyebrows, all redolent of mid-century conservativism. She complains to Joe about hippies that are camping on her land and invites him out for a meal at her home. She seems fully aware of the death of Joe's father, and Joe knows that she has a pig that lives in a pick-up truck. Her eccentric speech and manner, along with her fluttering her eyes excessively when she invites Joe to 'come play' with the pig, aligns her with the residents of the hidden world of the Delmar Hotel and Arbus's work.

In Penn's narrative schema, the worlds of Columbus, Ohio, of Robert Frank-like images in the jail waiting area and of Diane Arbus in the Delmar Hotel – that is, the worlds of Franky – are distinct from the world that Joe belongs to; the isolated, slumbering town, emphasised by the languid landscape imagery, including slow-motion aerial shots of ice-laden forests, where Joe is lauded for his patrolman work and his wife and child provide him with hope in the future. Figuratively, Frank and Arbus invoke two distinct yet interrelated critical strands in the lineage of American photography that are apparent in *The Indian Runner*.

Harry Crews

In the opening sequence, Joe returns to the patrol station visibly upset by the death of the escapee (Jimmy Intveld) he has just shot in the pursuit that commences the film. As Roberts sits and attempts to gather himself, the escapee's mother and father, Mr and Mrs Baker, played by Southern author, playwright and cult figure, Harry Crews and Penn's mother, Eileen Ryan, come to harangue him about their son's death. As the couple are escorted outside and the scene begins to close, Crews breaks into a hollowed out, death-rattle version of 'John Henry' as if he's putting a curse on Roberts:

> Captain said to John Henry, 'Oh Bring my Steam drill 'round
> Bring my Steam drill out on the job, I'm gonna hope that steel 'an down,
> Oh Lord, I'm a hope that steel'm down'
> Henry said to Captain, 'Man ain't nothin' but a Man…'

The use of Harry Crews is a characteristic case of casting and performance in Penn's body of work. Crews is a formidable figure in American underground literature, Southern identity and friend of Penn's whose appearance in a film set in smalltown Nebraska may seem an anomaly given Crews's southern roots.[4] Crews brings not just a jarring rendition of a traditional song but also a persona wrought over many years beginning with the autobiographical book, *A Childhood: The Biography of a Place*. As this title suggests, Crews' work could be seen to fit into the clichés about Southern writing and its sense of place. As Flannery O'Connor wrote: 'the anguish that most of us [Southern writers] have observed for some time now has been caused not by the fact that the South is alienated from the rest of the country, but by the fact that it is not alienated enough, that every day we are getting more and more like the rest of the country' (O'Connor quoted in Moss 1983: 36). The point about Crews' fiction is less to do with clichés about southern identity and more to do with the way that each of his novels, including *A Feast of Snakes* (1976), *Scar Lover* (1992) and *Florida Frenzy*

(1982), has a particular sense of place. As Jack Moore states in 'The Land and the Ethnics in Crews' Works':

> ... each of Crews' novels is located in a very specific place, and though people come to these places from elsewhere, one always has the sense that, as was true of his home region in *A Childhood*, 'where we lived and how we lived was almost hermetically sealed from everything and everybody else'. That is, the place of each book possesses a definiteness, with clear boundaries and a distinct physical nature. (1983: 48)

Yet there are some things to be gleaned from Crews' role in relation to the traditions of Southern literature and that is the theme of a Southern sense of loss concomitant with a strong sense of localised identity, of modernity effacing the sense of place.

An important part of this configuration is Crews' persona, mirrored in the scene at the opening of *The Indian Runner*, a great example of the Southern grotesque, and a persona that Crews has utilised in other arenas such as Andrew Douglas's *Searching for the Wrong Eyed Jesus* (2003) and Tyler Turkle's *Harry Crews: Survival is Triumph Enough* (2007). In this persona, Crews embraces the figure of the Southern freak or lunatic, but only as 'a departure or displacement from an accepted standard', as William Moss tells us. Like his 'physically or spiritually grotesque' (1983: 38) characters, Crews performs a version of his persona in *The Indian Runner*, summoning his Southern extremity of character to curse Joe Roberts, as a representative of the Law, whom Franky calls 'Brother Man', who has brought about the loss of his son as just another rod for his back.

John Henry

Of course it is also the use of the song 'John Henry' here that adds to this sense of loss; in this case, of humanity to mechanisation. According to Scott Nelson (2005), the song is based on a tale that emerged from a West Virginian railroad clearing about a worker who challenges one of the new steam-powered drills that threatens to replace him on the job. John Henry prevails in a marathon contest but eventually dies. The song accompanied a legend that spread throughout the United States and the world, becoming a story about workers and unions versus bosses, corporations, new technologies and modernity. It is in this sense of loss attended by working-class values that it is possible to see how the song sits well with Harry Crews' Southern persona and Penn's film about two brothers grieving over the loss of their place in modern society.

The loss of the Roberts farm and Franky going off to war are twin components of the forces of modernity, the unsettling of a localised community. In this way Crews' performance of 'John Henry', tied to his Southern persona, externalises and broadens these themes in a rupturous, raging against the machine of modernity which, following the death of his son at the hand of Joe Roberts, the lawman, is a summing up of the themes that course through the rest of the film. In a further continuation of this lineage, Springsteen would go on to record 'John Henry' on the 'We Shall Overcome:

The Seeger Sessions' (2006), his interpretation of American folk songs recorded by Pete Seeger.

Charles Bronson

The Indian Runner also includes a characteristically underplayed performance by Charles Bronson as the father of Joe and Franky, a farmer whose land is lost in the economic downturn. In a role purportedly offered, according to David Morse in Richard T. Kelly's biography of Penn, to Gene Hackman and Jon Voight (2004: 249), Bronson's character and performance in an 'art cinema' film could be seen in contrast to his low-brow action films of the 1970s and early 1980s. However, this claim misses the point of Penn's choice and use of Bronson in this role. Bronson made a career out of subdued performances simmering with underlying rage. This way of understanding Bronson in *The Indian Runner* sits comfortably within Penn's worldview, making Bronson an ideal choice for Joe and Franky's father.[5]

A key scene has Bronson's character allude to the lineage he and, particularly, Franky belong to, which, as well as drawing in the notion of America's original sin coupled to ideas of masculinity includes one of the slightest of intertextual links in the film. At the wake following the funeral of Franky and Joe's mother (Sandy Roberts), Joe and his father are sitting out on the veranda talking. After Joe's wife Maria (Valeria Golino) asks them both if they 'need anything', Bronson's character continues the conversation saying: 'You know, Joe, it didn't sit with me right when you married a Mexican woman, but I look at her today, she's beautiful. She's a beautiful and good woman. But was I wrong, I was dead wrong.' The pair discuss Franky's whereabouts and the father admits to receiving a card from Dorothy saying that 'Frank hit me. My Daddy said he had to go to jail. But don't worry because I'm here to take care of him.' Joe replies that 'he's a likeable son of a bitch'. His father asks 'Where does he get it Joe?', which is followed by a quick cut to Joe's response of 'I don't know' and then a lengthier shot on Bronson that implies he is the source of Franky's problems. We then cut to Joe's profile and then to his point of view in what is ostensibly a shot of Maria and his son on the floor watching a western on television. This idealised image has a tremendously sophisticated condensation of meaning emanating from the *mise-en-scène*.

The film on TV is John Ford's *Rio Grande* (1950), a quotation that extends the themes of father/son relations and the attendant issues of masculinity tied up with Mexican/US border issues and immigration and of hope for the frontier in the figures of children captured by American Indians. John Wayne is Lieutenant Colonel Kirby Yorke, a Union Officer leading a training outpost close to the Rio Grande. He is sent a group of new recruits, including his son Jeff (Claude Jarman Jr.) who he hasn't seen in fifteen years. At the same time, his wife arrives to retrieve her son from service but remains to become incorporated into the outpost and to fall back in love with her husband. The captured Apache Indian prisoners are broken out of the compound in which they are held and the outpost is attacked. The decision is made to send the women and children to safety by wagon train but they are attacked and the children taken captive across the Rio Grande into Mexico. The capture of the children forces

Kirby Yorke to set out illegally across the border to rescue the children, aided by his son, Trooper Tyree (Ben Johnson) and Trooper Daniel 'Sandy' Boone (Harry Carey Jnr.).

This scenario of US/Mexican relations is imbricated in the 'ancestral sins: the criminal past of the settlers in the United States' in relation to the American Indian race relations, and the ways that Penn has proposed that these have has 'inhabit[ed] our consciousness … by our fathers, and their fathers … a sort of shared disease in the culture', is wonderfully played out in this intertextual link.

As distinct from some of Bronson's earlier films such as *The Magnificent Seven* (1960), *The Great Escape* (1963), *The Dirty Dozen* (1967) and *Once Upon a Time in the West* (1968), his films made with Michael Winner such as *Chato's Land* (1972), *The Mechanic* (1972), *Hard Times* (1975) and the *Death Wish* series (1974, 1982, 1985, 1987, 1994) saw Bronson and the director develop a slow-burn, reticent masculinity derived from his characters turning to violence under extreme duress (*Chato's Land*, *Death Wish*) or merely as a way of making money (*Hard Times*). Upon its release, *The Mechanic* was noted for having no dialogue for the first sixteen minutes. In *The Indian Runner*, Bronson's inactivity and the film's emphasis on his measured, timely, yet clipped, lispy speech, serves to hold the seething masculinity in check. Yet there is also a sense of his physicality, the way he sits, eats, moves his head, that evokes the violence in him as a figure in 1970s filmmaking and, as already noted, is revisited in the Franky character. Oddly enough, it is Harry Crews that provides the best description of Charles Bronson in a report that he wrote from the set of *Breakheart Pass* (1975) entitled 'The Knuckles of Saint Bronson'. Crews describes Bronson walking across one of the train trestles:

> The trestle was very uneven, with crossties and broken rock. But Bronson, coming across it, could have been walking over a ballroom floor. He came as smoothly as a model with a book on her head. And he never looked down. He never does. No matter how rough the ground. And yet his feet go unerringly to the place where they need to be. No bounce. No wobble. No hitch in his gait. But he does not glide. Or float. He seems to be suctioned to the earth. Growing from it. Joined to it even when he's moving over it. And he comes straight toward you, you see that his center of gravity is very low in his body. Truly, his center of gravity must be his cock, or directly behind it. He does not smile. He rarely does, and when he does, it looks like it hurts him. Since his features are so distinct – heavy, even – you'd think they would also be mobile. Not so. No expression is his habitual expression. (1979: 103)

Crews' description expresses the groundedness of Bronson's persona, his ability to be at one with his surroundings, connected to the land he finds himself on. In these ways he is a mirror to the style of actor David Morse, whose reticence and measured monotone speech sits within a hulking frame (Morse is 6' 4") and who has a slow and deliberate movement similar to Bronson's. Penn, according to Morse in Kelly's biography, had seen the actor in Richard Donner's *Inside Moves* (1980); then, on the set of the television series *St. Elsewhere* (1982–88), where Leo Penn was directing Morse, Penn Sr. passed on Sean's regards and set up a meeting (2004: 243).

Joe Roberts is his father's son, once a farm owner. Like his father, Joe is a solid, calm, dependable, yet perhaps defeated figure, the ultimate in emplacement and belonging to the local community. He attempts to rekindle the sense of community and the place of family within a network by caring for eccentric neighbourhood characters, but also through digging a vegetable garden in his yard, getting his hands dirty with the earth, even finding a Native American arrow head in so doing.

Dennis Hopper

Like Bronson, Dennis Hopper brings a lot of baggage via a host of rebel roles from *Rebel Without a Cause* (1955), *Giant* (1956), *Easy Rider* and *The Last Movie* (1971); or those crazed, wasted roles in rearview nightmares such as *Apocalypse Now* and *River's Edge* (1986). Hopper's own oeuvre and the concomitant roles of actor-director (*Easy Rider* and *The Last Movie*) bolsters the claim for him as embodiment as well as chronicler of the 1960s, usually at the tail-end of that decade represented by Altamont, Charles Manson and the Vietnam War. As Adrian Martin points out in 'The Misleading Man', Hopper is 'a creature, product, of the 1960s' (2007: 34).

> Hopper is, all at once, the 1960s without apology or smothered in regret, a post-Beat relic or a pre-punk role model, the living spirit of an era or its haunted ghost. Through him, different social interest groups can work out – in that strange, imaginative space provided by cinema – something of their relation to the 1960s. […] Hopper, in the long run, is less an emblem of the 1960s, frozen in time, than an embodiment of the continuing legacy of that era, of the wear and tear visited by the vicissitudes of personal and public history upon its dreams and ideals, a living test of its ability either to survive as inspiration, or die pathetically, as if to reveal its original bankruptcy. (2007: 34–5)

Like Bronson, Dennis Hopper's appearance as the barman Caesar in *The Indian Runner* is brief – maybe five minutes screen time in total – yet his presence is significant in Penn's oeuvre. Caesar is a figure aligned with Franky, exhibiting a camaraderie or empathy with Mortensen's character. Caesar seems to be an ex-military man (tattoos, buzzcut), which brings with it an empathy with unexplained violence and anxiety.

In a telling scene late in the film, Franky has gone to Caesar's bar to avoid Dorothy's giving birth to their child and is locked into a close conversation with Caesar. The scene commences with images of the rioting at the 1968 Democratic convention on the bar's TV set and Caesar's monologue begins over an image of a bloodied face of a youth amongst the rioting:

> Did you ever want to kill someone, out of rage? And you don't do it, cause you're afraid? It's all about fear. Fear of the law coming down, sure, but mostly fear like in sin. Sin with God. Yeah, almighty God. What if he ain't almighty?

Caeser (Dennis Hopper) ranting in *The Indian Runner*

What if he ain't sacred? You might as well have done the fella, right? Goodness [chuckling], maybe he never met fear.

Later, we return to the bar that night and Franky, set off by Caesar's cleaning of his brother Joe's blood from the bar, wails on the barman with a chair, in a bloody closure that is interspersed with the birth scene, two images that bring together Penn's words about 'ancestral sins, this hustled land [being] passed on by our fathers, and their fathers' (Kelly 2004: 242).

Caesar's ranting, complimented by Hopper's fixed-eye stare recalls a host of monologues, from *Blue Velvet* (1992) to *The Blackout* (1997); what Martin describes as 'a Beat poetry – or jazz music-inspired – way of breaking down and repeating the parts of a line in several phrases or sentences … and a wholly individual way of stretching out certain syllables or words in a phrase' (2007: 10). Hopper's photojournalist in Francis Ford Coppola's *Apocalypse Now* is the apotheosis of this stream of consciousness ranting, bringing to his role in *The Indian Runner* a ready-made association with filmic Vietnam.

As we have seen Hopper also played the real-life role as a photographer. Tony Shafrazi, in 'Double Standards: An American Education', positions Hopper in a lineage with Robert Frank's 'haunted, lonely scenes of an American landscape and life seen through the eyes of an outsider', Diane Arbus's 'shocking and neglected lives of dysfunctional and bizarre disparities' and Lee Friedlander's 'fragmented partial shots of the occasional stranger, the car, the road … In contrast Dennis Hopper's photographs are iconic images of a dynamic America at a crucial time of upheaval and change, infused and charged with rebellion and vitality. Populated with great figures, signs, and symbols, they celebrated the act and play of life glowing with natural light' (2011: 65–6). Shafrazi provides an encapsulation of Hopper's documenting of the 1960s in what could be an overview of *The Indian Runner*:

> Scenes of the changing times, a young couple dressed in unusual Northern California hippie-style outfits – the saintly look of a biker boy, wearing denim vest and handcuffs, soon to end up with a bullet in his head – a dignified moment between a biker couple – the mythic Brian Jones, James Brown, and all the upheaval and unrest leading to the March from Selma, Alabama. Black

kids holding American flags, demanding full employment, and the future presidency to come. (2011: 66)

Franky

Mortensen's Franky belongs to a lineage which includes figures from Robert Frank's *The Americans,* but also, as Tony Shafrazi suggests above, Dennis Hopper's photos from the 1960s, in particular his 'Biker Couple' (1961). Penn's producer Don Philips told Richard T. Kelly how

> Sean had a really interesting book of photographs from the sixties [*Out of the Sixties*] by Dennis Hopper, just plain ordinary folks across the country. There was a picture of a guy at a diner, with his hair up in the air, wearing a white shirt with the cigarettes rolled up in the sleeve and a tattoo on his arm. And Sean said, 'That's Frankie!'[sic.]. (2004: 242)

Replete with torso tattoos, lengthy quiff and sideburns, Mortensen belongs to a collection of similar figures across cinema, from Marlon Brando in *The Wild One* (1953) and James Dean in *Rebel Without a Cause* to Hopper himself in *Easy Rider*, performances that also link him to a history of acting that has been associated with the Method as it emanates from Konstantin Stanislavski and Lee Strasberg's Actor's Studio. For Brando this could involve talking with his mouth full, or with a matchstick in his mouth or utilising seemingly distracted moments and pauses.

As James Naremore points out in his *Acting in the Cinema*, 'the Method … seems most useful when it points to something at once broader and more specific than either [Marlon] Brando or the teaching of the Actor's Studio – that is, when it indicates a stylistic or ideological leaning within fifties culture, which has left its traces on contemporary Hollywood' (1988: 201). In exploring Brando's performance in *On the Waterfront* (1954), Naremore utilises three 'nonconformist patterns' that are useful in examining Mortensen's performance as Franky. These are the use of a 'naturalistic setting', 'the acting out of an existentialist paradigm' and a deviation from 'a classical rhetoric'.

Naremore locates the first of these in relation to a series of independently produced, post-World War II 'social problem' films, shot mostly on location and often directed by Elia Kazan featuring mostly Actor's Studio people (1988: 200). Naremore mentions *A Face in the Crowd* (1957), *A Hatful of Rain* (1957) as well as *Marty* (1955) and *The Sweet Smell of Success* (1957) but we could also include films that Sean Penn's father, Leo, acted in such as *The Best Years of Our Lives*, *Fall Guy* and *Not Wanted*. In some ways *The Indian Runner* reflects these social problem films although utilises a Vietnam 'coming home' narrative in order to get at the deeper, societal and cultural roots of violence.

The use of location shooting is important in this context in that *The Indian Runner* strives to imagine Franky in motion, unsettled and anxious not only in the world of mid-west Nebraska (place) but of 1968 America (time). Importantly for this discussion, Naremore draws on Raymond Williams' conception of 'naturalism' to emphasise how 'authentic naturalism' is opposed to mere 'bourgeois physical representation'; 'naturalism ... was always a critical movement, in which the relation between men and their environments was not merely *represented* but *actively explored*' (1988: 200, 201; emphasis in original). Penn's realist mode is utilised not only to critique masculinity in crisis but to critique this masculinity in relation to the conditions from which it emerges and is constrained – until it erupts in the figure of Franky.

A lengthy sequence prior to Franky's return to his home town provides a sense of foreboding for the collision of Frank with the forces of patriarchy and his own dislocation from the place and time in which he finds himself. Penn cross-cuts between four scenes to signal the collision between Franky's itinerate, restless violence and the staid, familial *ennui* into which he is being beckoned. Franky hotwires the Ford Mustang convertible of a couple attending a lavish Hawaiian-themed party, replete with lei necklaces, whole suckling pig and hula dancing, to which the sequence intermittently returns. Accompanied by Jefferson Airplane's affecting 'Comin' Back to Me', Franky drives around downtown in the stolen Mustang, robbing and assaulting a gas station attendant and then dousing the Mustang with petrol and setting it on fire by dropping a lighted lei on it in an industrial setting. Meanwhile Dorothy sits with her mother and father, watching *Gilligan's Island* on television, waiting for Franky to call.[6] The fourth scene has Joe sitting up in bed smoking, with Maria asleep beside him, watching footage of the Vietnam War on television. The fifth component of this sequence has Joe and Franky's father, in his basement, watching home-movies of Joe and Franky (dressed as a cowboy) playing, the shadows of the projector spools flickering over his face. Although we subsequently learn that this sequence leads to their father's suicide, it is mostly about setting out Franky's character, and what it will bring external to the kinds of familial, domestic environs imaged in the other parts of the sequence.

Our introduction to Franky occurs when he arrives early one morning after being discharged from service in the Vietnam War and breaks into Joe and Maria's home only to be confronted by Maria holding Joe's pistol. Later Joe presumes that Franky would want to visit their parents only to witness the first of many abrupt shifts that Franky brings to the narrative. On their way to their parents house Franky unexpectedly jumps out and commences a mock chase in front of Joe's patrolman car, then enlists the help of a group of children to rain snow-balls down on his brother and his car in a memory play of the brothers' own childhood. In a telling shot Franky is shown on the top of the hill – 'king of the mountain', as he calls himself. With a slight twist of the head he recognises the factory in the background and something shifts. Possibly responding to the factory's siren call (or the train whistle that accompanies the image) to stable employment and a stultifying life back in his hometown, Franky stumbles down the hill and collects his belongings. When Joe asks him what he is doing, Franky announces that he won't be coming to see their parents, that he isn't saying 'goodbye' but 'see you later'. When Joe asks 'where are you going, you got a place to stay?' Franky motions towards the freight train emerging in the background, and tells his brother that he's already taken $40 from his brother's wallet. This dialogue and shot/reverse-shot is interrupted by the car of an older townsperson segmenting the two brothers, obscuring Franky while Joe is congratulated on the 'good job' of apprehending the escapee in the opening scene. When the car moves on Franky says, 'You know, if I can figure out the difference 'tween what gets you a kiss on the ass and gets me locked up?' As Franky departs on the back of the train, Joe, in his narration, invokes the questions of identity that oscillate between him and his brother: 'I used to know my brother like I'd always know I'd be a farmer'; and 'in the last few years before going overseas Frank had become branded the hell-raiser of town. That he'd come to no good.' Against Joe's obdurate solidity, Franky is a wild, sinewy and explosive character, a renegade, 'hell-raiser', 'junk-yard dog' leaving as soon as he has appeared. Franky is the blue-collar spirit of Vietnam with its restlessness and displacement and the attendant forces of damage, violence and change.

Mortensen's Franky invokes another tragic Vietnam figure, his Lalin in Brian De Palma's *Carlito's Way*. Like Franky, Lalin has just returned from the Vietnam War, yet unlike Franky, Lalin is wheelchair-bound, destitute, unable to work, 'can't get it up, pisses in a bag' and resorts to wearing a wire for the police to attempt to arrest his old friend Carlito (Al Pacino). Lalin is not only physically defeated but morally as well, resorting to the betrayal of his friend, presumably for payment. Later Mortensen played Tom Stall, the owner of a smalltown diner, whose appetite and proficiency for killing erupts in David Cronenberg's *A History of Violence* (2005).

In returning to Naremore's second and third patterns, the 'existential paradigm' and 'the deviation from classical rhetoric', these are closely related and can be understood in relation to its two major practitioners, Brando and James Dean. Like the protagonists familiar from *The Wild One*, *On the Waterfront*, *Rebel Without a Cause* and *East of Eden*, Naremore states that these two patterns involve an inarticulateness born of 'an uneasiness with official language and no words for his love and rage' while the simmering emotion and deep-set violence are often set off by seemingly minor or unrelated events (1988: 201). Naremore quotes Fredric Jameson: 'the agonies and exhalations of method acting were perfectly calculated to render [an] asphyxiation of the spirit that cannot complete its sentence' (ibid.). Similarly, the use of mumbling, colloquial dialect and a kind of 'self-consciously loose body'. Naremore describes Brando, as a working-class or outlaw persona 'allowed him to mock the "good manners" of traditional theatre' (ibid.). These characteristics associated with the Method return in the character of Franky in explicit and uncompromising ways and are best exemplified in Franky's first explosive outburst redolent of Brando, of Hopper and of Sean Penn himself.

Later in the film Dorothy and Franky are having dinner in Franky's parents' home. Frank mentions that he has 'some squita' bites that need scratchin'' and 'how 'bout you and me go and fiddle with the hydraulics', to which Dorothy replies, 'Frank, don't talk like that', pushes his face and leaves his lap to sit back down to finish her meal. As Dorothy giggles and turns to Franky when she drops a pea from her fork, we cut to Franky's stone face signaling another abrupt shift in tone. Franky continues the silent, uncomfortably long stare until Dorothy says, 'Come on Frank, you're scaring me', which she repeats after Franky rises, points back to his left, holding Dorothy's gaze and leans, after taking a handful of peas, against a sink. With the camera over Dorothy's right shoulder, in mid-shot, Franky asks, 'Did I say the wrong thing?' and

Franky (Viggo Mortensen) explodes in 'the pea scene' from *The Indian Runner*

throws a pea at Dorothy. 'Is it you don't know me when I say something nice? You don't know how to see good things from bad things?' asks Franky, still throwing peas. 'That it, that we're strangers? We're not strangers.' Dorothy then says with tears in her eyes, 'Lets eat.' Franky moves into close-up in front of Dorothy puts a handful of peas in his mouth, chews and spits them at her before saying 'You eat', twice, while repeatedly spitting. As Dorothy breaks down crying Franky's face in mid-shot drops into a wide-eyed innocent look before he departs, leaving Dorothy in mid-shot covered in peas and crying 'Where are you going?' then telling her unborn child, 'It's OK, baby, he's just restless that's all.'

Immediately following this scene, through a direct cut to a man with a bloodied face being counseled by Joe's patrolman friend Randall (Jordan Rhodes), we witness the aftermath of the 'pea scene'. Franky is handcuffed to Caesar's bar, his victim trying to get back in to square up with Franky for 'blindsiding' him. The 'pea scene' also provides a link to the other, subtler aspect of the Method as it emanates from Brando's performance in *On the Waterfront* which is the 'introspective manner and a sensual delicacy and sweetness that are all the more attractive for the way they coexist to generate a remarkable sense of adolescent beauty and pathos' (Naremore 1988: 205). Naremore describes Brando in *On the Waterfront* in words that pertain to Mortensen:

> His shy but streetwise remarks, the sway of his walk, the absent-minded look in his eye as he chews gum, the way he sprawls on a pile of gunnysacks and flips through the pages of a girlie magazine – all these things function to establish him as a sort of child, in appealing contrast to the stereotypical and sententious 'adults' who surround him. (Ibid.)

Unlike Brando's solidity and muscular heaviness, we are constantly reminded of Franky's childlike, even feminine qualities. Mortensen is lithe, sinewy, fleet-footed and slippery, dancing in front of his brother's car, jumping freight trains, stealing cars, running through the cornfields, riding his boyhood bicycle around the high school grounds. These images are reinforced by the home movie footage of young Franky and Joe playing cowboys interspersed in the film and watched by their father before he takes his own life. In these ways Franky is a spirit figure, in motion.

Mortensen's performance contains 'the remarkable sense of adolescent beauty and pathos' that Naremore mentions, yet here it is more about Franky maintaining an adolescent resistance to the settling and subjectification of adulthood, more in tune with James Dean's inarticulateness and restlessness in *Rebel Without a Cause* than Brando. Mortensen's Franky is contrasted with David Morse's 'brother man' as it represents the Law, an acceptance of the patriarchal structures of family, work and community which Joe is comfortable with. Franky's momentary incorporation back into the fold of the town including his marriage to Dorothy and work at the construction site is short-lived until the imminent arrival of his and Dorothy's child leads to the explosion of violence that necessitates him fleeing town with his brother on his tail.

The 'pea scene' scene in *The Indian Runner* is like a masterclass in the acting style associated with the Method, in the tradition that Naremore points out: 'Newman in *The Left-Handed Gun* (1958), Beatty in *All Fall Down* (1962), Pacino in *Serpico* (1973), Stallone in *Rocky* (1976), Travolta in *Saturday Night Fever* (1977), Gere in *Bloodbrothers* (1978), or indeed any of Hollywood's proletarian sex symbols down to the present day (a more recent example is Sean Penn in *At Close Range* [1985])' (ibid.), which can be traced back to Brando in *On the Waterfront*. We could include more recent performances: Hopper's Frank Booth in David Lynch's *Blue Velvet*, Nicholson in *The Crossing Guard* and Penn in Clint Eastwood's *Mystic River*, among others.

In all this Mortensen's Franky, Bronson's father and Hopper, as Caesar, recall the eruptive violence associated with their own bodies of work, yet somehow their characters in *The Indian Runner* are not without the seething anger that Franky is unable to contain, rather, they are acknowledging and accepting of it, not so much in themselves but all around them, recalling Penn's own divining of American 'original sin'. In this regard Bronson as the father and Hopper as Caesar, are both survivors, yet both ending in violent deaths (Bronson's in a spectacular, bloody way) 'as if to reveal its originary bankruptcy' (Martin 2007: 34). This notion of 'original sin' is powerfully played out in the film's closure, cross-cutting between the graphic birth scene and the scenes which lead up to and include Caesar's death in the bar at the hands of Franky.

Sandy Dennis

In contrast to the masculine roles of Franky, Joe, their father and Caeser, Sandy Dennis's Mrs. Roberts draws on a lineage of performance, across film, television and stage, and genre closer to melodrama, although with a New Hollywood flavour and derived from the Herbert Berghof Studio and Actors Studio in New York. Dennis is best known for *Splendour in the Grass* (1961), *Who's Afraid of Virginia Woolf?* (1966), for which she won an Academy Award for Best Supporting Actress, *Up the Down Staircase* (1967), *That Cold Day in the Park* (1969), *The Out-of-Towners* (1970), *The Four Seasons* (1981) and *Come Back to the 5 and Dime, Jimmie Dean, Jimmie Dean* (1982). Dennis's Mrs. Roberts, like Hopper's Caesar, has little screen time yet her performance is memorable due to its intensity and idiosyncrasy. Producer Don Philips, in Richard T. Kelly's biography, states that Dennis was Penn's inspiration for the figure of the mother and that he wanted her for the role but was told she was dying of ovarian cancer, which she did in March 1992 (2004: 250). Her biographer Peter Shelley speculates that Dennis took the role because it was to be shot in Nebraska, her home state, a home she shared with Fred Astaire, Marlon Brando, Montgomery Clift, James Coburn, Henry Fonda, Dorothy McGuire and Robert Taylor (2014: 154). In *The Indian Runner*, Dennis's Mrs. Roberts appears worn out at the same time as she is on edge and anxious, waiting on the return of Franky, which doesn't eventuate. In 'Missing Sandy Dennis', Viggo Mortensen tells us of an eight-page scene between himself and Dennis:

> Frank is taken by Joe to visit their parents for the first time since returning from a three-year tour in Vietnam. Frank is ill-at-ease from the start, and we gather that his relationship with his parents is not a very good one. Joe tries to keep the peace, as is his wont, but Frank rejects their hospitality and attempts at small-talk, insults them and eventually storms out of the house. This is particularly devastating to his ailing mother, who dies not long after. (1995: 315)

Dennis's performance is suitably intense, appearing, initially, in a mirror hung behind a photograph of Franky holding a shotgun in one hand and a felled duck in the other. The camera pans across to the left, past figurines, a stuffed pheasant, rifles on the wall and a Christian religious tapestry, before settling on her lowering herself onto a chair, eyes closed, mouth quivering, low noises, catching her breath, accompanied by the film's theme on piano. She is suitably dowdy, in pearly earrings and navy blue cardigan over a patterned dress. This twenty-second or so shot is interspersed with the scene where Joe and Franky are travelling through town and immediately prior to the snowball scene mentioned above. In her next scene, after Franky has jumped the freight train to avoid meeting his parents, Dennis, now with Charles Bronson and David Morse, continues the nervous, stumbling performance before she and Morse return to the lounge setting close to the previous scene where she commences a monologue as a rejoinder to Joe's explanation of Franky's sudden departure: 'I just thought he hated cops.' She responds, 'Don't, don't, say that.' She says directly into Joes' eyes as they both sit facing each other on a couch: 'Listen to your momma … you are a good man. You hear me? You are a good man. That don't exempt you from a time when you're going to have to kill a man. Can't regret it. If it hadn't been him, it might have been my son. No sir, no sir. Don't you regret it. You just keep saying the serenity prayer and you get on with…' The emotion catches her breath and Penn cuts to a close-up of Joe's hands cupping hers. This scene of thirty seconds or so is given further emphasis by a fade to a slow-motion aerial shot gliding over snow-covered ground and deciduous forest, as Joe narrates, 'We didn't hear from Frank for a good six months, when our lives took a turn', as the camera pans down a church spire with bells ringing on the soundtrack. A funeral procession enters the sunlight and Joe and his father are carrying a coffin with others. The brevity of Dennis's appearance, compared even to Hopper's, is disproportionate to the role Mrs. Roberts plays in the relationship between the brothers, accentuated by Dennis's halting, hesitant lines, given extra emphasis. Walter Kerr is quoted by Peter Shelley, describing her delivery:

> she has developed a habit of treating sentences as though they were poor crippled things that couldn't cross the street without making the false starts from the curb, breaking in midflight, shying back in terror, starting over bravely, hesitating in the middle of the traffic … what she's doing is jaytalking, and it's illegal. (2014: 21)

Like Hopper and Bronson, Dennis brings to this performance an intimacy and domesticity gleaned from deeply emotionally interior figures in the likes of *Who's Afraid of Virginia Woolf?* and *That Cold Day in the Park*, terribly house-bound roles where stultifying locales intensify the character's lives and interrelations. In Penn's film this intensity is reconfigured as familial love, echoed in Joe's nuclear family and in contrast to the outsider figures of Franky and Caesar.

Sandy Dennis's presence alongside Valeria Golino's Maria and Patricia Arquette's Dorothy provides some respite from the repressed (Joe) or exploding masculinity of Franky, Caesar and Mr. Roberts. These feminine characters also, in Penn's worldview, provide hope in a world assailed by modernity. While Mrs. Roberts represents a domestic world away from the bars, jails and flophouses of Franky's life, Maria and Dorothy are also figures of transcendence. Maria gives language (and life) lessons to her Mexican clients such as Miguel (Benicio Del Toro) and brandishes the gun when Franky arrives at the house; and Dorothy gives birth to her and Franky's child which, although it is inter-cut with Franky's murder of Caeser and his fleeing town pursued by his brother, is ultimately a figure of hope, for a new chance at life.

Notes

1 Christopher Connelly tells us that Penn's then fiancée at the time of *Nebraska*'s release, Pamela Springsteen, Bruce's younger sister, facilitated the approach to her brother, to make a film from the song, 'Highway Patrolman' (1991: 62).
2 Sean Penn also directed the music video for Springsteen's song 'Highway Patrolman' which is a version of *The Indian Runner* edited down to 5 minutes 40 seconds. Springsteen also contributed the song 'Missing' to the credit sequence of the soundtrack of Penn's *The Crossing Guard*.
3 Robert Bashlow and Tuli Kupferberg's *1001 Ways to Avoid the Draft* (1966) was a satirical pamphlet republished with illustrations in 1967 by Grove Press. This is the version used in this scene.
4 Crews dedicated his book *Scarlover* (1992) to 'my main most man, Sean Penn'.
5 Bronson was born in in Ehrenfeld, Pennsylvania, in the Allegheny Mountain Coal region just north of Johnstown.
6 Dorothy's name, of course, invokes Victor Fleming's *The Wizard of Oz* (1939) and the phrase 'there's no place like home' that attends that figure.

CHAPTER FOUR

The Crossing Guard

> The continual reconstruction of the city as a movie set has been reciprocated by the cinema's use of the city as a set, so that over the city's places are superimposed the shadows of their roles in old movies and new shows.
> – David E. James (2005: 9)

Penn's second feature, *The Crossing Guard* from 1995, is, like *The Indian Runner*, an interior-focused narrative, utilising, in the main, Brentwood, San Pedro and Long Beach in California. It also presents one of the strongest images of hope in Penn's oeuvre. Freddie Gale (Jack Nicholson) has been waiting for John Booth (David Morse), the drunk driver who killed his daughter, to be released from jail so that he can kill him. At his second attempt, Booth leads Gale on journey by foot and bus across Los Angeles, to Emily's grave, which Gale, due to his grief, has been unable to visit. As they both kneel at the graveside, Gale takes Booth's hand and Booth whispers, 'Here comes your daddy, he needs your help.' With these lines the camera cranes up to take in a Los Angeles cityscape, projecting the reconciliation of the protagonists onto the city, as a larger, societal concern.

    The Crossing Guard belongs to a tradition of imagining Los Angeles, including that city's *film noir* tradition as well as the Los Angeles films of independent maverick John Cassavetes. The primary cast members – Jack Nicholson, Anjelica Huston and David Morse, who appears in both *The Indian Runner* and *The Crossing Guard* – provide links to a host of roles and associations in New Hollywood cinema. *The Crossing Guard* can also be understood as a remake of Cassavetes' *The Killing of a Chinese Bookie* (1976), as well as being influenced by the work and figure of LA novelist and poet Charles Bukowski.

Jack Nicholson

In the previous chapter we saw how Dennis Hopper, Charles Bronson, Sandy Dennis, Viggo Mortensen and others provide links with other personas, performances, films and written texts that, in turn, contributed to the intertextual web which holds down the rendering of the places of Omaha, Nebraska and Columbus, Ohio. Jack Nicholson's performance in *The Crossing Guard* brings to his role of Freddie an extensive career emerging from the New Hollywood of the 1970s. In his films *Easy Rider*, *Five Easy Pieces* (1970), *The Last Detail* (1973), and in Roman Polanski's *Chinatown* (1974), which is quoted in *The Crossing Guard* and also concerns the rendering of Los Angeles as place, Nicholson developed a complex acting style, which is useful in examining his role in Penn's film.

Despite the significant presence of David Morse as John Booth, Penn's film is dominated by the performance of Nicholson as Freddie Gale. While *The Indian Runner* featured a more balanced couple of central performances from Morse and Mortensen, Nicholson's Freddie is magnetic, partly to do with the power of the role, a depressed, anxiety-ridden, violent alcoholic unable to recover from his daughter Emily's death at the hands of Booth, leading to the demise of his marriage to Mary (Anjelica Huston) and his relationship with his twin sons (Michael and Matthew Ryan). He is in limbo, waiting for Booth's release from prison, to resurrect himself. Nicholson brings to Freddie a host of previous roles that are major contributions to the New Hollywood that impact this film.

While Dennis Hopper and Viggo Mortensen, as we have seen, can be understood with recourse to the Method, this is only part of the story with Nicholson. Although he undertook some training, as James Naremore points out, alongside James Dean, Paul Newman, Bruce Dern, Al Pacino and Jane Fonda, in Lee Strasberg's version of the Stanislavksi System, Nicholson, across the 1960s and 1970s, developed one of the most distinctive styles in post-war cinema (1988: 198n). While in later films, such as

Freddie Gale (Jack Nicholson), masculinity at the breaking point in *The Crossing Guard* (1995)

Batman (1989), *Mars Attacks!* (1996), *A Few Good Men* (1992), *As Good as It Gets* (1997) and *The Departed* (2006), Nicholson has developed a formidable, larger than life, self-referential style, something Dennis Bingham in *Acting Male* calls 'ironic, self-aware' (1994: 115), his earlier films are marked by a naturalistic style as outlined by Naremore and examined in the previous chapter in relation to Viggo Mortensen.

In developing his study of Nicholson's straddling of New Hollywood and classical Hollywood filmmaking in this period, Bingham turns to Bertolt Brecht's theory of epic theatre in relation to Hollywood, whereby Nicholson 'italicizes the idea of himself as actor and of his characters as actors' (1994: 100):

> Nicholson's characters often mistake performance for competence. Since competence, the ability to get things done, is key to male subjectivity, their identities depend on role-playing of the sort that masculinism generally represses and displaces onto woman. One of the functions of most film acting, like that of classical realist film, is to mask signs of its artifice. For the actor this actually means masking the mask, making stylization appear real. What Nicholson does is to deny the 'naturalness' of masculinity and stress the mask. (Ibid.)

This 'paradoxical' style, according to Bingham, arises where Nicholson 'superimpose(s) awareness onto an unaware character ... dramatizes, acts out, misrecognition, in that a little man thinks that his gender gives him special powers and abilities' (ibid.). He extends this notion further, arguing that by 'performing "masculine" aggressiveness, rituals, and self-presentation, Nicholson turns an individual man into a representation of "Man" ... breaking down unitary masculinity, in Brechtian fashion ... with the paradoxical result that the coherence of the character is in fact shown by the way in which its individual qualities contradict one another ... emphasizing the character as a social and narrative construction' (1994: 101). In this regard Nicholson's performance, as part of Penn's cinema, can be understood in the lineage of the social problem film to which we saw *The Indian Runner* belongs. In *The Crossing Guard*, Penn's social problem is the masculinity that lies at the heart of the film.

As Bingham recognises, this invocation of Brecht in relation to a performance in what is ostensibly a Hollywood film, or at least a film that sits astride indie cinema and Hollywood, is problematic but is instructive in considering the degree to which Nicholson's style simultaneously articulates a naturalistic and an ironic masculinity. As we will see, this is particularly instructive in relation to Nicholson's performance of Freddie, in relation to Morse's John Booth and Huston's Mary. Bingham again:

> Nicholson then becomes a subversive force in 1970s films that adhere basically to the classical narrative paradigm but at least imply criticism of the dominant order, often largely through Nicholson's highly prominent role-playing. [...] It can be said that Nicholson's initial Hollywood films, *The Last Detail* and *Chinatown*, set up a dialectic between the modernism of Nicholson's performance and the classical cinematic form that parallels the dialectic between subversion and restoration of gender and race issues ... when he speaks of trying 'to drip

acid in the nerves' [Rosenbaum 1986], he seems out to alienate the audience from the class complacency reaffirmed by classical film while still 'immersing' them in an affecting diegetic experience. (1994: 107)

Not only is Nicholson's performance redolent of an ironic masculinity, the characters that he plays also contribute to the awkwardness we feel in this 'affective diegetic experience'. Freddie Gale stumbles his way through his life trying to negotiate the space between, on the one hand, his depressive, anxious, alcoholic self, mourning for the loss of his child and family, and, on the other, his determination, his drive, to kill John Booth. This space between the two recalls the gulf between the performance of masculinity, that Freddie can carry off, and the competence that is said to define masculinity. Freddie, embodies all the hallmarks of a masculine figure at breaking point, constantly attempting to manage a façade of control, at the same time as it escapes his grasp. In this schema the killing of Booth, as an end game, a goal to be achieved, a masculine competence whose consequences are undetermined, is understood by his character to be a way of resolving his crisis and to 'to be a man', as he says. But in his mission to exact revenge for his daughter and family, Freddie is woefully inept.

In the scene where he visits Booth's parents' house (accompanied on the soundtrack by Dead Can Dance's 'The Ubiquitous Mr Lovegrove' – 'I thought you knew it all / well you've seen it ten times before / I thought you had it down / with both your feet on the ground'), Freddie displays both sides to his dilemma. Penn sets this up with a few simple shots complimented by Nicholson's performance. In the blue wash of night, Freddie approaches Booth's suburban house to search for him. Freddie's approach is smooth and silent accompanied by Jack Nitzsche's *noir*-like atonal strings and tinkling piano. Unable to enter the house due to the locked front door (which shouldn't be a surprise), he moves around to the space between the house and a trailer home. In long-shot with his back to the camera, he looks in the window of the trailer and, it seems, locates Booth's whereabouts. As Nicholson turns to face the camera in long-shot and pulls his pistol, the film cuts to a close-up on the gun, pans up to a close-up on Nicholson's face in slight profile across the frame of which he moves his head, following his eyes to the door of the trailer. Penn then cuts back to the long-shot as Nicholson raises his left hand to the door handle with the pistol in his right. As he opens the door, Penn cuts on this action, to a shot of the inside of the trailer into which Nicholson falls with the music raising in volume to an abrupt stop. The sound switches to diegetic location effects, and Freddie, groaning, awkwardly crashes on to the floor. Penn cuts to Booth peering at the comic spectacle over his blanket from his bed. Freddie then jumps to his feet, puffing and sweating, raising the pistol, which misfires. His face drops, exclaiming 'God dammit!' as he reloads. He misfires again. 'God dammit. Fuckin', fuckin' thing's empty!' We cut to Booth as he slowly moves his right arm across from his bed asking, 'Alright if I get a cigarette?' We cut back to Freddie, legs apart, left arm raised, crouched, half lit from the light entering the door, pointing his unloaded gun at Booth. In the same shot Booth raises himself carefully to sit on the side of the bed, turns on the lamp, which allows us to see his hulking physique and asks, politely, 'Would you mind closing the door? I don't want to wake my parents.' The next cut back to Freddie in mid-shot has Nicholson, sweating profusely, eyes shifting side-to-side, mouth soft and slightly open mumbling ('wake his fuckin' parents') as he obediently shuts the door, still holding the unloaded pistol, while Booth nonchalantly lights a cigarette. As Booth commences his monologue – 'When the thing happened…' – Freddie, in mid-shot, stares at the pistol in his hand in disbelief, lowering it in a sign of realisation, shaking his head, then gripping and shaking it in two hands sucking air between gritted teeth. As Booth continues – 'I didn't want your forgiveness' – Nicholson sets into the familiar expression, his head tilted down, a slight frown and mouth ajar, an expression of incredulity. He then raises the gun again, briefly, then concedes and lowers it to the floor, out of shot, until Booth gets to his feet and walks toward Freddie, emphasising his large chest and arms, to which Freddie, almost hysterically, raises the pistol and retreats to the back corner of the trailer. Booth responds reassuringly with 'It's alright, sit down' and, after a pause, more firmly, 'sit down'. With Booth standing, Freddie, in close-up, still pointing the gun, lowers himself, self-consciously, now looking up to Booth, mouth agape, as Booth tells him, 'I'm not going anywhere. I'm not calling any cops. I'll just be here. Trying to get on with things. Would you maybe take a couple of days and, maybe, think about not taking my life?' Freddie then responds, in characteristic pointed and eccentric manner. 'Look, I'm a jeweller. I got a jewellery store. That's all I got. That's it. That's what I am. Do you understand what I'm talking about?' Booth replies 'I think I do.' Freddie snaps – 'Shut up, because you don't understand' – and, pointing the gun, yells 'You don't!' Booth calmly replies 'Alright.' Freddie rises to his feet and points the gun again, remembers it's not loaded and lowers it, then says 'I'm gonna' give you three days', then, emphatically, 'Three days' and as he leaves mumbles, 'Maybe I can remember the fuckin' clip for this gun, son of a bitch.'

In this scene Booth quickly imposes a masculine air, shifting the tone of the encounter with his prison-honed muscularity, even-toned voice and deliberate manner, slightly mocking Freddie by asking permission to get a cigarette from a man with an unloaded pistol. In relation to Booth, Freddie is slapstick comical, his mood, his masculinity, like his eyes and body, swinging widely as if he is unable to reconcile the way he had always imagined this encounter with the way it eventually plays out. This scene also delays the narrative drive of the film in that Freddie and Booth have to wait three days before Freddie can come back to kill Booth. This delay sets the film up to enter into a series of vignettes or episodes where Penn delves further into Freddie's relationships with Mary, Vera, Mia and others.

Anjelica Huston

Nicholson's and Penn's construction of masculinity, following Bingham, is not only done in relation to the figure of John Booth, as a means to extend 'into a representation of "Man" … breaking down unitary masculinity' but also in relation to his former wife, Mary. Played by Anjelica Huston, the casting invokes a past, a history, in the film's diegesis, but also, instructively, points outside of the film to the real-life relationship between Nicholson and Huston which had ended just prior to the shooting of *The*

Crossing Guard, as well as Huston's own belonging to a Hollywood dynasty, stemming from her father John Huston which opens up a plethora of further intertexts. The demise of the real-life relationship between the film's protagonists, played out against the production, brought to the film's release an aura that can be understood in relation to traditions in melodrama. In an interview with Richard T. Kelly, Huston describes the shoot, tongue in cheek, in a manner recalling a film narrative:

> Jack and I had split up some two or three years previous. So for me … well, it was a choice [laughs]. There are a couple of things you can do with bad endings: you can try to remake them a little or you can put them away. But one of the blessings of what I do for a living is that it can be very cathartic: it can give you a new way to look at things. I thought it was an audacious idea, and that Sean would be a trustworthy person to do it with. Plus, the part contained sufficient vitriol on my character's part – and Jack's – for it to be playable, and resonant. It was a passionate part, someone who'd been abandoned – by her daughter, by her husband. And I knew about that, on several levels. So I thought, 'Yeah…'. (2004: 276–7)

Huston's recognition here, of how her relationship with Nicholson would be 'resonant' for audiences, and how her role, as Mary, would provide for a kind of retribution, or, at least, a therapeutic aspect to the shoot, displays a remarkably nuanced awareness of her figure in popular culture as well as the manner in which her real-life history is taken up in the film.

Having emerged from a number of minor roles in *The Last Tycoon* (1976), *The Postman Always Rings Twice* (1981) and *Frances* (1982) to become an Academy Award winner for Best Supporting Actress in *Prizzi's Honor* (1985) and be critically feted for her role in *The Dead* (1987), Anjelica Huston's Lilly Dillon in Stephen Frears' *The Grifters* (1990) sets in train a figure that sits in a nexus of public persona, roles and

Mary (Anjelica Huston), a stoic, time-worn figure in *The Crossing Guard*

the Hollywood star system that flows into her performance as Mary in *The Crossing Guard*.

Huston's Mary is a stoic, time-worn and fatigued figure against which, like John Booth, we consider the figure of Freddie. Huston, we might recall, comes from Hollywood royalty, courtesy of her father John, screenwriter, actor and director of *The Maltese Falcon* (1941), *The Treasure of the Sierra Madre* (1948), *Key Largo* (1948), *The Asphalt Jungle* (1950), *The African Queen* (1951), *Beat the Devil* (1953), *The Misfits* (1961) and *Wiseblood* (1979) as well as *Prizzi's Honor* and *The Dead* that featured his daughter. Huston was also a character actor in *Casino Royale* (1967), *Candy* (1968), *Myra Breckinridge* (1970) and *Chinatown*. In the popular press, much has been made of Anjelica's relationship with her father, her long-time partner Nicholson and her performances. David Thomson sums up Anjelica Huston's persona:

> Tall, strong, forthright, gentle and so incidentally handsome, she seems more a subject for Matisse, say, than a cultured smear of attractiveness waiting for a lens. The beauty comes out of her life, casually; it does not surround it or intimidate it. The camera has never quite caught this yet; she may be a little impatient being photographed or not comfortable watching the results, one does feel she is more interested in life, and that larger curiosity and impatience will only look better as she grows older. (1990: 28)

In this world-weariness, Huston brings to her roles a similar understanding and experience that Thomson identifies in her public persona. He explains a particular scene from *The Grifters*:

> Huston's character, a small-time character, is tortured by her boss in punishment for a mistake. He has to do it, to keep up appearances: he burns her hand with a cigar. What is most terrifying is the ordinariness, the way she accepts the necessary fate and talks to the man afterwards – small talk. (Ibid.)

In response to Thomson, Huston characterises this scene, in what could be a description of her role as Mary in *The Crossing Guard*:

> This is my father; this is my life. My character doesn't come through in my part of the operation – these are the rules, this is the game I play. When I mess up, that's it. […] It's not like he burns my hand and I run off into the blue horizon. This guy's on her like a tick on a dog. Given the situation, rats will behave accordingly. Finally, the fox will eat off its own paw to get out of the trap. We see it up in Harlem, where the seven-year-olds are selling crack to support their mother's habit. It's everyone who's struggling to stay out of the soup. (Ibid.)

In this regard Thomson understands Huston's persona in relation to the figure of her father, telling us 'at 40, John Huston was a lean, gangling, ugly, attractive, battered kid still. Before he died, he could have played the wisest man on earth, pitched somewhere between benevolence and iniquity, Anjelica Huston might reach a point where her face knows so much, it is frightening' (ibid.). This transfer of her father's maturing to her own persona could include her long-term relationship with Jack Nicholson, whom she was with from the early 1970s when Nicholson fashioned himself out of those New Hollywood roles, in particular his Jake Gittes in *Chinatown*, a film in which John Huston performed his most acerbic and resonant role; that of the patriarch Noah Cross. Uncannily *Chinatown* also drew substantially on Huston's early directorial works for the figure of Gittes, in particular Humphrey Bogart's roles as Sam Spade in *The Maltese Falcon* or Frank McCloud in *Key Largo*. In a 'life imitating the movies' vignette characteristic of David Thomson, we are told of an encounter:

> There was a day early on in her relationship with Nicholson when Anjelica visited the set of *Chinatown*. [Huston continues] 'Oh, that was the day I showed up and Dad said, "Come and sit down." Polanski was there and Jack and my father. And I sat down, being lunchtime, and my father looked at Jack and said, "Have you been sleeping with my daughter ... Mr Gittes?"' (1990: 32)

This inclusion of Anjelica Huston in a joke about Nicholson's character Jake Gittes' relationship with Evelyn Mulwray (Faye Dunaway), and to her father's character, Noah Cross's, incestuous relationship with Evelyn, his daughter, further complicates the intertextual nexus that surrounds *The Crossing Guard*.

This nexus is also invoked in Penn's film with a reference to *Chinatown*. As the cat and mouse routine has John Booth being chased by Freddie across Los Angeles, along freeways, main and back streets, through houses, including a child's bedroom, Booth leaps up on to a high fence, Freddie fires at him and he drops into a culvert full of running water, before recovering, in slow-motion, and continuing to lead Freddie in the chase.

In *Chinatown*, after Hollis Mulwray's (Darrell Zwerling) body is found in the spillway of the Oak Pass Reservoir and, he learns from the mortician (Charles Knapp), that Leroy Shoehart, the 'local drunk ... drowned too', Gittes visits the largely dry LA River bed right under Hollerback Bridge where Shoehart was found. Gittes discovers from a boy on horseback (Claudio Martinez) that the water, 'when it comes, it comes in different parts of the river'. Gittes returns to the reservoir at night and is shot at. As he hides from the gunman, water hurtles down the culvert, washing him up against a cyclone fence. He manages to climb the fence and escape drowning. It is immediately after this scene that 'the Man with the Knife' (Roman Polanski) – or 'the Midget', as Gittes calls him – and Mulvihill (Roy Jenson) appear and try to warn off Gittes by slashing his nose in the most infamous scene in the film.

The Crossing Guard's unexpected reference to *Chinatown*, in particular the subtext that motivates Polanski's film, the conspiracy to fraudulently obtain the water rights to Los Angeles by Noah Cross and his cronies, is a textual interlude that further draws on the John Huston, *film noir*, Jake Gittes, Freddie Gale, Jack Nicholson, Anjelica Huston, Los Angeles emplacement intertextual net that involves *The Crossing Guard*.

With this in mind it is possible to return to the figure of Freddie Gale, comparing him to the luckless figure of Jake Gittes.

In what could be a description of Freddie Gale, Dennis Bingham tells us, 'nothing could better describe the self-image of Nicholson's Gittes, a careful, self-confident, glib detective who dresses immaculately, parts his (sparse) hair down the middle, and does business in a smartly furnished office, with Venetian blinds ... "that were just installed on Wednesday"' but by the end of the film, 'the cool Gittes is shown up as a kind of prize fool, with virtually every deduction he's made proved disastrously wrong' (1994: 127). While Freddie is less of an investigator of events than a jeweller with a single-minded strategy to restore things to their correct order by killing John Booth, he is just as powerless, at the mercy of the events he finds himself in, despite his quest to control these circumstances with his single-mindedness. In *Chinatown*, as Bingham points out, Gittes is subject to the overwhelming figure of Noah Cross, who, like John Booth, overwhelms his attempts at masculine assertiveness, as we saw in the trailer-home scene. 'Huston's screen presence,' Bingham writes, 'is so overwhelming that it almost obliterates a strong personality like Nicholson' (1994: 132). While Bingham argues that the confrontation between Cross and Gittes is a matter of 'duelling male egos', which it may be in narrative terms, it is also the weight of film history that overpowers Gittes. Nicholson's performance of a detective in 1930s Los Angeles unavoidably recalls Bogart's Sam Spade and he can't compete. Following this intertextual logic, Nicholson's Gittes is just as much a 'mask' as Bingham terms Nicholson's style, but this time, a Bogart mask that sits between him and his performance of Gittes. In the same way, Nicholson's Freddie incorporates his own Gittes, and as we have seen, opens up a portal to *Chinatown* at the same time as it seeks an engagement with the localised, vernacular Los Angeles, in particular its majority location shooting and the myth of the city's origins as its subject.

Another film that is concerned with the life of Los Angeles, involves a protagonist of a strip club, a journey across town to commit a murder and several set pieces that are recalled in *The Crossing Guard*, is Cassavetes' *The Killing of a Chinese Bookie*. Cassavetes is a significant model for Penn's directorial work, having, like Cassavetes in the 1960s and 1970s, negotiated acting in some of the biggest films of the 1990s and 2000s while managing to direct his own films at the edge of Hollywood. Penn's early script workshopping with Cassavetes in an earlier incarnation of the Nick Cassavetes-directed *She's So Lovely* (1997) and his later influence on the production of that film, including his performance, and that of his then wife Robin Wright Penn, who also appears in *The Crossing Guard*, provides a more direct link to that director's work. Before pressing on with a comparison between *The Crossing Guard* and Cassavetes' cinema it is useful to look again at the opening of Penn's film.

The Crossing Guard's interest in the localised, intimate stories of Los Angeles, is announced by the opening of the film, or more correctly, by the way in which the film avoids announcing itself, directly, as a film concerned with a 'generalised' Los Angeles. It also indicates the activist, pragmatist dimension of the film. The 4:39-minute title sequence features cross-cutting characteristic of Penn's cinema. The opening six-second shot is an extreme red-lit close-up of a flaming torch moving over a dancer's leg before fading to black. This image is accompanied by an audible hum until it is overlain with the voice of a woman in a group therapy session: 'To lose an 18-year-old brother. He didn't get a chance to graduate from high school. It was a blow. It destroyed me. It made me feel like … [cut to an extreme four-second close-up of a lit cigarette in a person's hand, and fade to black] I was afraid to love anybody. I was afraid to let people get close to me [cut to a frame of three women's faces in close-up, the central one in focus, talking] … I felt like if I loved somebody, deeply, like I do my family, they would be taken away.' Mid-sentence the camera pans up to a extreme close-up of Mary (Angelica Huston) in profile with her finger between her lips before fading to black. The sequence returns to a four-second shot of the red-lit dancer now lying on her back in a nightclub passing the flaming torch over her naked chest, with a dancing pole and downlights and a few men at tables in the audience in the background until it fades to black. This image is accompanied by the orchestral theme of the film which continues until the 'Miramax Films Presents' title appears with a black background which fades to black, followed by a three-second medium close-up of the dancer, this time sidelong in the frame, bent backwards moving her hands over her torso before fading to black and 'Jack Nicholson' appears as a credit, fades to black, then is followed by the dancer in a three-second extreme close-up moving the lit torch between her breasts up to her neck before again fading to black. The film's title follows.

The next sequence emerging from the title sequence continues this cross-cutting between the strip-club and the group therapy session in longer shots. As *The Crossing Guard* title holds on screen, the soundtrack cuts to a masculine voice belonging to the strip-club comedian Sunny Ventura (Richard Sarfian) telling a joke before cutting to a medium close-up: 'Where did you learn to do that? She says, "I've been practicing on an old flame for 16 years"'; and 'Look at this guy here. He's looking at me and beating his meat. I like that. And there she is … Miss America 1912. Ina. Alright, comes here every night. Right sweetie? Right? Come here let me have a kiss.' The woman says 'Let me at him,' to which he replies 'Somebody throw a net over this broad.' The shots in the strip club focus on the men, in close-up, that inhabit a particular booth including Freddie (Nicholson), Coop (Bobby Cooper), Silas (Jeff Morris) and Buddy (Buddy Anderson) in a smoky, dim-lit, blue-hued interior, while the therapy session is captured utilising close-ups and extreme close-ups in bright fluorescent light with crowded frames and a variety of angles with several participants speaking, often over each other's images.

Penn cuts directly to a group shot of the men in the booth laughing at Sunny's antics as a voice from the therapy group begins before cutting to the face of one of the members. 'The Steve I've always known was 18. He, um … [cut to woman speaking] was killed by a drunk-driver, just a month before he was to graduate.' The sequence cuts to a shot of Bobby (John Savage) and holds in close-up while another woman begins talking. 'It's alright when you have two policemen come in and say "your daughter's dead". I open the door and I saw them there and I said "Mandy's dead isn't she?"' We then cut to a close-up of Mary over which the woman continues, 'A mum knows.'

Penn then cuts back to the club as a dancer in pink and blue lighting enters the stage to dance to Adam Ant's 'Room at the Top' intercut with a couple of scenes of customers at the club before cutting back to the booth where Coop says 'Freddie's coming over here [Freddie enters the frame] ... you better slide in.' The comedian Sunny slides into the booth from the left next to Freddie as the camera pans back to include both of them in the frame and cuts to the other men. The banter between the men continues along the lines of 'How would you like to spank her?'; 'Yeah, but softly.' Sunny begins his story in profile while the men, including Freddie listen. 'You know my wife Joan. We got a step down to our living room. It's like two steps down so the bitch doesn't want to walk. She wants me to raise it. She don't want to walk down two steps.' Penn cuts back to a close-up of Bobby in the therapy group, partly obscured in the frame and the first woman in the group, who is then in close-up, continues '... its something you have to work with on a daily basis'. As we cut to Bobby, he commences a monologue in response to this first woman, turning his head upper frame right. He is framed with two others. 'He's not going to come back. It's yours. It's like your body. You've lost something inside, or something of yourself.' This direction also includes Mary who is framed upper right with Booby out of focus in the left foreground before cutting to a reverse-shot of Bobby over Mary's shoulder just as he says the film's signature lines, 'I miss me'... [extreme close-up of Bobby] 'It's five years now. I look in the mirror. Where's Bobby? My family drives me up the fuckin' wall.' The editing then returns to Mary fuller in the frame, with a slight zoom, upper left with Bobby in the left lower out of focus. 'But they still think I'm me, Bobby' [cut to a woman and man in close-up followed by another woman in profile then back to Bobby in close-up, speaking to screen right]. 'They joke about it. They call me sibling number three. Right. And its like a nick-name for Bobby depressed' [cut to extreme close-up of second woman]. 'It's my older brother Danny that we lost and he was sibling number one. And did they forget, I don't know.' Over this last sentence Penn fades to a direct close-up of Freddie in the booth drawing on a cigarette with the title 'The Father' in the lower left of the frame in a deep blue light. As he turns to his right, Bobby's monologue continues over the image of a naked dancer, in eyeline match, placing dollar notes into her nipple ring. 'I'm gone.' Bobby says. We cut back to an extreme close-up of Bobby as he says 'I miss me.' Penn cuts to a close-up of Mary with a tear rolling down her cheek and the title 'The Mother' in lower left of the frame. The shot holds as Bobby asks emphatically, 'Who's running this fuckin' place?'

These scenes maintain an interiorised coupling of realist modes that stall the films opening on to narrative, delaying the 'establishing shot' of the film until nearly twelve minutes into the film when we see Booth, with his parents, re-enter Los Angeles signaled by a freeway sign.

This use of two realist modes operates as a kind of dialectic that motivates the whole film. The images and dialogue of the group therapy session, according to Angelica Huston in her interview with Richard T. Kelly, were taken in a Mothers Against Drunk Drivers meeting:

> It was a real MADD meeting. These people agreed to conduct it as such and to allow us to shoot. Very upsetting. But then my mother was killed in a car

accident, so I didn't feel entirely bogus being in that room – not that she was killed by a drunk driver, but I could relate. Sean just shot it as you would a documentary, very simply, very quietly; one barely noticed the camera and yet it was moving around as people were speaking. And it was solemn, quiet, intense… (2004: 277).

One way to understand the MADD meeting scenes within Penn's oeuvre is as a reflection of the Omaha sequence of *The Indian Runner* where Penn asked his camera operator to film the extras 'unawares' after yelling 'cut', yet in relation to the strip-club scenes it recalls the cinema of John Cassavetes, in particular his *Faces* (1968) in its raw, crowded frames and overlapping dialogue in relation to the club setting which recalls *The Killing of a Chinese Bookie*.

In close-ups, overlapping dialogue (in the main monologues) and dialogue at a variance to the images, the MADD scenes Penn has reproduced the documentary feel of Cassavetes' cinema. While Penn inserts documentary footage and sound into his narrative film, he has also inserted the narrative, via Mary and Bobby's participation in the documentary of the MADD therapy sessions. In this way *The Crossing Guard* not only remakes *The Killing of a Chinese Bookie* but it also seeks to remake Cassavetes' oeuvre.

George Kouvaros, in *Where Does it Happen?: John Cassavetes and Cinema at the Breaking Point*, draws on Jean-Louis Comolli in describing the means by which we can understand the documentary feel, the relationship between its documentation and its fiction. For Comolli, Kouvaros states, direct cinema, particularly Richard Leacock's films such *Chiefs* (1969), relied on a process of uncovering the truth through 'a model of operation and exposition' (2004: 58). For Comolli, this presumption of a hidden truth available for the makers of direct cinema to be able to reveal is not only unsophisticated but (recalling Jean Rouch) disallows a more intricate notion of truth which is available through the self-reflexive documentary well aware of, and including, in its own representation, the means by which these events are being represented:

> For Comolli, Direct Cinema is no longer understood as a means to uncover or gain access to the real. It is framed as actively engaged in the production of its own specific meanings and effects. In 'le detour par le direct', a two-part article published in February and April of 1969 (in *Cahiers du cinéma*), Comolli describes this change in the way cinema relates to the events it records in terms of a shift from a process or reproduction to one of 'reciprocal production': 'Through direct cinema the point is reached when the cinema is linked to life according to a system, which is not one of reproduction, but of reciprocal production so that the film … is simultaneously produced by and produces the events and situations.' (2004: 60)

For Comolli and Kouvaros, this 'reciprocal reproduction' involves the 'moment of mutual implication when the process of filming acts upon the material it records and is, in turn, acted upon and constituted by this material' (2004: 61) as Comolli proposes.

According to Kouvaros, Comolli proposes that *Faces* is an example of a 'nonidealist, reflexive Direct Cinema', pointing to the constraining environs the characters find themselves in, they 'put on a show' (2004: 63) or a performance about the issues that confront their lives, or, we might say, *Faces* is a document of a fiction, each of these components impressing on each other.

This notion of 'mutual implication' is played out in the MADD scenes that open *The Crossing Guard* but in a different manner to *Faces*. Penn's film relies on the documentary effect (following Anjelica Huston's affirmation above) of the therapy session not so much to 'life according to a system ... of reciprocal production' but more specifically to 'one of reproduction'. The scene is staged in a documentary manner, with non-actors performing their roles as real-life, second-order victims of drunk drivers. This allows for two things. First, these actors link the whole film to a real-life political and social issue, the Mothers Against Drunk Driving advocacy group, utilising the structures of Direct Cinema connecting the scenes to the history of observational documentary that Comolli and Kouvaros address. Second, in inserting Anjelica Huston (as Mary) and John Savage (as Bobby) into the documentary-like scenes it also contaminates the documentary effect with fiction. In this way these scenes, interspersed as they are between the scenes of Freddie and his buddies, connect the documentary-like footage, in a dialectical manner, to the masculine world of strip clubs and booze. This non-too-subtle dialectic, we know, is to be played out across the ensuing drama, as a kind of response to the question Bobby poses: 'Who's running this fuckin' place?'

The insertion of actors Anjelica Huston and John Savage into the otherwise documentary-like scenes also allows for a distinction to be made between what the film understands as reality and as fiction, or more precisely, melodrama. As we have seen, it is not until well into the scene that we happen upon Mary's face, a jolt which results from the delay in its appearance amongst the other faces present in the scene and our knowledge of Huston's visage. In this scene, Huston's face is knowing, stoic and tearful. While Savage's is a face less familiar than Huston's, it is nonetheless recognisable as an actor's, and therefore non-documentary. The distinction between documentary and fiction in this scene, is, as we have them linked, by the title 'The Mother', screen bottom left, with 'The Father', screen bottom left, providing a clue to the response to Bobby's question as well as the relations that form the drama about to unfold.

The Killing of a Chinese Bookie

Nicholson's Freddie physically resembles Ben Gazzara's Cosmo Vitelli in Cassavetes' *The Killing of a Chinese Bookie*, in his open-neck shirts and suits, his gold jewellery, slicked-back hair and sideburns, and constant imbibing of alcohol, as well as his nervous motion, his constant comings and goings.[1] While Cosmo is the owner of the Crazy Horse West nightclub, Freddie is a regular at Sunny's, to the point where, like Cosmo, he is well known to the other regulars as well as the girls and staff who work at the strip club. Penn's Sunny also has a mirror in Cassavetes' Sonny (Salvatore Aprile). At the same time, Nicholson's performance recalls another Freddie, that of Fred Draper as Freddie in Cassavetes *Faces*, in his intonation, particularly the pauses between lines that Nicholson has come to make his own, as well as the timbre of voice; a thin, nasal, sound with deeper, serious tones and accentuated 'r's in his pronunciation.

Settings

In their semantic elements, both films oscillate between downtown Los Angeles and the suburbs, maintaining an interiority to the worlds of the films, largely absent of location establishing shots such as aerial or grand city shots. While the Crazy Horse West in Cassavetes' film is bathed in a red light and peopled with groups of men and women, overall Cassavetes' film adopts a distinct blue tone for the night-time exteriors and for the entrance-way to the Crazy Horse West. The club in *The Crossing Guard* is doused in blue light, as are the night-time exteriors, the club a contemporary location (if slightly dated representation) for the date of the film's release in 1995. Sunny Ventura's club is largely blue-lit, darker and sinister, featuring a more masculine crowd. While the Crazy Horse West features an odd mix of pantomime and striptease, Sunny's club is predominantly 'straight' striptease to contemporary 'new wave' music. Both

Freddie (Jack Nicholson) from *The Crossing Guard* mirroring Cosmo Vitelli (Ben Gazzara) in John Cassavetes' *The Killing of a Chinese Bookie* (1976)

films feature location-shot exteriors, the opening of *The Killing of a Chinese Bookie*, with Cosmo arriving by taxi to The Melting Pot café mirrored in Freddie's long walk through the jewellery district to his shop. Both films also use *noir*ish lighting and settings when the protagonists are journeying to their shootings.

Narrative

As examples of the syntactic variations between *The Crossing Guard* and *The Killing of a Chinese Bookie*, both films feature their protagonists, Freddie and Cosmo respectively, setting out across town to shoot men; Cosmo to kill the bookie and Freddie to kill Booth. Both films also feature extended sequences where the protagonists venture out with three female companions, one of whom is a girlfriend. Freddie takes three girls from Sunny's club – his girlfriend Verna (Priscilla Barnes), Jennifer (Jennifer Leigh Warren) and Tanya (Kellita Smith) – out to a bar recalling the extended sequence in *The Killing of a Chinese Bookie* where Cosmo takes girlfriend Rachel (Azizi Johari), Sherry (Alice Friedland) and Margo (Donna Gordon) to the Ship Ahoy casino which ends in tragedy when Cosmo loses all his money and racks up a debt of $23,000. Similarly Freddie's night out with the girls ends in him being jailed for starting a fight in the bar when Joe (Joe Viterelli) tries to join his group. Both films feature a freeway scene, where the cars of Cosmo and Freddie, both on their way to commit murder, are stopped on a freeway. Cosmo's car breaks down with a tyre blowout, which he abandons and calls a taxi. Freddie is pulled over by the police for driving erratically, is tested for driving under the influence of alcohol, and before he can be detained, grabs his revolver and runs to kill John Booth.

Film Noir

These night scenes, in both *The Killing of a Chinese Bookie* and *The Crossing Guard* have a distinct *film noir* style, shot through with blue tones, asphalt and men alone on their missions to murder. After picking up the hamburgers from the bar, Cosmo is shown in a shadowy suburban street while the laneway to the bookie's house is also lit with streetlamps, Cosmo's figure a mere shadow against the entrance to the compound. As Cosmo walks toward the compound, key lights shine from above and rear, throwing a strong shadow ahead of him. As he feeds the dogs, he is almost totally in shadow and remains so through the red gate into the dark stillness of the compound, lit from below and side in a classic chiaroscuro effect.

In *The Crossing Guard* after Freddie has fled the police, the soundtrack is a cacophony of strings, jazzy saxophone and urgent drum effects. The images of Freddie running from the police down an alleyway and across a cyclone fence to a suburban streetscape is captured on a wildly swinging camera frame and handheld shots. Almost immediately Freddie breaks into a house full of shadows and dull-lit surfaces until he seeks refuge in a child's bedroom. After this interlude, while the police search for Freddie with helicopters and spotlights, he moves along a drainage culvert against a concrete wall, shown in close-up, back-lit and sweating profusely. An image of a helicopter spotlight and a police car, stop lights on, drenched in blue light and a dog barking in the distance completes these *noir* traits. As we have seen, this kind of style alludes to *Chinatown* but also more broadly to the *film noir* cycle.

In *Film Noir and the Spaces of Modernity*, Edward Dimendberg points to New York and Los Angeles as two of the iconic *noir* cities, tracing a Cornel Woolrich/Raymond Chandler diad in representing these cities. For Dimendberg this tradition of imaging the West Coast city is emblematic of a 'uniquely Chandlerian approach to the space of Los Angeles', particularly in films such as *Murder My Sweet* (1944), where 'the action of the film is inflected by Los Angeles, where the boundaries between interior space and the metropolis remain permeable' (2004: 167–8).

> The city serves as a character or agent throughout his fiction, its isolated particulars derailing the reader from the plot. Juxtaposing long shots and close-ups, Chandler's prose functions as akin to cinematic montage by alternating different scales and perspectives. Had they never been adapted for the screen, his narratives still would remain illustrious screenplays of twentieth-century Los Angeles. (2004: 167)

These words could also be a description of *The Crossing Guard*, particularly the chase scene that stretches from Freddie's meeting with Mary, to his encounter with the police, his confrontation with Booth at the trailer and on to the Children's Cemetery. It is difficult to trace the geography of this journey. Can Freddie have chased Booth from downtown LA to the Forest Lawn Memorial Park where the Children's Cemetery lies? Is it possible to view the docks of San Pedro from Forest Lawn? Part of these questions is to do with the compartmentalised nature of Los Angeles, what Dimendberg terms its 'centripetal space' following Fredric Jameson's characterising of Chandler's work as reflecting the 'logic of modernism' (2004: 166). Penn's goes to great lengths to include locations as disparate as the suburban greenery of Mary and Roger's house, Freddie's dark, oppressive apartment, the Jewellery District, the docks of San Pedro, Sunny's downtown (it would seem) nightclub and a downtown diner where Freddie and Mary have coffee.

Melodrama and Family

At the time of *The Crossing Guard*'s release much was made of the scene where Nicholson and Huston face off in a diner in the small hours, just prior to Freddie heading off to kill John Booth; in the main, due to it being understood in terms of bravura performances and the subject of the discussion being the breakdown of a relationship, of fiction imitating life. There is an earlier melodramatic scene that brings together the film's deepest themes in a simple confrontation between these two actors. A significant difference between Penn's film and Cassavetes' is the way in which Penn uses melodrama in an inverse way in *The Indian Runner* and *The Crossing Guard* and *The Pledge*, particularly the domestic setting, redolent of family and middle-class values, to criticise the outside figure of Freddie in relation to John Booth and Mary.

In another dialectic favouring Penn's neo-traditionalist ideals, Freddie's apartment, with its black patterned wallpaper, black satin sheets and dim lighting is contrasted with Mary's light-filled suburban house. At the same time Booth's parents Stuart and Helen (Richard Bradford and Piper Laurie), in a reflection of the roles of Mr. and Mrs. Roberts in *The Indian Runner*, represent the domesticity of the nuclear family from which Freddie has been estranged. To get at the ways in which Penn articulates this suburban ideal, recalling Sandy Dennis's role in Penn's previous film, utilising the signs of melodrama, it is useful to look closely at the scene where Freddie unexpectedly drops in to visit Mary and Roger (Robbie Robertson) and Freddie's children.

The scene opens with an extreme close-up of a finger pressing a doorbell button, and cuts to a shot of a green glass door with the figure of Freddie behind it. Another figure in the foreground opens the door to Freddie in sunglasses and suit with a verdant, sun-filled garden and house with a breeze moving the branches of the trees behind him. The second figure greets Freddie, 'How's it going?' to which Freddie responds with a firm 'Roger, good to see you.' Roger asks Freddie to 'come in' and closes the door before leading Freddie in to an open-plan kitchen/dining area with a mix of light and shadow marked out on the rear wall. Freddie sidles up to the side of the area against a shelving area containing a European-looking ceramic figurine in a boat with a duck amongst family photos. Freddie gestures and, over a close-up of his hand and the figurine, says 'Emily really loved this thing.' As we cut to a close-up of his face he continues in a weary voice and expression, 'We used to keep it over there on the counter', using his eyes to suggest both the direction and disappointment that it is now in another position. 'Stretch her whole body out trying to reach it. Last joint on her little finger.' He then bounces on his toes, sighs and look down in discomfort. There is a shot/reverse-shot sequence between Freddie and Roger, in silence, and then a cut to a shot of both characters in a mid-shot, both with their hands in pockets looking at each other uncomfortably. Freddie grins with embarrassment and asks 'What?' Roger replies 'Nothing' as he moves out of shot left. 'Come sit down, Freddie,' he asks out of shot. Freddie looks back to the figurine and to where Roger had been standing and moves across frame left towards Roger, picking up a framed photograph in both hands saying 'Boy, you really look like a natural family, you could be their father,' before sitting down next to Roger on a couch. We then cut to a close-up of the photo over Freddie's shoulder. It is a photo of Mary, whom we know as 'The Mother' from the opening sequence, Roger and two small boys. Freddie comments, 'Spectacular looking family, really.' Roger uneasily asks, 'Um … what can I, ah, do for you, ah.' Freddie replies, 'Well, I really came to see Mary.' Roger says, 'Well, I don't mean to be nosy Freddie, but, what about?' Freddie – 'Well I'd rather talk to Mary about that.' Roger – 'well'; Freddie – 'well, well, well.' Penn cuts back to the two men sitting on the couch in mid-shot, Freddie holding the photo, grinning, and Roger, facing screen left, also grinning. Roger asks again, 'Can I get you something to drink?' Freddie replies 'No, no.' We then hear a key in a door and Freddie points in that direction stating 'Well, maybe they're here.' Roger rises toward the sound of people, leaving Freddie on the couch. Nicholson raises his eyebrows with a mock grin on his face as we cut to Mary entering the area with shopping in her hands and the two boys from the photo behind her. The boys call out 'Hi Dad, Hi Freddie!' as Roger moves across the room to kiss Mary, dressed in a suit, white top and pearl earrings and necklace. Mary and Freddie exchange looks as Freddie rises from the couch and walks toward her, carrying the photo and replacing it on the sideboard. He puts his hands back into his pockets and continues over to Mary. 'This ... my own kids call me "Freddie",' and continues to Mary, in a two-shot sequence, saying 'You look wonderful.' Mary replies, 'Wonderful, I think, would be pushing it.' Freddie says 'No, you do, you look wonderful.' 'Thank you,' she says.

As she moves frame right and around behind the kitchen bench Mary asks, 'So, how's business?' As the camera follows her Freddie replies 'So-so.' As she opens cupboards to put away the groceries Freddie says, 'Its only a jewellery store, what can I say, business. What about you, still doing real estate?' Mary – 'Well, it's a tough market right now, I'm still representing some properties. But Roger's been doing so well, I've been able to back off a little ... spend more time with the kids.' With the mention of Roger's name Freddie jumps a bit, recovers his composure and grins to himself then looks at the floor commenting 'Wonderful, that, yep, that's um, really um, really wonderful.' Freddie sighs, collects himself, takes a deep breath and commences: 'Um ... um, Mary there's something you should know, the reason I came here.' Cut to close-up of Mary looking concerned, holding Freddie's gaze and replies 'Freddie?' Freddie – 'I've got something I wanna' tell you.'

> Mary – 'You made me a promise, I hope you're going to keep it.'
> Freddie asserts himself holding up two fingers and holding the tension in his mouth.
> Freddie – 'I made you a promise. That's one. And I have great news. That's two. Now you gonna' let me speak or not?'
> Mary – 'I'm sorry, what's your great news?'
> Freddie – [nervously] 'It's really great news. It's spectacular news, I'm telling you. You wanna' hear it or not? Are you sure, are you ready? He's out, John Booth is out [grinning] I'm gonna' kill him.'
> Mary – [moving towards Freddie] 'Get out of here, Freddie, get out!'
> Freddie – 'I'm not going anywhere until I see you courageous enough to tell the truth.'
> Mary – 'The truth? What truth, Freddie? You promised you wouldn't.'
> Freddie – 'Wouldn't what, Mary? Mention our daughter, why? So you can blackmail me?'
> Mary – 'Blackmail...'
> Freddie – 'If I ever, ever want to speak to the mother of my children I must never mention my daughter.'
> Mary – 'Get out of our house.'
> Freddie – 'My house, by any natural law this is my house.'
> As he walks back toward the sitting area stabbing the air with his fingers, he fans his arms out to the side in exasperation.

Freddie – 'If my children live here, my children, then who's to say I can't come here to see them any fuckin' time I want to?'
Roger – [appearing in the doorway] 'You had to do it didn't you, huh?'
Freddie – [shouting] 'Nobody's talking to you!'
Mary – 'Do you want me to call the police?'
Freddie – 'Call whoever the fuck you want!'
Mary – 'Where do you get off calling them your children? You haven't been a father to those kids. You stopped with our daughter.'
Freddie – 'Emily, is her name.'
Mary – 'Yes, Emily, Emily, and she is dead…'
Cut to Freddie, eyes pained, eyebrows raised and mouth tense.
Mary – '…but I owe those two little boys up there all the love I've got and it kills you that I can give it to them and you can't.'
Freddie has his back turned, nods and then marches toward Roger and Mary, furious. Roger steps in front of him and Freddie grabs him in a headlock behind his back while he pushes Mary.
Freddie – 'Tell me the truth, you want me to kill John Booth?'
Mary – 'Let go of him…'
Freddie – 'That's my job in life and your job is to go on like nothing has happened!'
Mary – 'Let go of him!'
Freddie sneers, grimaces, his face strained across his jaw and teeth.
Roger – [muffled, out of frame] 'Why don't you let me go? I'll make us some coffee.'
Freddie stares into Mary's eyes until he lets Roger go and relaxes.
Freddie – 'Yes, I'd like some coffee.'
Roger – 'Why don't we all sit down and have some coffee and talk about this civilly'.
Freddie – [mid-shot, half obscured by Mary's shoulder] 'You know what, I don't want any coffee. I don't like coffee, it makes my heart, you know…' [thumps his chest and walks out of frame].
Mary – 'You just said you wanted coffee.'
Roger – 'Are you sure?'
Freddie – 'Yes, no, I, ah, I'm gonna go' … [breathes deeply]… 'I feel good.'
Freddie walks out of the room towards the front door. Roger then walks around to comfort Mary. They are hugging when Freddie re-enters the room pointing, and addressing Mary:
Freddie – 'I just want to say this. I've done a lot of things for you. You know, a lot of things. And I think it's cheap of you that you won't hear me out on things… [pleading]…I really do.'
Roger – [comforting Mary] 'Mary's just upset.'
Mary – 'Excuse me, I'm not upset, and if you think I'm gonna' keep score with you on who's done what to who then you're very fuckin' wrong. And if you think that's cheap then fuck you. Now I don't know whether you're serious

about killing this man or not but I do know this, it has nothing to do with our daughter. Our little girl is gone, Freddie, and she's not coming back not matter what you do. You've never been to the cemetery Freddie. You've never even been to Emily's grave'.

Freddie – [through gritted teeth] 'Why? Because I didn't go to your little party. Your funeral. In my own time, Mary. In private.'

Mary – [shaking her head] 'Oh, really? Then you're a braver man than I thought… [accusingly] What's the inscription on the stone, Freddie?… [the camera slowly zooms in on a sullen Freddie]… 'What colour is it? Is it on a hill? Is it under a tree? Does it lay flat or does it stick up out of the ground?'

The slow zoom in continues as Freddie shakes his head, rocking on the balls of his feet as chiming notes enter the soundtrack. Cut to Mary with a tear running down her face, shaking her head.

Mary – 'That's what I thought.'

Freddie – 'Roger, man to man, when you two read in the newspaper that John Booth has been shot dead, will you look into her face, and tell me if you don't see pride and relief? Pride and relief, Mary.'

Freddie leaves, Mary and Roger embrace as the camera pans frame right and down to the figurine within a dream sequence with rocking shadows and a child's hand activating a mechanism. The figurine moves its head and foot, the camera zooms in further as a chorus of nursery rhyme-like whistling increases on the soundtrack, undercut by a few deep bass notes which link to the next sequence commencing with a distorted image of a stripper dancing, soaked in red light, replete with an Eastern-sounding music track.

This scene is comparable to an early scene in *Faces* where Freddie and Richard 'Dicky' Forst (John Marley) accompany Jeannie (Gena Rowlands) back to her house where the two men compete for Jeannie's affection. After some time Jeannie returns from changing into 'something more comfortable' and Freddie greets her with his rendition of 'I Dream of Jeannie with the Light Brown Hair', which all three sing while dancing and holding each other. As he comes to realise that Jeannie and Dicky are becoming closer, Freddie's tone shifts as he asks Jeannie how much she charges, implying she is a prostitute. While both Dicky and Jeannie attempt to restore the festive mood to the party, they all come to realise that the moment is lost and Freddie leaves. This scene, particularly the shift in mood between three characters facilitated by Freddie's outburst, is like a number of scenes in *The Crossing Guard* where Nicholson's Freddie, due to a small trigger, shifts his tone and that of the scene, to a point where it cannot be recuperated. In some ways, Cassavetes' Freddie is also a similar character, unable to deal with the forces that dominate him.

This scene with Freddie, Mary and Roger, while it recalls the kind of interplay between characters and the abrupt emotional shifts we see in Cassavetes' cinema, can also be understood in relation to theories of melodrama, another set of genre conventions that are utilised in Penn's cinema, as a means to get at the deep cultural and historical forces which underlay his films. *The Crossing Guard*, like all his films, and in the tradition of the social problem film, delves into the cultural forces which motivate its characters, giving rise to the narratives.

One of the ways in which this scene draws on the family melodramatic tradition is early on, where Freddie fixates on the figurine that was Emily's favourite. This scene, along with the suburban, verdant outlook and the sunbathed, spacious living area, includes the bourgeois crowded shelves of photos and knick-knacks. These symbols are harbingers of loss for Freddie, recalling the domestic spaces of *The Indian Runner*. Thomas Elsaesser states:

> Pressure is generated by things crowding in on them, life becomes increasingly complicated because cluttered with obstacles ... and objects that invade their personalities, take them over, stand for them, become more real than the human relations or emotions they were intended to symbolize. (1972: 13)

Penn re-emphasises the way that the grief of Emily's death is embodied in the figurine, and how this has 'taken over' Freddie's life and personality, by ending the scene with a slow-motion image of the figurine accompanied by the nursery rhyme-like whistling and then the cut to the stripper bathed in red light. In this instance Penn, none too subtly, draws the comparison between the figurine, an image of Emily's death, and the depiction of women in the strip club. In the schema of Penn's social problem cinema, what lies at the heart of the problem is the alcoholic, sexist, repressive nature of American masculinity.

As we have seen, Penn's films are primarily concerned with masculine, outsider figures striving to find their way in the modern world. But these figures are also understood in relation to the figure of the family, often represented by a character, such as Joe in *The Indian Runner*. As Elsaesser states:

> The family melodrama ... though dealing largely with the same Oedipal themes of emotional and moral identity, more often records the failure of the protagonist to act in a way that could shape the events and influence the emotional environment, let alone change the stifling social milieu. The world is closed and the characters are acted upon. Melodrama confers on them a negative identity through suffering, and the progressive self-immolation and disillusionment generally ends in resignation: they emerge as lesser human beings for having become wise and acquiescent to the ways of the world. (1972: 9)

In *The Crossing Guard* Freddie is waiting for John Booth to be released from prison so he can kill him and release the grief that has imprisoned him in a life of loneliness, darkness, bitterness and alcohol. Booth too is looking for a way to heal his guilt which impedes his ability to return to life after prison. In what Steve Neale sees as a 'blockages, barriers and bars to the fulfillment of desire' (1986: 12), both men are blocked from achieving their goals. Freddie's comic/tragic attempt to kill Booth in the trailer-home with an unloaded gun is one example of this, as is the perceived lack of support he receives from Mary in his quest and being arrested for drunk driving on the freeway on his way to kill his daughter's murderer. John Booth is blocked from laying flowers on Emily's grave by the presence of Mary and her sons and from forming a relationship with Jojo (Robin Wright Penn), who provides him with a choice when she says to him after they have made love, 'Your guilt is a little too much competition for me. You should let me know when you want life.'

In both cases, in what could be seen as dramatic, rather than melodramatic resolutions, these men take journeys to heal themselves which Booth combines to provide the solution. His leading of Freddie to the Children's Cemetery at Greendale is initially a resolution of his guilt and Freddie's grief by taking both men to visit the grave they have both previously been unable to visit. It is also another blockage to Freddie's quest to kill him, a quest that eventuates in the shot that grazes Booth's neck, a quote from *Chinatown* more than a serious intention to murder. While this scene provides a resolution to Freddie's grief and Booth's guilt, their isolation and loneliness, not to mention Freddie's crimes, still remain.

In Penn's schema, drawing on Cassavetes' dramaturgy, the scene at Mary and Roger's house, with its emotions rising and falling, and rising again, is melodramatic, even though its violence is comic, alongside Freddie's childish return to the scene after the tensions have dissipated. But these are not just melodramatic effects but another way in which Penn draws the many dialectical relations put into play by the film's intertextuality into this climactic scene. Elsaesser spells this out in what could be an appropriate description of the scene:

> The emotional extremes are played off in such a way that they reveal an inherent dialectic, and the undeniable psychic energy contained in this seemingly so vulnerable sentimentality is utilized to furnish its own antidote, to bring home the discontinuities in the strictures of emotional experience which

Emily provides hope to John Booth (David Morse) and Freddie (Jack Nicholson) in *The Crossing Guard*

give a kind of realism and toughness rare if not unthinkable in the European cinema. (1972: 12)

The film's dénouement is also transformed by Penn's use of the final crane shot to extend what are basically melodramatic sentiments out onto, following Rorty, a communitarian, pragmatic image of, first, the Los Angeles cityscape, and then onto an image of the docks and harbour of San Pedro, replete with the dedication to Bukowski. The first is the strongest image of hope in Penn's oeuvre with the two men seeking forgiveness from Emily who lies in her grave at their feet. It is also an image of the future, the two men, holding hands on a hill overlooking the metropolis. As the second image replaces the first, the cranes and docks of San Pedro come into focus, with the dedication, 'For My Friend Henry Charles Bukowski, Jnr. I miss you. – SP', honouring the port's most famous inhabitant.

Charles Bukowski

In novels such as *Post Office* (1971), *Factotum* (1975), *Women* (1978) and *Ham on Rye* (1982) and collections of short stories such as *Erections, Ejaculations, Exhibitions and General Tales of Ordinary Madness* (1972), *Notes of a Dirty Old Man* (1973) and *South of No North* (1973) and books of poetry such as *Dangling in the Tournefortia* (1981), *Hot Water Music* (1983) and *War All the Time: Poems 1981–1984* (1984), Bukowski fashioned a distinct individualist, outsider worldview.

Penn and Bukowski's friendship, as Howard Sounes in *Charles Bukowski: Locked in the Arms of a Crazy Life* tells us, evolved from Penn's interest in playing the writer after reading the screenplay to *Barfly* (1987), a film based on Bukowski's life featuring his alter ego, Henry Chinaski:

> When he saw the *Barfly* screenplay, he was so enthused about the film that he offered to play Henry Chinaski for the minimal fee of one dollar. He loved Bukowski's writing, and began composing poems of his own. His only stipulation was that Barbet Schroeder relinquish the director's chair to *Easy Rider* star Dennis Hopper, a good friend of his. (1998: 207)

Bukowski and Schroeder declined Penn's offer but Penn became close friends with Bukowski, as well as with Mickey Rourke who would play Chinaski and whom he would cast in his next film, *The Pledge*. Bukowski is another outsider author who became fast friends with Penn, like Harry Crews, as mentioned in the previous chapter.

Penn's closing dedication is more than a personal note. It is another means to keep *The Crossing Guard* grounded in the life-ways of Los Angeles, to the life, stories and poetry of Bukowski, whose work depicts the everyday working life, bars and streets in what Tamas Dobozy has called 'dirty realism' (2001: 43). However, it is possible to see an earlier reference to Bukowski. In a scene at the strip club, Mia (Kari Wuhrer) emerges on stage in a kewpie-doll dress, bow in her hair and holding an oversized lollipop and dances to Shirley Temple's rendition of 'The Good Ship Lollipop', which Coop provides a kind of narration to: 'This is what I hate. I hate this fuckin' number. I timed it. Takes four or five minutes to get the flash off before we can see a little titty. And in the meantime I gotta' listen to this music. I hate this fuckin' number.' Freddie, drunk and swaying replies, 'I like it. It's traditional. Without tradition, new things die.' His friends reply in consternation, '"New things die"? The son of a bitch's a poet. A jeweller poet. First goddam' jeweller poet I ever saw, a Jew jeweller poet.' Freddie then leans in to one of the men and says, 'I'm gonna' kill a guy.' Mia then calls from the stage, 'Freddie, come dance with me!' while taking her dress off. Urged on by his friends and the crowd, Freddie takes the stage to perform a drunken, awkward dance while trying to follow Mia's lead in side-steps and a swing around a pole.

This scene represents Penn's reimagining of *The Killing of a Chinese Bookie*, with Charles Bukowski as its protagonist. The appearance of Mia in a kewpie-doll dress, singing the Shirley Temple song, recalls the pantomime/burlesque of the Crazy Horse West while the figure of Freddie in this scene, as a 'Jew, jewellery poet', reconfigures the Cosmo character as a regular, alcoholic customer of the bar, and a poet, like Bukowski's, character Henry Chinaski and Bukowski's own public persona.

Bukowski represents a romantic masculine, left-leaning, proletarian figure, not unlike Penn himself, whose representations of Los Angeles, are generally localised and alcohol-fuelled and probably not too far from the Beats. Elizabeth Young puts it well:

> Wet rings on bar counters; the swish of the barman's dirty cloth, rotgut whisky and paint-stripper wine. Misanthropy. Despair. Women with big swaying bottoms and very high heels. A touch of misogyny. Barflies, bums, floozies... (Quoted in Madigan 1996: 447)

For Penn it is also about bringing together the very personal, a close friendship, with the kind of storytelling he was attempting in *The Crossing Guard*, although Penn's worldview is tempered, as we have seen, by hope in the future.

Note

1   It is also worth noting that Leo Penn performed alongside Gazzara in Elia Kazan's theatre production of *Cat on a Hot Tin Roof* in New York City in 1955.

CHAPTER FIVE

The Pledge

> Whenever a good child dies, an angel of God comes down from heaven, takes the dead child in his arms, spreads out his great white wings, and flies with him over all the places which the child had loved during his life. Then he gathers a large handful of flowers, which he carries up to the Almighty, that they may bloom more brightly in heaven than they do on earth.
> – 'The Angel', Hans Christian Andersen

In *The Pledge* (2001) Jack Nicholson plays Jerry Black, a retiring police officer who, on his last day, becomes involved in the investigation into a child murder that he comes to believe is the work of a serial killer. Having discovered a cartographic pattern in the murders, he buys a gas station, and eventually, it seems after the case has diminished, takes in a young mother, Lori (Robin Wright Penn), and her daughter, Chrissy (Pauline Roberts). Jerry eventually comes to suspect a local preacher and sets a trap for the killer using Chrissy as bait. When Lori discovers the trap (after we discover that Jerry had suspected correctly) and her daughter's involvement, she disowns Jerry, leading to his apparent breakdown. The film ends with an aerial shot of Jerry, some time later, as a mumbling alcoholic, alone in the run-down, disused gas station.

The Pledge uses distinct location shooting in British Columbia to render a Nevada of forests, mountains and lakes, which Penn termed a world at once coherent and distinct. Penn has described his divergence from the screenplay:

> The Kromolowsky version was set in a *Fargo*-esque landscape: flat, white lakes. It lacked religion to me. I wanted a much more vertical landscape. And I was trying to locate it in a real place to me, which would be the Sierras, where you had flatlands and mountains. For economic reasons we scouted Canada, and I found

places that looked right. I did a rewrite on the script that made me feel like I owned it by the time I was going – I'd convinced myself of that, anyway. (Penn quoted in Kelly 2004: 370)

At the same time Penn employs a host of performers, such as Vanessa Redgrave, Mickey Rourke, Harry Dean Stanton and Sam Shepard, fairytales, intertexts and remakes to, again, utilise a personal cultural web that constitutes the elements of this film and his oeuvre.

Adaptation

Penn told Terry Lawson, 'when I was making *The Crossing Guard* with Jack [Nicholson], I saw he was always reading thrillers on the set to relax. I knew I wanted to make another film with Jack and that started me thinking about making a thriller. So I asked my business partner Michael Fitzgerald to look for something that would be, uh, suitable' (Lawson 2001). Fitzgerald brought Penn *The Pledge: Requiem for the Detective Novel* (1958) by Friedrich Dürrenmatt because it represented a work that Lawson calls 'something beyond by-the-numbers suspense, and even beyond the usual definition of a thriller' but also 'whose recurring themes of injustice, guilt, revenge and helplessness mirror those in Penn's original screenplays for his first two films, *The Indian Runner* and *The Crossing Guard*' (ibid.). Penn originally brought in Jerzy Kromolowski and Mary Olson-Kromolowski to write a screenplay based on the novel. Jerzy Kromolowski followed up this screenplay with another for Bertrand Tavernier's *In the Electric Mist* (2009), an adaptation of James Lee Burke's *In the Electric Mist with Confederate Dead* (1993). Burke is another distinct location-based writer. Like Dennis Lehane or George Pelecanos's use of place, as we have seen, Burke is best known for his use of Louisiana in his Dave Robicheaux novels.

Penn also sent Nicholson a copy of Dürrenmatt's *The Pledge*, and later the screenplay. Nicholson recalled the difference between the two to Richard T. Kelly:

> When Sean brought me the Dürrenmatt book, I read it and I told him, 'I don't see any movie in this Sean.' Because I had read so many. And the novel's a flashback: we know the cop is now a derelict. That's an easy adjustment to make in a film – you just don't make it a flashback, end of problem. But because of the flashback there isn't a lot of suspense in the novel. Then when I read the script, I felt there were a lot of strange things in it that could have gone a lot of ways, and if I feel that reading something, then I always think that's the way an audience will see it. So I thought, 'Oh, all right, I see that there's a *difficult* movie here. But there *is* a movie.' And then I read an essay that Dürrenmatt had written about writing the novel. He wrote it in reaction because he was furious with the form – the way the good man follows the clues and inevitably catches the bad man. Given the tough existentialist that Dürrenmatt is, he was aesthetically offended by this completely dominant aspect of the form and wrote the book in rebellion, really. So this is the one where the good guy follows the clues, he's

right; and then he doesn't get the guy, and he's the one who is punished. So that in itself gives it a certain literary uniqueness. (2004: 367)

It Happened in Broad Daylight

Here Nicholson may be referring to what is said to be Dürrenmatt's dissatisfaction with the screenplay he wrote, with Hans Jacoby and Ladislas Vajda, for Vajda's *It Happened in Broad Daylight*, a Spanish/Swiss/German co-production from 1958, that, according to Theodore Ziolkowski, was envisioned as

> a warning for parents about the dangers of sex crimes against minors. In the film the monomaniacally persistent detective, who makes a promise to the murdered child's parents, sets a trap and ultimately captures the murderer. But Dürrenmatt was uneasy with this neat conclusion, Accordingly he rewrote the story with a different ending: the murderer is never caught and brought to justice but is killed in an automobile accident: Matthau, the brilliant detective who has given up his a career and tried for years to entrap him, thinks he has failed and drinks himself into oblivion. (Ziolkowski n.d.)

Ladislas Vajda was a Hungarian-born film editor, art director, writer of screenplays and director who made films from the 1930s to the 1960s in many countries including Hungary, Germany, Portugal, the United Kingdom and Spain. His best known directorial works alongside *It Happened in Broad Daylight* are *The Miracle of Marcelino* (1955) and *The Man Who Wagged His Tail* (1957).

The title sequence of Vajda's production of *It Happened in Broad Daylight* states that the film is based on a novel by Friedrich Dürrenmatt. It has Inspector Matthäi (Heinz Rühmann), an obsessive and highly regarded detective, preparing to take up a position in Jordan to restructure the police force there. As he is preparing to leave he receives a phone call to tell him that a peddler that he once convicted for a minor offence, Jacquier (Michel Simon), has requested his presence in Mägendorf, a small Swiss village where the mutilated body of child, Gritli Moser, had been discovered by Jacquier in the forest and who has been subsequently charged with the murder. Matthäi accepts the request and travels to Mägendorf, where he quells an agitated crowd accusing Jacquier, participates in a preliminary investigation, including discovering a drawing by Gritli of a giant who hands hedgehogs to children, drives a large black car and makes a promise – or pledge – to the murdered girl's parents that he will find the killer, before Jacquier, under interrogation confesses to the crime and hangs himself in his cell. Following the preliminary investigation and the suicide of Jacquier, and with some doubt in his mind as to Jacquier's guilt, Matthäi heads to the airport to take up his new position in Jordan. At the airport the Inspector witnesses a large group of children waving Swiss flags and handkerchiefs and takes his seat on the plane next to a man eating chocolate truffles. These two images cause him to leave the plane to continue the investigation rather than leave for Jordan.

Unable to return to his former position as Inspector, Matthäi, working on a map he has devised based on the three existent child murders in the area, takes over the running of a gas station and asks Lotte Heller (Maria Rosa Salgado) and her daughter Annemarie (Anita von Ow) to live with him in the residence attached to the gas station in order to set a trap for the real murderer whom he knows is a 'giant', gives hedgehogs as presents and drives a large black car. It is revealed that this giant is Schrott (Gert Fröbe), a simple man-child himself, dominated and psychologically abused by his mother, Fraue Schrott (Berta Drews) and who drives a large black, American car. Matthäi sets a trap for Schrott in the forest where he has met with Gritli previously, using a life-size doll. Schrott appears, attacks Matthäi with a razor before being shot and killed by the other police lying in wait.

Later, the screenplay formed the basis for two other productions, a German telemovie also entitled *It Happened in Broad Daylight* directed by Nico Hoffmann in 1997 and a Dutch version entitled *The Cold Light of Day* (1996) directed by Rudolf van den Berg and starring Richard E. Grant and Lynsey Baxter.

In 'Popular Genres and Cultural Legitimacy: Fassbinder's *Lola* and the Legacy of 1950s West German Cinema', Tim Bergfeldern includes Vajda's *It Happened in Broad Daylight* amongst the '*Problemfilms*' of the period:

> Another subset of the West German *Problemfilm* of the 1950s could be constructed around the topos of the corrupt community that in traumatic encounters with the outsider (for example the occupation forces, returning emigres, or refugees from Germany's lost provinces such as Eastern Prussia, Pommerania and Silesia) closes in on itself in spasms of guilt and paranoia. Here *Rosemarie* sits side by side with films such as *The Golden Plague, Town without Pity, Es geschah am hellichten Tag/It Happened in Broad Daylight* and *Kirmes/Carnival*, as well as more highbrow cultural texts of the time such as Friedrich Dürrenmatt's play *Der Besuch der alten Dame/The Visit*. (2004: 34)

Following traditional criticisms that these *Problemfilms* "failed" to resolve their chosen problems or that it provided "hypocritical" or "pseudo-realist" answers to "real" issues', as Bergfelden puts it, Dürrenmatt rewrote the screenplay for *It Happened in Broad Daylight* as the novel *Das Versprechen* [*The Pledge*] in 1958. Ladislas Vajda, Hans Jacoby and Friedrich Dürrenmatt's film is an example of a German *Problemfilm* coterminous with the social problem films we saw Penn's father Leo involved with in 1950s America, a film cycle which it is possible to understand Sean Penn's cinema as recounting.

Friedrich Dürrenmatt's Das Versprechen/The Pledge

Ladislas Vajda's version of *It Happened in Broad Daylight*, running at 96 minutes, lacks the complexity of Dürrenmatt's novel, in particular the framing story that the latter version provides. The novel is framed by a first-person recounting of a story by the author who is announced as giving a lecture in Chur, the capital of the Swiss canton of Graubünden, 'on the art of writing detective stories', in parallel to a lecture on Goethe being presented by Emil Staiger, which is a much better attended event (Dürrenmatt 2006a: 1). The narrator then meets a former chief of police, Dr H., who offers him a lift to Zurich in his car. Early on in this trip the two men stop at a gas station, which, the narrator tells us,

> struck me as peculiar, perhaps because it stood out from its neat and proper surroundings. It was a wretched-looking thing with streams of water flowing down it sides. [...] Next to the open door sat an old man on a stone bench. He was unshaven and unwashed, wore a pale smock that was smeared and stained, and dark, grease-spotted trousers that had once been a tuxedo. Old slippers on his feet. His eyes were staring, stupefied, and I could smell the liquor from afar. The pavement around the stone bench was littered with cigarette butts that were floating in puddles of melted snow. (2006a: 5)

As the story concludes we realise that this character is Matthäi at his derelict gas station.

As suggested above, the conclusion to the book differs in two ways to the original film. First, Matthäi is unable to snare the killer despite setting a trap for him in the forest. Like Penn's film the detective in the novel convinces the local police to accompany him as he lays in wait for the killer for five days to rendezvous with Annemarie, to no avail. Matthäi and the police, frustrated that Annemarie won't tell them who she is to meet, eventually lose patience 'grabbing the child's arm and shaking her, "now tell us what you know!" And we all shouted with him, senselessly, because we had simply lost control of ourselves; we, too, shook her, and started to hit her, beat that little body lying there in ashes and red leaves among rusty tin cans, beat her cruelly, furiously, shouting and yelling' (2006a: 140). The child runs off into her mother's arms.

Second, it is the coda to the novel that provides the dénouement. Some time after the episode with Annemarie in the forest, the detective, in his own story, tells of receiving a call from a Catholic priest who was attending a dying woman, Frau Schott, whom, he presumes, would like to make a bequest to the police. Eventually she tells the story of her adopted son Bertie, who 'a voice from heaven' had told to kill several girls in the surrounding district including Gritli Moser and two before her, all children with blonde braids and red dresses. Bertie drove a black Buick car and 'had suddenly started taking chocolate truffles from the candy box' (2006a: 166). His mother noticed that he had a razor in his pocket and 'there were truffles missing in the bonbon box' (2006a: 168). She confronts him: 'I can't allow this, where is the girl? Not far from here, near a gas station.' He runs out 'with the truffles and the razor to the Buick, and just fifteen minutes later [Frau Schott] receives a call telling [her] he had collided with a truck and died' (ibid.).

Friedrich Dürrenmatt's oeuvre, as Timo Tiusanen suggests, is difficult to encapsulate. He wrote plays, novels, short stories, theories of dramaturgy, as well as being a painter. Across and within all these forms and the sizeable cultural shifts in his lifetime has seen the possibility of defining his work further complicated. Tiusanen describes this quandary:

He plays several contradictory roles with equal gusto. He is a comedian, a religious mediator, a moralist; a child of nature and a theoretician of literature; a dramatist and a prosaist. There is not just one Dürrenmatt, there is a host of them. (1977: 6)

In response to this difficulty in identifying an underlying cohesiveness in Dürrenmatt's works, Tiusanen, drawing on Wolfgang Kayser, identifies 'the grotesque' as a 'relevant concept' of use to Dürrenmatt research such that the 'typically grotesque phenomena listed by Kayser are to be found in Dürrenmatt' and that the grotesque is 'the basic structure' (1977: 14–15). Tiusanen defines the grotesque for us:

They express a breakdown in the categories we need for finding our way in the world. Grotesque disharmonies include the mixing up of separate conceptual spheres, abolition of the laws of statics, loss of identity, deformation of natural proportions or historical chronology. (1977: 14)

As Tiusanen points out, this notion of the grotesque borders on the absurd, 'employing grotesque and other stylistic elements to question the world order, sometimes with the implication that the world is more empty of meaning than is commonly assumed' (1977: 20). In Dürrenmatt's novel the distinctly Swiss location is given a strong sense of foreboding, marked by a magical sense of place. This is particularly so in the early passages where the author sets out in the morning with Dr H. for Zurich. It is worth quoting from the novel at length here:

The day seemed still dark, though the sun had risen a while ago. There was a patch of metallic sky gleaming somewhere through a covering of dense, sluggishly lumbering, snow-filled clouds. Winter seemed unwilling to leave this part of the country. The city was surrounded by mountains, but there was nothing majestic about them; they rather resembled heaps of earth, as though someone had dug an immense grave. Chur itself was quite evidently made of stone. Gray, with large government buildings. It seemed incredible to me that this was a wine-growing region. We tried to penetrate into the old inner city, but the heavy car strayed into a network of narrow lanes and one-way streets, and only a complex manoeuvre in reverse gear got us out of the tangle of houses. Moreover, the streets were icy, so we were glad to have the city behind us at last, although I had seen almost nothing of this old episcopal residence. It was like a flight. I dozed, feeling leaden and weary; vaguely, through the low scuttling clouds, I saw a snow-covered valley gliding past us, rigid with cold. I don't know for how long. Then we were driving toward a large village, perhaps a small town. Carefully, and suddenly everything was illuminated by sunlight so powerful and blinding that the snowy planes began to melt. A white ground mist rose, spreading imperceptibly over the snowfields until, once again, the valley was hidden from sight. It was like a bad dream, like an evil spell, as if I was not supposed to experience these mountains. (2006a: 3)[1]

In this framing story of the novel we are then introduced to Matthäi in the condition described above. As the author and Dr H. continue on their journey after visiting the gas station, Dr H. commences his story about the child murder and the fall of Matthäi by describing the imposing figure former police detective made:

> He was a lonely man, always neatly dressed, impersonal, formal, aloof; he didn't smoke, didn't drink, but on the job was as tough as nails, downright ruthless, and as hated as he was successful … he was extremely bright, but the all too solid structures in our country had made him emotionless. He was what you'd call an organization man, and he used the police apparatus like a slide rule. He wasn't married, he never spoke of his private life – probably he didn't have one. (2006a: 10)

The characterisation of Matthäi in Dürrenmatt's novel is starker, more mechanistic than that of Jerry Black in Penn's film. The performance of Jack Nicholson along with other distinct changes from the novel and *It Happened in Broad Daylight* are cross-cultural adaptations that significantly transform Penn's film from the novel and the film.

Penn's The Pledge

In their screenplay, Jerzy Kromolowski and Mary Olson-Kromolowski eschew the framing story of Dürrenmatt's novel for framing scenes of Nicholson as Jerry Black.

The opening shot, following a white/blue screen is a fade into an overhead of an ankle and boot with a hand lifting a trouser leg to scratch (the earth) which fades into an image of two birds winging their way across the blue sky, then fades back to an overhead shot of Nicholson and then into a further mid-shot of him with his light blue shirt and brown trousers and his cut head singled out against the stony dirt of the gas station driveway. This image fades back to an image of birds in the blue sky and then again to a side-on shot of Nicholson, unkempt with moustache and a cut on his forehead grimacing and talking to himself. The film then cuts to a mid-shot, front on, of Nicholson gesticulating, seated against the faded signage of the station and then fades back to a superimposition of birds and Nicholson continuing to talk to himself. A singular (angelic) voice and solid, deep drum sounds commence the film's theme. This scene then fades to blue again, then into the white of an iced-over lake ringed by trees with a solitary figure close to mid-shot. As the film's titles appear, a series of cuts move into what emerges as a small ramshackle fishing hut on the ice right of screen. We then cut to an interior shot of a hole in the ice and a trout on the end of a line, with another cut to a fishing rod being reeled in.

This opening with its images of isolation and outsiderness in a pristine landscape is further emphasised with the film's use of slow-motion images that are scattered throughout the film, or when Jerry observes the characters in the bar in which Lori works or the provincial nature of his approach to business when he closes the gas station when a rain storm approaches. Following Penn's use of clocks and other time pieces in *The Indian Runner* and *The Crossing Guard*, there are two scenes where Jerry

Jerry's (Jack Nicholson) breakdown that opens *The Pledge* (2001)

checks his watch. First, in the already mentioned ice fishing scene we see a close-up of his watch sitting at 11.05am. Second, when he is waiting to board his plane for the fishing trip to Baha his work colleagues gifted him on his retirement, Jerry glances at a clock ticking loudly in the airport concourse, amongst, as we have already seen, the clamour and fast-motion images in which he is immersed; the clock in a series of close-ups is ticking towards 11.00am. This scene not only intensifies the pressure on Jerry to remain and investigate Ginny Larsen's murder but it also further 'locks off' the possibility to leave the place to which he belongs, and following Dürrenmatt, the local knowledge that he believes is needed to catch the murderer.

It is clear that the opening shots of Jerry Black, alone, dishevelled and crazy, recalling Dürrenmatt's description quoted above, invokes the police procedural in providing a query, an unexplained figure, which the film will investigate. In its use of the figure of Jack Nicholson, it also signals a certain utilisation of a sympathetic protagonist, in the Hollywood tradition, an adaptation of the figure of Matthäi for a mainstream film, which affects much of the *mise-en-scène*. Compared to the figure of Matthäi in Dürrenmatt's novel, Jerry Black is a much softer, retiring and diffident character. While Matthäi was preparing for a secondment to Jordan to transfer his systematic police work to that country, Black is simply retiring, albeit reluctantly, with an emphasis on his fishing prowess as an analogy for his detection abilities. In these ways Black is a less starkly defined character than Matthäi. The fading in and out of his image and the sky, presumably in an attempt to delineate between the brown and the blue, the earth and the sky, and to foreground the film's insistence on Black's affinity with location, serves to blur his character in relation to his surroundings rather than the distinction made between Matthäi and his surroundings, or at least between Matthäi and Dürrenmatt's imagining of the world that he encounters. Penn's film asks us to read Black in amongst, as part of, the locale rather than the opposite, which serves to diminish the moral distinction, as a mirror of the fantasy and rational dyad that Dürrenmatt proposes constitutes the grotesque in his worldview.

The second scene of the film continues this blurring. The currently unknown figure from the fishing hut drives through a snow-covered landscape, similar to the ones that open *The Indian Runner*, with horses running in paddocks, cattle herds in a paddock, and fir trees. The musical soundtrack employs an ethereal rendition of the theme, emphasised by the hollow sound design of the car noises and a bass hum as the SUV passes through a tunnel accompanied by tunnel lights tracking across the beige tones of the hood of the truck with the lights flickering across windscreen. It isn't until this moment that we see Nicholson's face. The screen then flashes to a startling white, emphasising the truck emerging into the daylight from the tunnel with the city of Reno in the background – arid land without snow. This slow reveal and imperceptibility of Black, with the aforementioned fades, contribute further to this characterisation.

Compared with his performances in contemporary films of the late 1990s and early 2000s, such as *As Good as It Gets* (1997) or *About Schmidt* (2002) or even the lower-key role as Freddy in *The Crossing Guard*, as we have seen, Nicholson's performance in *The Pledge* is at odds with the 'ironic, self aware' characteristics that Dennis Bingham has identified (1994: 115). Here Nicholson avoids even the stinging aggressiveness that appears unexpectedly, or even the physicality that is apparent in his performance in Penn's previous film. In many ways Black appears as more of a domestically wholesome character, exhibiting a comfort with himself, a warmth and understatedness missing from his other roles at this time and also from Matthäi in *It Happened in Broad Daylight* or in Dürrenmatt's novel. In this regard, Penn's emphasis on place, in seeking to invoke a natural world of Nevada, and of Jerry Black as a component of it, works against the stricter definition of the detective that is important to the earlier film and novel. While Jerry is an outsider, alongside Franky from *The Indian Runner* and Freddie from *The Crossing Guard*, his immersion, in the natural world, as a fisherman, a facet of his character that is foregrounded in a way that isn't in Dürrenmatt's novel or Vajda's film, his capabilities as a cook and in assembling Ginny's swing set, strengthen his domestic credentials.

Further to this emphasis on Nicholson's star quality and that of Jerry's protagonist role, *The Pledge*, following on from the opening shots replacing the framing story, is a reconfiguring of the airport scenes, adapting a plot point common to all versions of the story. In Dürrenmatt's novel and Vajda's film, following the death of the peddler, Matthäi is waiting at the airport ready to board the plane for Jordan when he reads about the murder of Gritli Moser and the suicide of the peddler. Dürrenmatt writes:

> A man at the pinnacle of his career. But when he stepped onto the runway, his raincoat over his arm, he noticed that the terrace of the building was full of children. Several school classes had come to visit the airport – girls and boys in colourful summer clothes. There was much of little flags and handkerchiefs, whoops of amazement as the giant silver machines descended and took off. The inspector halted, then walked on toward the waiting Swissair plane ... he looked at the crowd of children, who were waving, happily and enviously, at the plane that was about to start. 'Miss', he said, 'I'm not flying' and returned to the airport building. (2006a: 72)

Here Matthäi is struck by the innocence and vitality of the children, an overwhelming experience, exemplified in Vajda's film by the flurry of Swiss flags, and a soundtrack filled with children's voices, that causes the detective to abandon his career in Jordan, telling his superior that he believes the murderer is 'still alive and free' and that 'if the possibility of such a danger exists … it is the duty of the police to protect the children and prevent another crime' (2006a: 75).

Jerry watches his own image on television at the airport in *The Pledge*

In Penn's film this scene is transformed so that Jerry Back is sitting at a bar in the airport where he watches a television news report of the murder. In the report following a segment on the suicide of Toby Wadaner (Benicio Del Toro) and a smaller discussion between Black and a bar attendant, the television footage shifts to location imagery from the crime scene, interspersed with extreme close-ups of Black, his hand running over his mouth and moustache, intently watching the report. Attending these scenes is a mix of diegetic location sound and a looped vocal sound which increases in level as the image of Black, alone in the snow at the crime scene, is included in a brief montage of Black's face in a tighter extreme close-up, and cutaways of slot machines, a ticking wall clock and individuals crossing the frame in front of Black in a medium shot, all of this as the sound level increases. Overwhelmingly this sequence serves to position Black, and his mental disturbance, as the central figure in the fiction. While Dürrenmatt's detective is swayed by the images of children, in a communitarian, yet obsessive psychological trigger, Penn's Jerry Black is subjected to an internalised, personal characterisation redolent of classical Hollywood at a variance to the grotesque worldview of Dürrenmatt.

An Angelic Point of View

As Timo Tiusanen points out, Dürrenmatt's novel alludes to fairy tales whereby 'Annemarie's world is governed by them, they are told to her by Matthäi', and Schrott tells her story, 'as if she were telling a fairy tale to two children' (1977: 174n). In Penn's film the figure of the fairy tale is amplified, to include scenes where Jerry reads Hans Christian Andersen's 'Thumbelina', The Grimm Brothers' 'The Elves and the Shoemaker' and the English fairy tale 'Jack and the Beanstalk', while Ginny's Grandmother, Annalise Hansen (Vanessa Redgrave) recites Andersen's 'The Angel' to Jerry Black. Penn has taken the fairy tale as a guiding principle for *The Pledge*, seeking to invoke Andersen's 'The Angel' as a structuring principle. Numerous times Penn utilises overhead and aerial shots to render, in filmic terms, the idea that 'whenever a good child dies, an angel of God comes down from heaven, takes the dead child in his arms, spreads out his great white wings, and flies with him over all the places which the child had loved during his life'. One scene in particular makes this explicit.

On leaving the airport Jerry travels in his SUV to a snow-covered streetscape. Penn employs a direct aerial shot of Jerry parking his car in the street next to a deciduous tree amongst footprints in the snow. In the same shot, as the camera tilts forward, Jerry

An angelic point of view in *The Pledge*

exits the vehicle on to the sidewalk to the right of the frame, past a Sears sign, as the frame tilts to the lower right and cuts to the interior of the 'Land of Christmas' gift store, with a close-up of a mannequin's hand holding a gold trumpet. Jerry enters the frame through the shop window amongst the tinsel and gold furnishings. When he enters the shop through a glass door, bells are struck by the door causing him to look up, screen left; he looks up before gazing into the shop and glimpsing a grey-haired male and the sound of a voice calling 'Customer, Oliver', before the camera pans left as an eccentric lady (Kathy Jensen, who also starred in *The Indian Runner*) appears, adorned in a Santa hat. After asking for directions for Annalise Hansen, Jerry is told that she 'lives above the electrical store', while the soundtrack plays ethereal strings and bell-like piano music. As Black leaves the shop we see an abrupt cut to an overhead of bells being struck by the door and again he looks up, this time directly into the camera. In the scene with Annalise Hansen, Jerry is told that Ginny 'loved Andersen' and she recites a version of 'The Angel' to him.

Another key scene is an 'angel's point of view' aerial helicopter shot when Jerry revisits the crime scene in summer with yellow police containment tape littering the ground. He sits on a log shaking his head and staring at the earth as Annalise's voice-over reprises the lines from 'The Angel' which commences and continues as the shot fades into an aerial shot of a forest-rimmed lake. The camera pans over the lake, a forested area and onto a playground with swings and slides as Annalise uses the specific words 'and flies with him over all the places which the child had loved' before moving on and fading into a brief shot of Jerry's truck travelling on a highway.

These overhead and aerial shots are peppered throughout the film such as when Jerry ducks under a barrier at the police station, and the lift he is a passenger in raises upwards from the floor in front of camera; or when Jerry looks out of his office window several stories above the street where he views, from on high, two elderly men, one with a walking frame accompanying each other on the street. These scenes, as suggested above, are all designed to invoke an 'angel's point of view' prefiguring the places associated with the young girls, Ginny Larsen and Chrissy. In this way Penn has designed a *mise-en-scène*, adapting Dürrenmatt's allusion to fairytales, and in tandem with a narrative that features a delineation between reality and fantasy in which Jerry Black is caught. Again it is Jerry's slipping between a belief in fantasy that characterises the worldview of Ginny and Chrissy on the one hand, and the objective, rational world of a policeman on the other.

Vanessa Redgrave

An important component of Penn's attempt to adapt Dürrenmatt's novel to the screen is the allusions to the Europeanness of the environs in which the story occurs, particularly the characters of the Larsen family, Ginny's parents as well as her grandmother, Annalise. While it appears that the Larsen name is of an indistinct European heritage, it is the performance by and the figure of Vanessa Redgrave that emphasises this heritage. Redgrave, of course, belongs to English acting royalty as the daughter of Sir Michael and Lady Rachel Redgrave, mother of Natasha Richardson and Joely Richardson and sister of Lynn Redgrave. She is known for her roles in films as diverse as *Blow Up* (1966), *A Man for All Seasons* (1966), Camelot (1967), Isadora (1968), *The Devils* (1971), *Julia* (1977), *Howard's End* (1992), *Little Odessa* (1994), *Mission: Impossible* (1996) and *Mrs Dalloway* (1997) but is also well known for her many roles in the theatre. Throughout her career Redgrave has developed a formidable persona based on stoicism and a quiet solidity emphasised by her diction and intonation.

As well as these acting roles Redgrave has become well known for her radical politics. She has stood for the British parliament for the Trotskyist Workers' Revolutionary Party, 'never gathering more than a few hundred votes on a platform that included nationalization of major industries without compensation and that warned that a Conservative victory in the 1970s would lead to dictatorship and concentration camps in England' (Schemo 1994). It has been her support for the Anti-Zionist cause, including her financial support for a documentary about the Palestinian Liberation Front in Lebanon and a 'cultural boycott that would have banned British actors from performing in the Jewish state or having their work shown there' as well as associations with campaigns to end apartheid in South Africa and to promote peace talks in Northern Ireland, amongst others, that have made her a figure of progressive politics internationally (see Schemo 1994). In this way it is possible to see, alongside her figure of Europeaness, an alignment with the kind of left-wing activist politics that Penn identifies with, as we saw in chapter two.

Sam Shepard

Another actor who brings to *The Pledge* an air of rebellion as well as a sense of ease with himself is Sam Shepard as Jerry's boss, Eric Pollack. As Blanch McCrary Boyd states in 'The Natural', Shepard hung out with Patti Smith in the early 1970s and had his first acting role in Bob Dylan's *Renaldo and Clara* (1978), lending a connection to the Beats through Allen Ginsberg's association with Dylan and that film (1984: 25). A teenage playwright, Shepard has written many plays, poems and screenplays including Wim Wenders' *Paris, Texas* (1984) and acted in Terrence Malick's *Days of Heaven* (1978), Daniel Petrie's *Resurrection* (1980), Jack Fisk's *Raggedy Man* (1981), Philip Kaufman's *The Right Stuff* (1983), Richard Pearce's *Country* (1984) and Robert Altman's adaptation of Shepard's own play *Fool for Love* (1985), amongst others. Shepard is a slim-hipped cowboy type, often wearing 'his Sam Shepard uniform' as Boyd describes it: 'faded jeans, worn boots, a leather buckle and a western shirt … the face he'd like to keep anonymous is lean and weathered with high cheekbones and brown eyes that slant slightly. His hairline is receding from a widow's peak. Although he's not conventionally good looking, his rough elegance is compelling' (1984: 23).

Shepard brings to the role of Eric Pollack his familiar angularity in suit, vest, white shirt and tie, his hair slicked back, a kind of authoritative unease that befits an officer ambivalent about Jerry pursuing the murder case while retired from the force. In comparison to the loudmouth recklessness of Aaron Eckhart's Stan Krolak and the other police, Shepard's Eric is warm, composed and understanding, providing a rational medium between Stan's dismissive ebullience and Jerry's obsessive zeal for the case. In his demeanour and attire Shepard's Eric is closer to Dürrenmatt's Matthäi than Nicholson/Penn's Jerry Black is.

Mickey Rourke

In a series of roles including *Body Heat* (1981), *Diner* (1982), *Rumblefish* (1983), *The Pope of Greenwich Village* (1984), *Year of the Dragon* (1985), *Nine ½ Weeks* (1986), *Angel Heart* (1987), *Barfly* (1987) and *Homeboy* (1987) Rourke has made a career out of playing people who have lost things, people who are at the end of things, washed up, finished, and losers. As Keri Walsh points out, Rourke emerged around the same time as a new generation of Hollywood actors including Tom Cruise, Robert Downey Jr., Mary Stuart Masterson, Matt Dillon, John Cusack, Kevin Bacon, Molly Ringwald, Andrew McCarthy, Demi Moore, Emilio Estevez, Keifer Sutherland, Robe Lowe, Judd Nelson, Ally Sheedy and, of course, Sean Penn, in what has come to be termed the 'Brat Pack'. While these actors were known for their youthful and adolescent characters accompanying the resurgence in the teen film such as Harold Becker's *Taps* (1981), Francis Ford Coppola's *The Outsiders* (1983), John Hughes' *Sixteen Candles* (1984), *The Breakfast Club* (1985) and *Pretty in Pink* (1986) and Joel Schumacher's *St Elmo's Fire* (1985), Rourke was more rough hewn, acne-scarred, greasy hair, mumbling intonation. In his full-lipped, lispy, halting delivery, conveying an uncertain, damaged interior and a rumpled, unkempt exterior, Rourke was very much the mystery man. As Walsh points out, Rourke can be understood in contrast to the Brat Pack:

> Although Rourke may have pioneered the flippant smile that came to define the eighties leading man, he was never in tune with the Brat Pack, for his angst went far beyond the suburban kind. He was an anti yuppie because amidst all the prosperity he relished the opposite trajectory: downhill all the way. Tom Cruise built a career out of the roles Rourke turned down (hotshot parts in *Top Gun* and *Rain Man*), while Rourke preferred to play the beautiful loser – addict, masochist, extremist. In an age of accumulation, all of his roles documented loss: of parents, lovers, bets, fights, and finally, in *Angel Heart*, his immortal soul. (2010: 137)

Amongst these teen films Rourke emerged as a slightly older figure bringing with him an updated Method, something Walsh terms an 'intersubjective realm':

James Olstadt (Mickey Rourke), at the end of things in *The Pledge*

a way of reading and responding to other actors, an openness, a curiosity, an empathy so extreme that he seemed to become the other. It overcame all self-protection or self-interest, leading him to acts of extraordinary renunciation. The compulsion to watch him, it seemed, came from this casual throwing away of the self. [...] Rourke specialized in moments when a totally submissive character suddenly lashes out or a dominant one suddenly buckles. And those exchanges, always held in reserve beyond the point when you might expect them, were his dramatic thrills, the electrical jolts his performances always gave. He had no middle register, no small talk, but vacillated between scenes of extreme intimacy and sudden, violent retreats, always pulling away just when he got closest. (2010: 136)

Rourke's cameo role as Jim Olstadt, father of a missing child in *The Pledge*, is an example of this 'intersubjectivity' that Walsh proposes. It is also a cameo, like that of Harry Crews and Dennis Hopper in *The Indian Runner* or Anjelica Huston in *The Crossing Guard*, that draws on a whole oeuvre of roles that make up the Rourke persona.

In Penn's film, an odd episode features Jerry Black visiting Olstadt (Rourke) at what seems to be some kind of a hospice. As Black arrives at the facility, he pulls up alongside three elderly men on a park bench where he learns that James Olstadt is not a patient, as Black believes, but 'he is the custodian, sir' and is told he might be 'mopping in the building'. We cut to some pick-up shots of the shadows of a wheelchair, budgerigars and elderly patients until we cut to a shot of Black approaching from the other side of the glass door with the words 'Solarium Smoking Lounge' printed on his side of the door. Black opens the door and enters the room, addresses a space close to straight on to the camera and asks 'James Olstadt?' We then cut to a long shot with Nicholson in the rear and the back of Rourke's head. In the brief interlude before he introduces himself with 'I'm Jerry Black, a police detective. Just like to talk to you about your daughter', birds fly around the room and Nicholson follows their flight with an open mouth and a roll of the eyes. We then cut to a close-up sidelong shot of Olstadt exhaling cigarette smoke. He is unshaven, his longish hair greying and swept off his face. He is seated in a plaid shirt and denim jacket. 'What daughter?' Rourke responds. 'You did have a daughter that went missing a few years ago didn't you?' Black continues. Rourke then looks up, positioned far left in the 16:9 shot, with some window bars and wall filling the rest, at Nicholson with sad, watery eyes. 'Did you come here to tell me something … um … happened to her?' 'No sir,' Nicholson responds. Then Rourke strongly, 'Something happen to her? D'you find her dead or somethin'?' Black pauses then says, 'No, we're still trying to find her.' We then cut to Rourke sighing and nodding in relief. Nicholson continues, 'Is there anything you might tell me about her? Could you describe her?' Cut to Rourke: 'Oh shoot, she must be, she must be different now' – cut to and from Black, and Rourke exhales smoke – 'She was so pretty.' The camera remains on Rourke as the silence lengthens and the pressure builds in his face. His eyes gather tears and his mouth twitches: 'I miss her so much', he says, sniffing, the words difficult to follow. 'We used to just, like, hold each other. I was supposed to take care of her. She was my little girl, you know?' Then with a sharp twist of the neck and a strong sniff, he recomposes himself, tears still in his eyes. 'Where's my little girl? Where's my baby?' We then cut abruptly to the next scene.

Here Rourke, appears grief stricken yet holding on to the hope of his daughter returning. His performance embodies this oscillation between grief and depression verging on violence on one hand and, on the other, an overwhelming tenderness for a lost daughter. Because of this scene's brevity (just over two minutes), there is little time to give due regard to the violence being kept in check by Olstadt. But it is there. It's there in Rourke's snapping 'What daughter?' but more so, it is in Rourke's cinematic history, in the figure he has built in his body of work, which is less a history of explosive characters committing momentary violence as it is characters having to deal with the aftermath of violence, moments often overcome by existential world-weariness.

This scene is a strange interlude in the development of Black's investigation in that we learn about the Olstadt murder much earlier in the film and this scene is directly preceded by one where Black visits the Monash County police station and learns about the death of Louanne Rancy. In some ways the scene with Rourke mirrors the episodes in *The Crossing Guard* that occur while Freddie waits three days to kill Booth.

While this scene contributes to Jerry's moral confidence in continuing the investigation, his belief that there were other murders of young girls, it also, employing the setting of an asylum of sorts, provides a reference to Milos Forman's *One Flew Over the Cuckoo's Nest* (1975) where Nicholson played the perfectly sane yet anti-authoritarian and criminal, Randle Patrick McMurphy in a battle of wills with Nurse Ratched (Louise Fletcher) for control of the mental asylum. McMurphy succumbs to the institution and is lobotomised, but inspires Chief (Will Sampson), who stages an escape with the now comatose McMurphy giving hope to the remaining inmates. In relation to *The Pledge*, the New Hollywood *One Flew Over the Cuckoo's Nest* acts as an intertext about moral values in the face of institutional constraint as well as in relation to the decline of Jerry's own mental health which, despite his correct assessment of the serial murder pattern, leads to his complete breakdown by the film's end.

Harry Dean Stanton

Although his appearance in *The Pledge* is extremely brief, perhaps less than a minute screentime, Harry Dean Stanton brings to the film a long history of roles that culminate in a defeated, or at least a compliant, eccentric mode of American masculinity as well as an immediately recognisable character actor's face to the role of Floyd Cage, the owner of a gas station. Ian Penman describes Stanton's face:

> The head seems both shrunken and outsize – as if decomposition had set in, but been arrested; and quite possibly this is the case. You try and get an angle on it, but it already contains too many. On paper – enervated but heightened by fax and xerox – a press shot makes him look like an early photographer's cowboy: one of those gauche, toughing Frontier emulsions. It's a physiog he shares with his buddy Dennis Hopper, and Sam Shepard: ghosts of the uncivil dead. (1998: 42)

Another outsider in the Brat Pack era, fifteen years older even than Rourke, Stanton forged a name with mostly character actor roles in numerous television shows and New Hollywood films, including *Two Lane Blacktop* (1971), *Cisco Pike* (1972), *Pat Garrett and Billy the Kid* (1973), *Dillinger* (1973), *Cockfighter* (1974), *Farewell My Lovely* (1975), *The Missouri Breaks* (1976), *Wise Blood*, *Alien* (1979), *One from the Heart* (1981), *Repo Man* (1984) and *The Last Temptation of Christ* (1988). In Wenders' *Paris, Texas*, Stanton's singular visage is redolent of hard living and impassivity. As Danny Leigh puts it:

> In Wenders' evocation of endless freeways and half-empty diners through whose windows the actor is shot, his face is a mask of sombre remorse, as much an expression of the film's elegiac Americana as a pulse of flashing neon by a roadside motel. The near-25 minutes of catatonic silence with which he begins the story is a period in which he nonetheless has to develop a clear sense of his character's identity, so that by the time Travis speaks, we already know him. (2006: 53)

In a career of small roles, Stanton is often understood in relation to more assertive figures on the outskirts of Hollywood: Nicholson, Warren Oates, Marlon Brando and more recently Penn himself.

> Stanton was best man at [Nicholson's] wedding to Sandra Knight in 1962 and it was into Stanton's Laurel Canyon apartment that Nicholson moved after his divorce six years later. Then there was Brando, who would often call at 3am to discuss the I Ching, run through *Macbeth* or just to share 'three or four minutes' of absolute silence. The three men were united onscreen in Arthur Penn's flawed but absorbing *The Missouri Breaks* ... in which Stanton and Nicholson, like everything else, are overshadowed by the grand derangement of Brando's performance. (Leigh 2006: 51)

Stanton then appeared with Penn and Elvis Costello, as themselves, in the 'Back off Mary Poppins' (2004) episode of Lee Aransohn and Chuck Lorre's *Two and a Half Men* where the three friends smoke cigars and drink scotch at a kind of men's support group at Charlie's (Charlie Sheen) house to which Alan (John Cryer) is not invited. Penn asks 'All right. How do I say this? Do any of you get up in the middle of the night to pee?' The men reply affirmatively except Stanton who says, 'Sometimes I don't even get up.' When Alan stumbles upon the gathering, offended that he hasn't been invited he asks, pointing to Penn and Costello, 'is that … and is that …?', then pointing to Stanton, 'and that?', to which Charlie replies 'he used to be … not any more'. This gathering of outsider Hollywood figures to talk over their fading machismo is a comic undermining of their masculine media representation. In this scenario Charlie is admonished by his friends for not supporting or admitting Alan to the group, and Stanton, who plays the eccentric elder statesmen, delivers kooky advice in a comic take on his reputation as a sage-like figure. He says, 'Let me tell you something about sharing kid. Sharing is a two-way street. When you share with another human being you always get back more than you gave. Assuming that you are smart enough to share with someone who has more stuff than you had in the beginning.'

But it is probably as Oates's sidekick that Stanton commenced forming the obdurate figure with the resonant baritone voice that endures. Leigh again:

> Born within a couple of hundred miles of Stanton in rural Kentucky, the balding, gap-toothed Oates followed a path into Hollywood that was uncannily similar. But Oates broke through after exposure in 1967's *In the Heat of the Night*, which gained him top billing in a series of low-rent minor classics during the early 1970s, four of which featured support from Stanton. In Monte Hellman's road movie *Two Lane Blacktop*, John Milius's gangster biopic *Dillinger*, and Thomas McGuane's *92 in the Shade* (1975), Stanton and Oates mesh beautifully whenever called on to share a scene. But the most compelling moment between them comes in Hellman's *Cockfighter* (1974), a strange, rambling movie doomed by its title and protests from the American Society for the Prevention of Cruelty to Animals. Typically, Stanton's role is limited in terms of screen time, but integral to the story and essential for the mood. At the film's outset, Oates's obsessive cockfighter Frank Mansfield meets his nemesis Jack Burke (Stanton) to negotiate a contest. Mansfield, however, has taken a vow of silence and so while it is Oates's litany of glances and gestures that catches the eye, Stanton's meticulously focused cues and responses are what gives the scene its energy and rhythm, all the while directing the audiences attention to Oates. (2006: 53)

Leigh's comparison of Oates and Stanton here translates well to the interaction between Nicholson and Stanton in *The Pledge*. As Jerry Black, sitting in his truck, discovers a cartographic pattern between the three murders of young girls in Monash County, he marks a spot on the map, a junction between the Monash and Becker Counties, before heading down the road to a gas station. The station is raggedy and unkempt with stores, wood and an ice machine out front and an ungainly faded construction including a residence recalling Dürrenmatt's description from his novel. As Black

Floyd Cage's (Harry Dean Stanton) defeated, eccentric masculinity in *The Pledge*

pulls up outside, the film cuts to what we eventually see is Stanton's Floyd Cage's point of view followed by a medium close-up of him nestled in a chair reading a newspaper in an open-neck shirt and baseball cap, reading glasses, obligatory cigarette in his right hand and a two-day growth on his face. Immediately following this shot, indicated by Cage's glance to his left, is a medium close-up of his daughter Alma Cage (Lucy Schmidt) who is seated behind the counter also reading. She is a little overweight with lank blonde hair. Black enters the store and asks for 'a pack of lights' from her before asking, with a nod of his head 'That the owner?' to which she responds 'My daddy' with a pointed finger. Stanton is seated low, half obscured by a counter, surrounded by fishing lures, and other supplies, now wearing his glasses. 'What can I do for you,' he asks. Black responds: 'Well, I was just having a look around. How long you had this place?' 'Oh, about thirty years,' Cage replies as Penn cuts to a shot of Stanton, Nicholson and Schmidt in the one shot, the latter eating a sandwich and drinking as she giggles when Cage says to Black that the station is not for sale. Black gives Cage his number at the resort he is staying at and leaves asking Cage to 'think about it'. The final shot of this scene is a close-up of Stanton, glasses dangling from his hand and a pensive look on his face as he looks off screen in thought.

When Black returns to the gas station to say farewell to Cage and his daughter, Stanton is on his feet, dealing with the real estate agent (J. J. McColl), shown with the wind in his hair, a cigarette in his mouth and dust blowing across the screen. He is in a cream jacket and another open neck shirt and trousers offering to call when he gets a number down in Arizona if Black 'forgets something or wants to know where something is' before shaking hands and climbing into his car with a U-Haul trailer. In these scenes Nicholson is all assertive sociability, a large figure, an ex-policeman, in contrast to, or perhaps supported by the smaller, inexpressive Stanton. It appears as though Cage wouldn't have sold up unless he was made a very generous offer yet there is also a sense in this scene that Cage is thinking of his daughter, trapped (their surname is no accident) in the gas station alongside her father and moving on now. Ian Penman characterises Stanton's consistency in his roles:

> Harry Dean has embodied this marginal spirit in every possible guise and period. [...] With Stanton the demarcation 'loser' is never securely circumscribed. Unlike Lee Marvin, he nearly always elicits sympathy: always the stiff, and never the pallbearer. (1998: 43)

Both Stanton and Rourke, following Nicholson's Freddie Gale in *The Crossing Guard*, bring their past to bear on their roles as fathers; Rourke with despair and grief for his lost daughter, Stanton with deadpan hope for his daughter and a new life away from their stultifying, isolated life running a gas station. This hope for the future, embodied in the figure of a daughter, rhymes with the eternal figure of the child that we saw in *The Crossing Guard*, with Freddie's daughter Emily haunting him and eventually, through the agency of John Booth, leading to his salvation, and the figure of Chrissy in *The Pledge*.

The next chapter will consider Penn's short film 'U.S.A.', his contribution to Alain Brigand's omnibus film *11/09/'01–September 11*, which utilises the distinct place of Lower Manhattan in conjunction with the figure of Ernest Borgnine in order to propose a moral question – and a hopeful answer – in the face of nationalist fervour and global fear following the 2001 attacks on the World Trade Center.

Note

1   In Tiusanien's translation this last sentence reads: 'It was like a bad dream, like witchcraft, as though a spell were upon this region, so that I could never come to know it' (1977: 167), which lends itself better to the ideas of the grotesque, particularly of the fairytale vs rationality dialectic at work in the novel.

CHAPTER SIX

Interlude: 'U.S.A.'

In *Omnibus Films: Theorizing Transauthorial Cinema*, David Scott Diffrient points out that Alain Brigand's *11/09/'01–September 11* (2002), which includes Sean Penn's 'U.S.A.', 'despite [its] textual schizophrenia, [presents] repeated images and themes throughout the film, giving it an *intratextual* – as opposed to strictly intertextual – density' (2014: 215; emphasis in original). While Diffrient is concerned with issues of authorship and genre he doesn't consider that the film's primary structuring principle is one of place at a particular time; the World Trade Center buildings of Lower West Side Manhattan, New York City on 11 September 2001. In these ways Penn's participation in the film continues the interest in the sense of place alongside the intertextual readings available in all his films. The subject of *11/09/'01*, like all omnibus films, provides a certain coherence to which contributing directors can build their films in relation, while employing very different approaches.

11/09/'01–September 11 includes eleven films by eleven different directors who were asked to make a short film lasting eleven minutes and nine seconds long – plus one frame. The film was produced by Alain Brigand with directors from different regions, including Ken Loach from the UK, Youseff Chahine from Egypt, Shôhei Imamura from Japan, Alejandro González Iñárittu from Mexico, Danis Tanovic from Bosnia-Herzegovina, Idrissa Ouedraogo from Burkina Faso and Penn from the United States. In this regard Penn becomes responsible for the United States of America, in a spatial sense, as well as being the central topic of all the films. In a formal sense, *11/09/'01–September 11,* like all omnibus films, operates across a sense of, on the one hand, cohesion, and on the other, fragmentation, and in the case of *11/09/'01–September 11,* as Maria Pramaggiore points out, utilising documentary avant-garde and narrative modes: 'the film's focus on the space of lower Manhattan and the attack on the WTC serves to unify a cluster of disparate events, and it also lends coherence to the inherently fragmented genre of the omnibus film [where the filmmakers] all interpret 9/11 through different genres as well as from diverse political, cultural, and geographical vantage points' (2010). As Pramaggiore also points out, Brigand employs a 'graphic device' in the film's title sequence as well as between the episodes, to cohere or, as Pramaggiore contends, 'contain' the omnibus:

> In the opening of the film, small luminous clockfaces, with sections of continents etched in them, glide across the dark background. After they move into place, forming the continents, all the clocks stop ticking. A bright red glowing dot illuminates New York City, signifying the moment of the attack on the WTC. The various times on the clockfaces record the same instant in different time zones. Finally, the clock and maps dissolve into the title. (Ibid.)

While this device is designed to bring together the components – of various structural and aesthetic qualities – of the omnibus, each episode, at the same time, resonates out of its surroundings.

As Pramaggiore also points out *11/09/'01–September 11* has significant forebears in the German New Wave's *Germany in Autumn* (1978), a collection of documentary and narrative works by Rainer Werner Fassbinder, Alexander Kluge, Volker Schlöndorff, Edgar Reitz and others, exploring the politics of West Germany around the time of the Red Army Faction's kidnapping and murder of industrialist Hanns-Martin Schleyer. Another omnibus precursor is the French New Wave's *Far from Vietnam* (1967) which includes contributions from Jean-Luc Godard, William Klein, Agnès Varda, Joris Ivena, Alain Resnais and others, addressing America's involvement in the Vietnam War (ibid.).

Interiority

Penn's 'U.S.A.', for our purposes, following the place-based yet intertextual workings of his oeuvre, is Penn's most interior film, at the same time as it seeks the grandest of his cinematic statements. 'U.S.A.' is concerned with L'Homme (Ernest Borgnine), mostly holed up in a jaded, stultifying and dull apartment, alone except for the faded memory of his wife whose dresses he sets out daily on their bed. Apart from two shots of him walking the street in hat and coat, L'Homme is imaged mostly within the confines of the apartment, chatting away to his wife as he goes through the routines of shaving, eating, drinking and vacuuming. The film opens in darkness with Borgnine's loud voice proclaiming amongst street sounds, 'I woke up before your alarm clock this morning, I get up early anyway. But usually I need your alarm clock to wake me.' The image of a faded, dying plant in a pot emerges from the dark and cuts to a close-up of a dripping tap in slow-motion, followed by items in a kitchen, a drain hole in a sink and a blade being removed from a razor and being placed in a slot, followed by an interior of the blade landing in a pile of other blades as the sound of a television set emerges on the soundtrack. The film then focuses on L'Homme in a singlet and boxer shorts, commencing his shave interspersed with still images of the apartment's interior: air conditioner, a woman's face in a framed photograph, a photograph of a man in military uniform in front of an American flag, a high-angle shot of the main room of the apartment, a close-up of an old ticking analogue clock at eight o'clock before the alarm rings. The shrill alarm continues over a slow-motion image of hands splashing water over L'Homme's face and back down into a sink before an overhead shot of the grey-green bathroom leads to another of the protagonist entering the main room.

This opening sequence is a condensation of many of the themes of Penn's earlier films, including some of the most extreme close-ups in Penn's oeuvre, marking out an interior space of a couple of rooms of an apartment in forensic detail, coupled with the stretching of real time and exaggerated sound effects. L'Homme's monologue continues in none-too-subtle mode, stating: 'There's not enough light. That's why your flowers are not doing so well. They're like me, you know. They need light to wake up, right?' As the screen splits to images of the clock and L'Homme sitting on the bed, he says, 'Maybe we should have taken that place out in the country, then you'd have plenty of light!' He finally recognises the alarm and rises to switch it off, saying 'I forgot all about you, didn't I?' before a cut to the interior of a closet where he turns the light on – 'And there was light!' – then sorts through hanging clothes. We return to an overhead shot of the main room as the musical soundtrack emerges.

Marty

The presence of Borgnine, with his loud sing-song voice talking to himself, depicted in oppressive, dull interiors, recalls the actor's breakthrough role as Marty Piletti in Delbert Mann's *Marty* (1955). Like Penn's films, Paddy Chayefsky's oeuvre, such as the screenplay for the tele-movie and film of *Marty*, featured loner figures struggling with family pressures, loneliness or societal demands. Like the protagonists of Chayefsky's *The Bachelor Party* (Delbert Mann, 1957), *The Hospital* (Arthur Hiller, 1971) and *Network* (Sidney Lumet, 1976), Borgnine's Marty, is a middle-class, hard-working individual, in this case a Bronx butcher, from an Italian Catholic family. Despite his apparent zest for life, encapsulated in his exclamations such as 'fabulous' and 'perfect', he has given up on marriage and is bored with his dull social life spent mostly with his friends, Angie (Joe Mantell) and Ralph (Frank Sutton), wondering what they will do for entertainment. His mother (Esther Minciotti), spurred on by his aunt Catherine (Augusta Ciolli), after at first suggesting that he should get out of the house and go to the Stardust Ballroom, is worried about the possibility of life without her son in the house and seeks to undermine his romantic prospects with the plain Clara (Betsy Blair), a girl he meets at the Ballroom after she is jilted for a more glamorous girl. After almost succumbing to the pressures from his mother and friends, Marty makes the promised phone call to Clara, who, in a scene recalling a similar one with Dorothy from *The Indian Runner*, is sitting at home watching television with her parents. The film closes with Marty apparently breaking free of the constraints of his situation with his Mother and friends and exclaiming, 'You don't like her? That's too bad!'

In *Marty*, much is made of the house that he shares with his mother, including his aunt's coming to live with them at the request of his cousin Tommy (Jerry Paris) and the number of empty rooms available. The interior of the house, despite its size, prefigures the décor of the apartment in Penn's 'U.S.A.', with small rooms, busy flock wallpaper, heavy dark-timbered furniture, wood-panelled walls, the kind of photographic portraits already described in 'U.S.A.' and little natural light. Marty also contains a scene with Borgnine in a singlet and trousers shaving at a sink. The narrative of *Marty* combined with the production design and characterisation could be transferred to 'U.S.A.' as if Penn's film depicts Marty years later, after Clara has passed away, struggling to deal with life without her, in the same way that his mother had to deal with the possibility of life without Marty.

Ernest Borgnine

The figure of Ernest Borgnine in American public life provides an intriguing intertext with Penn's 'U.S.A.'. Prior to this acting career Borgnine, served ten years as a gunner's mate in the US Navy during World War II and later in his life closely identified with his naval career, receiving the Lone Sailor Award and the Honorary title of Master Chief Petty Officer of the Navy in 2004 for services to the Navy and Navy families. He appeared as the reviled, violent, Sergeant 'Fatso' Watson in Fred Zinnemann's *From Here to Eternity* (1953), as Bart Lonergan in Nicholas Ray's *Johnny Guitar* (1954), as Coley Trimble in John Sturges's *Bad Day at Black Rock* (1955) and later as Dutch Engstrom in Sam Peckinpah's *The Wild Bunch* (1969), as Mike Rogo in Ronald Neame's *The Poseidon Adventure* (1972) and as a cab driver in John Carpenter's *Escape From New York* (1981). His most famous role is probably as Lieutenant Quinton McHale in the American Broadcasting Corporation's television series *McHale's Navy* (1962–66), where his character headed up a motley crew of naval misfits and raconteurs plying the seas of the Pacific Ocean. Borgnine's roles as a naval officer and ex-servicemen, his public life as decorated serviceman and his role as a likeable everyman in *Marty*, bring to L'Homme a reflection between his performances and his roles such as we have seen from Dennis Hopper, Jack Nicholson and Anjelica Huston in Penn's earlier films.

L'Homme's (Ernest Borgnine) interior monologue in 'U.S.A.' (2002)

Television

Borgnine's television career and its mirroring of his personal life provides a link with the manner in which 'U.S.A.' works with the televisual images of the World Trade Center attacks in relation to the interiorised domestic images just discussed. In a continuation of the ways in which Penn has utilised television images of the 1968 Democratic convention, the Vietnam War, *Rio Grande* on the television screen and *Gilligan's Island* in *The Indian Runner*, of news reports of the murder in *The Pledge* and, as we will see, President George H. W. Bush in *Into the Wild*, 'U.S.A.' includes the TV images of the burning and collapsing towers which infiltrate L'Homme's apartment despite the character's obliviousness to the real-life acts.

Later in 'U.S.A.', following a montage sequence including repeated images of the *Jerry Springer Show*, L'Homme shaving, eating, shining his shoes, and speaking to himself, with a rhythmic interlude in the musical soundtrack, he returns to the bed and to sleep. Once again, we return to images of the air conditioner, an extreme close-up of a tap dripping in slow-motion, the sink hole and a close-up on the alarm clock, then a refocusing to the face of L'Homme. The camera then pans down the length of his body, again in the singlet and boxer shorts, again past the air conditioner and the dying flowerpot to rest on the television set screening the burning Twin Towers as the sound of the ticking clock rises on the soundtrack. The film cuts to L'Homme asleep on the bed and then zooms in on the dark image of the Twin Towers until the screen is black, back to the bed, then to the doubled shot of the television screen and the flowerpot in the same image.

The next cut is to the outside of the apartment with light descending the wall and back to inside the apartment with light appearing on the flower pot and the photograph of the woman until it begins to creep up the bed towards the sleeping L'Homme. The bright light wakes him and he rises to look towards the flowers which are blooming in bright reds and yellows, exclaiming, 'The light. Your flowers, your flowers my dear, they're alive', while laughing loudly. He takes them over to the bed and notices that it is her dress he has been addressing not the woman, and begins weeping, holding the yellow dress saying 'You should have seen this my dear. You should have seen this.' The camera pulls back, outside the window frame, as he continues to weep, until the

'The light, your flowers my dear, they're alive'

outside of the apartment another shadow drops from the wall to illuminate another window bathed in light.

While Penn's previous films have included externalised television images to gesture to a larger outside world or to provide an intertextual link with another film or television programme, the Twin Towers images are proclaimed as 'LIVE' on the TV screen, signalling a temporal simultaneity as well as a geographic proximity to the (non-)events inside the apartment. Unlike the ways in which the images of Vietnam or the 1968 Democratic convention affect Joe in *The Indian Runner*, the images of the Twin Towers in 'U.S.A.', while depicting historical events just as significant, are depicted by Penn as being narratively and intimately involved (they affect the interior lives of individuals) in the most mundane of everyday lives, via the most banal of mediums: broadcast television. In the same way, we know that these events, unlike the spatial distance of the earlier television intertexts, are occurring in the same geographical space, downtown Manhattan. Penn's proposal about the effect of these events, however, is not contained by the domestic sphere, to the everyday lives of Americans but, within his oeuvre, seeks to broaden the events out onto the heart of American democracy, via an intensification of the temporal and spatial relations in 'U.S.A.' which, as seen in chapter one, following Richard Rorty, is the notion of hope.

Exteriority

L'Homme's waking to the light brought about by the elimination of the shadows that keep the apartment in darkness, prefigured by the incessant ring of the clock and the monologue in the second part of the film invoking the analogies of 'waking up' to the 'light', including L'Homme's use of the biblical phrase from Genesis – 'And there was light' – in tandem with the realisation that his wife is not there to see these events, is a distillation of the ongoing epic concerns that motivate Penn's work. Penn spells out the proposal in an interview with Duncan Campbell:

> I thought, what a wonderful chance to explore my own reaction, an opportunity I would wish for all people. After September 11, I cancelled a feature film I was about to make that, in context, was not relevant or had at least not been provoked by this new state of things. I wanted to take a deep breath and try to begin to understand what our new obligation would be. [...] The events of that day, tragic as they were, seemed to have been overwhelmingly co-opted by the media. And somewhere inside all of us, I think, is not only the recognition of the losses and impact of those horrifying events but also of the mother who lost a son to a drunk driver on that day, to an overdose, a daughter to a murder, a father to an illness. Loss comes every day and pain follows it. The question has always been how to be at peace with today and believe tomorrow can be better. (2002)

While *The Indian Runner*, *The Crossing Guard*, *The Pledge* and, as we will see, *Into the Wild*, can be understood as social problems films, addressing returned soldiers, colonialism and the violence at the heart of America, masculinity in crisis, the failure of a rational worldview and the search for identity amongst the nation's myths, 'U.S.A.' proposes that the events of 11 September 2001 offer an opportunity, at least, to reconsider what the events might mean, recalling Penn's activist politics, for the life of a democracy so much at the mercy of its own mediatised images.

CHAPTER SEVEN

Into the Wild

> There is a pleasure in the pathless woods;
> There is a rapture on the lonely shore;
> There is society, where none intrudes,
> By the deep sea, and music in its roar:
> I love not man less, but Nature more…
>
> Lord Byron (pre-title epigraph to *Into the Wild*)

> It's just not a mystery to me why he [McCandless] wanted to come here. […] It's so hard to explain. I know that there's a lot of people for whom it is a mystery but it's another one of those things. If you have to ask, you're never going to understand. But it's our job [he and Penn] to try to help people to understand.
>
> – Jon Krakauer, in *Iconclasts* (2007)

Of all Penn's films, *Into the Wild* (2007) is most interested in location. Although the film, in its earlier scenes, is set in various parts of the US, including Georgia, California, Washington, Oregon, Arizona and Nevada, it is principally concerned with Alaska, the place to which Christopher McCandless (Emile Hirsch), leaving behind a life of privilege and familial deceit, and a lost childhood, is heading and where he believes he will, in a transcendental manner, realise himself. It is difficult to over-emphasise the gravity of Alaska in the American imagination.

Into the Wild is based on Jon Krakauer's 1996 account of McCandless's death, expanded from his 1993 *Outside* magazine article. What generated and sustained Krakauer's interest in McCandless's death is the ways in which the story spoke to him personally and to what he understood to be broader cultural concerns. In his 'Author's Note' Krakauer tells us:

> I was haunted by the particulars of the boy's starvation and by vague, unsettling parallels between events in his life and those in my own. Unwilling to let McCandless go, I spent more than a year retracing the convoluted path that led to his death in the Alaskan taiga, chasing down details of his peregrinations with an interest that bordered on obsession. In trying to understand McCandless, I inevitably came to reflect on other larger subjects as well; the grip wilderness has on the American imagination, the allure high-risk activities hold for young men of a certain mind, the complicated, highly charged bond that exists between fathers and sons. The result of this meandering inquiry is the book now before you. (1998: x)

The romantic sentiment in these words, including the interest in masculine relationships, and the breadth of a concept such as the 'American imagination', as well as the overwhelming concern with place, would have made *Into the Wild* an obvious attraction to Penn.

At the same time, Krakauer's book maintains in interpersonal dimension that coheres the vast array of literary and cultural intertexts that the author marshals in order to make some sort of sense of the attraction that McCandless found in the life, and ultimate death, he chose. Figures as large as Leo Tolstoy, Nicolai Gogol, Henry David Thoreau, Ralph Waldo Emerson, Jack London, Mark Twain, Boris Pasternak, G. K. Chesterton and Wallace Stegner as well as Robert Nash, John Haines, Edward Hoagland, Paul Shephard are invoked through epigraphs to both buttress Krakauer's assertions as well as extend the story of McCandless out onto enormous, ineffable concerns.

This chapter will differ from previous ones in that the kind of adaptation that Penn undertakes involves a doubled intersubjective relationship, between Krakauer and McCandless and between Penn and Krakauer. Penn's identification with Krakauer and Krakauer's identification with McCandless, as well as the drawing on the already mentioned literary and cultural figures, is further complicated by including Penn's own particular use of performers, filmic style and thematic concerns.

Wilderness

At the heart of the American imagination that motivates Krakauer's book and Penn's film is the notion of wilderness. According to Roderick Nash in *Wilderness and the American Mind*, the notion can be traced back to the late nineteenth century where a number of factors brought into existence the lineage we can see persisting in recent times. In delineating between an earlier 'condemnation of wilderness', the 1890s saw the emergence of a shift from the negative connotations of wilderness being transferred to the urban environments, where 'cities were regarded with a hostility once reserved for wild forests' (1967: 143). This shift, according to Nash, was also apparent in an alteration in intellectual approaches. The 1890s saw the 'optimism and hope of the antebellum years partially yielded toward the end of the century to more sober assessments, doubts, and uncertainties' including 'a flood of immigrants ... diluting the American strain and weakening American traditions ... business values and urban living were felt to be undermining character, taste, and morality' (1967: 144). Alongside these concerns there existed a 'countercurrent' that perhaps 'the United States, if not the entire Western world, has seen it's greatest moments and was in an incipient state of decline' (ibid.).

Out of this malaise, according to Nash, emerged a 'wilderness cult' which reinvigorated the past association of wilderness with the frontier and pioneering spirit which had shaped the country. It also emerged as a source of 'virility, toughness and savagery – qualities that defined fitness in Darwinian terms' and, with the accompanying transcendental literary movement of the period, 'an increasing number of Americans invested wild places with aesthetic and ethical values, emphasizing the opportunity they afforded for contemplation and worship' (1967: 145). In these tenets it is possible to see a concomitant reaffirmation of the individual, in concert with the wilderness, as well as 'an applauding [of] savage virtues' (1967: 152). In this way wilderness offered an image, at least, of what the increasingly complicated urban modern life lacked. Nash makes this very clear:

> As the antipode of civilization, of cities, and of machines, wilderness could be associated with the virtues these entities lacked. In the primitivism specifically, many Americans detected the qualities of innocence, purity, cleanliness, and morality which seemed on the verge of succumbing to utilitarianism and the surge of progress. (1967: 157)

Jack London

A key proponent brought into this shift was the stories of Jack London, whose *The Call of the Wild* from 1903 was a runaway bestseller. The novel tells the story of Buck, a large dog stolen from his home to pull sleds on the frozen Klondike. Due to the savagery of his treatment at the hands of his keepers in combination with the harsh climactic conditions and his most significant trait, imagination, Buck develops in to what London calls 'the dominant primordial beast' defeating the legendary Spitz, a lead dog that London describes as 'from Spitzbergen through the Arctic, and across Canada and the Barrens, he had held his own with all manner of dogs and achieved mastery over them' (1987: 78). Buck in his ascendancy divests himself of the 'domestic habits'. He is shown at the close of the novel, as Nash relates, 'running at the heals of the pack through the pale moonlight or glimmering borealis, leaping gigantic above his fellows, his great throat a-bellow as he sings a song of the younger world' (1987: 156). For Nash, 'London left no doubt that it was also the song of a more vital, stronger and generally superior world, and his readers had little difficulty seeing the moral for their own lives in Buck's reversion to the primitive' (1967: 156). In the figure of Buck from *The Call of the Wild*, it is possible to see the aggregation of these ideas of wildness as an 'antipode of civilisation', of individualism, of 'savage virtues' and a morality in distinction from the oppressive urban centres of modernity.

Krakauer utilises two epigraphs from London. First, in the opening to the second chapter of his book Krakauer quotes from *White Fang*, London's 1906 follow-up novel to the story of Buck in which a wolf becomes a family dog which, as Nash points out, in the context of the 'wilderness cult ... never enjoyed the popularity' of *The Call of the Wild* (197: 156). Krakauer quotes London:

> Dark spruce forest frowned on either side the frozen waterway. The trees had been stripped by a recent wind of their white covering of frost, and they seemed to lean toward each other, black and ominous, in the fading light. A vast silence reigned over the land. The land itself was a desolation, lifeless, without movement, so lone and cold that the spirit of it was not even that of sadness. There was a hint in it of laughter, but of a laughter more terrible than any sadness – a laughter that was mirthless as the smile of the Sphinx, a laughter cold as the frost and partaking of the grimness of fallibility. It was the masterful and incommunicable wisdom of eternity, laughing at the futility of life and the effort of life. It was the Wild, the savage, frozen-hearted Northland Wild. (Quoted in Krakauer 1998: 9)

Second, as an epigraph to chapter five, entitled 'Bullhead City', Krakauer includes the lines, 'The dominant primordial beast was strong in Buck, and under the fierce conditions of trail life it grew and grew. Yet it was a secret growth. His newborn cunning gave him poise and control' from *The Call of the Wild*, in tandem with McCandless's own conflation of London and Melville – '"All Hail the Dominant Primordial Beast! And Captain Ahab Too!" ascribed to 'Alexander Supertramp, May 1999, Graffito Found Outside the Abandoned Bus on the Stampede Trail'. Krakauer's quotations are used to provide an authorised and historical companion to the preceding quote 'Jack London is King', apparently taken from 'a graffito carved into a piece of wood discovered at the site of Chris McCandless's death' (1998: 9). This strategy of drawing on evidence from McCandless's journal, correspondences and objects from the campsite further functions to enlist the nineteenth-century literature favoured by McCandless to support Krakauer's thesis. The quote from *White Fang* also serves as an illustration of the chapter entitled 'The Stampede Chapter', describing the trail and the expedition that led to the discovery of McCandless's body in the bus left in the area in the 1960s.

In this way Krakauer's employment of London functions as part of the intertextual network that holds the figure of Chris McCandless in place. Despite the invocation of such a mythical figure as London, Krakauer is, at the same time, able to point to McCandless's own hopeless romanticisation of London. Krakauer writes:

> McCandless had been infatuated with London since childhood. London's fervent condemnation of capitalist society, his glorification of the primordial world, his championing of the great unwashed – all of it mirrored McCand-

less's passions. Mesmerized by London's turgid portrayal of life in Alaska and the Yukon, McCandless read and reread *The Call of the Wild, White Fang*, 'To Build a Fire', 'An Odyssey of the North', 'The Wit of the Porportuk'. He was so enthralled with these tales, however, that he seemed to forget they were works of fiction, constructions of the imagination that had more to do with London's romantic sensibilities than with the actualities of life in the subarctic wilderness. McCandless conveniently overlooked the fact that London himself had spent just a single winter in the North and that he'd died by his own hand on his California estate at the age of forty, a fatuous drunk, obese and pathetic, maintaining a sedentary existence that bore scant resemblance to the ideals he espoused in print. (1998: 45)

Despite his own leavening of McCandless's romanticisation of London's Alaska, Krakauer, and Penn, are able to allow this canonisation of London to remain as part of the make up of the figure of the young adventurer in *Into the Wild*. In this way London becomes dispersed amongst the literary figures and their works listed at the commencement of this chapter.

Henry David Thoreau

As suggested above, alongside the rise of a popular interest in the wilderness in the late nineteenth century, emerged the transcendental movement in United States literature including Ralph Waldo Emerson, Walt Whitman and Henry David Thoreau, writers who figure prominently in the McCandless/Krakauer/Penn intersubjective triad.

In Krakauer's book and Penn's film, Thoreau remains a formidable life-force born of his singular presence in American culture, particularly that to do with the invocation of place. As Roderick Nash points out, Thoreau emerged from not just his two years at Walden Pond but also the mid-1900s amongst the Transcendentalists, as the preeminent figure that 'led the intellectual revolution that was beginning to invest wilderness with attractive rather than repulsive qualities' (1967: 95). Nash himself introduces Thoreau in terms of a significant individualism:

> On April 23, 1851 Henry David Thoreau, slight and stooped, ascended the lecture platform before the Concord Lyceum. 'I wish' he began, 'to speak a word for Nature, for absolute freedom and wildness.' Thoreau promised his statement would be extreme in an effort to answer the numerous champions of civilization. 'Let me live where I will,' he declared, 'on this side is the city, on that the wilderness, and ever I am leaving the city more and more, and withdrawing into the wilderness.' Near the end of the address, he concentrated his message in eight words: 'in Wildness is the preservation of the World'. (1967: 84)

In this dramatic character sketch and opening to the chapter 'Henry David Thoreau: Philosopher', it is possible to see the essence of the individualist, radical, pragmatic and philosophical figure that has remained such as force in conceptions of the wild in American thought. In this figure is realised 'the core of Transcendentalism ... the belief that a correspondence of parallelism between the higher realm of spiritual truth and the lower one of material objects' (1967: 85). This correspondence enabled natural objects to be understood in relation to, or more specifically as 'they reflected universal spiritual truths' (ibid.). This universe 'divided between object and essence' provided a place of surety for Humanity, although his physical existence rooted him to the material portion, like all natural objects, but his soul gave him the potential to *transcend* this condition' (ibid.; emphasis in original). As Nash points out, Transcendentalism was not entirely new but 'gave forceful expression to older ideas about the presence of divinity in the natural world' such as in English Romanticism (1967: 86). In Transcendentalism it is possible to see a means by which to shift the philosophical ground of the already mentioned emerging dissatisfaction with urban environments, on one hand, and, on the other, the idea of a dangerous, savage wilderness. This new attitude to wilderness, not only diminished fears of the wild but brought humanity closer to, or able to engage in a meaningful manner, with nature.

In Thoreau, as Nash points out, initially, this faith in wilderness was born of a concern with the cost of progress. The advent of modernity, with its 'bustling tempo and materialistic tone ... left Thoreau and many of his contemporaries vaguely disturbed and insecure' (ibid.). In relation to Krakauer and Penn's figure of McCandless, Thoreau operates as a signal characterisation in that the idea of 'self-examination' was central to his thinking and journeying through wilderness was paramount to his thinking and to understanding its value (see 1967: 87–8). While he looked to literature, in '*Hamlet*, *The Iliad*, and the Scripture' and in history such as 'Rome's founders being suckled by the wolf', it was in experience, in the affect of wilderness, where he found 'some grand, serene, immortal, infinitely encouraging, thought invisible companion, and walked with him' (1967: 88, 89). Importantly this conception of nature was superficial, what Nash terms 'a figurative tool' that Thoreau utilised as 'a metaphor for the human mind' (1967: 89):

> Wilderness symbolized the unexplored qualities and untapped capacities of every individual. The burden of his message was to penetrate the 'wildness ... in our brain and bowels, the primitive vigor of Nature in us.' In *Walden* (1854) he exhorted his reader to 'be ... the Lewis and Cark [sic] and Frobisher of your own streams and oceans; explore your own higher latitudes.' The essential frontier, in Thoreau's estimation, had no geographic location but was found 'wherever a man *fronts* a fact.' But going to the outward, physical wilderness was highly conducive to an inward journey. Wild country offered the necessary freedom and solitude. Moreover it offered life stripped down to the essentials. (Ibid.)

This slippage between the outward, physical journeying undertaken by Thoreau at Walden, the Maine Woods and Middlesex County and inward, philosophical and identificatory journeying that underlay the adventure, could be seen as opening up a space for a kind of individualistic pursuit of wilderness for the sake of realising the self, the kind of embracing of the wild to realise oneself, at all costs to relationships and community that is apparent in Krakauer and Penn's *Into the Wild*.

Yet, as Nash also points out, Thoreau's was not an unabashed embracing of wildness but a 'straddling' of the 'savage and civilized conditions of man' (1967: 91). Nash states that in 1846 Thoreau travelled from Concord to the woods of Northern Maine where 'the wilderness of Maine shocked [him]' (ibid.). Nash describes Thoreau's encounter:

> Climbing Mt. Katahdin, he was struck by its contrast to the kind of scenery he knew around Concord. The wild landscape was 'savage and dreary' and instead of his usual exultation in the presence of nature, he felt 'more lone than you can imagine.' It seems as if he was robbed of his capacity for thought and transcendence. Speaking of man's situation in wilderness, he observed: 'vast, Titanic, inhuman Nature has got him at disadvantage, caught him alone, and pilfers him of some of his divine faculty. She does not smile on him as in the plains'. (Ibid.)

For Nash, the Maine Woods experience 'sharpened Thoreau's thinking about wilderness's relationship with civilization' and led to him recalibrating his insistence on the importance of wildness, as a lived experience and a philosophical concept:

> The answer for Thoreau lay in a combination of the good inherent in wildness with the benefits of cultural refinement. An excess of either condition must be avoided. The vitality, heroism, and toughness that came with a wilderness condition had to be balanced by the delicacy, sensitivity, and 'intellectual and moral growth' characteristic of civilization. 'The natural remedy' he continued, 'is to be found in the proportion which the night bears to the day, the winter to the summer, thought to experience'. (1967: 92)

This rebalancing of the wilderness/civilisation dyad is one aspect of the writer's account of wildness that gets lost in what Lawrence Buell, in his 'The Thoreauvian Pilgrimage', has called 'the public reverence for Thoreau' (1989: 175). For Buell, it is not just the figure of Thoreau that looms large in transcendental conceptions of wilderness, but also 'Thoreau's Walden as a site of pilgrimage and as a prototype for imitation' (1989: 176). For our purposes it is the ways in which the figure of Thoreau is identified with by McCandless, and Krakauer and Penn. In many ways this identification springs from the ways in which Thoreau, according to Buell in *Literary Transcendentalism*, compared to, say, Emerson 'establishes himself as a more distinct character in his own books, telling far more about himself and almost never using an exemplary "I"' (1973: 297). Writing about the dearth of accounts of Thoreau's use of a persona, in a way that seems to preempt McCandless, Krakauer and Penn, Buell understands the attention given to 'Thoreau's use of nature, and particularly the symbolism of *Walden*' (1973: 297):

> To the extent that Thoreau's works are designed to replicate a universe in miniature, this approach is certainly a fruitful one, but it tends to distract attention

too much from the hero of the story. To most readers, I suspect, the metaphorical unity of *Walden* is really less interesting than the succession of exploits of its crusty, resourceful, unpredictable narrator: Thoreau hoeing beans, Thoreau nearly devouring a woodchuck, Thoreau throwing his limestone paperweight out the window, and so forth. (1973: 297–8)

Here, as Buell asserts, Thoreau's persona comes to the fore in *Walden*, 'more than in Thoreau's other books, where the persona plays a relatively passive role of mediator and reporter for the most part, the speaker in *Walden* becomes the main character in an action of his own making. Thoreau's masterpiece is thus the closest the transcendentalists came to creating a major work of prose fiction' (1973: 301).

While *Walden* stands as Thoreau's preeminent work, perhaps more of a symbol which we readily interchange for the author's name, providing us with a direct link to ideas of place which prefigure the manner in which McCandless is understood by Krakauer and Penn, it is through Thoreau's 'Civil Disobedience' that it is possible to better understand the radical individualism that constitutes much of what motivates the figure in the American imagination. As José Joaquín Sánchez Vera points out, Krakauer writes that McCandless 'took as gospel the essay "On the Duty of Civil Disobedience"' in the episode where McCandless abandons his yellow Datsun in the desert (2013: 1). Later when trying to understand McCandless's admiration for Ronald Reagan and his co-founding of the Republican Club in College, despite 'more and more of the classes he took [addressing] such pressing issues as racism and world hunger and inequities in the distribution of wealth' (Krakauer 1998: 123), Krakauer could argue,

> Chris's seemingly anomalous political positions were perhaps best summed up by Thoreau's declaration in 'Civil Disobedience': 'I heartily accept the motto – "That government is best which serves least".' Beyond that his views were not easily characterized. (Ibid.)

This pliability of Thoreau's thinking, able to encompass disparate positions, makes for easy philosophical underpinning, emboldened by the formidable figure of Thoreau. In his 'Henry Thoreau as a Mirror of Ourselves', Alfred Tauber tells us he first encountered *Walden* in the early 190s when it aligned with the social and cultural movements that were emerging at the time:

> When I read him again as a freshman in college, the sixties had provided a rich personal and cultural mulch. The Civil Rights movement had reached its zenith; feminism simmered; environmentalism renewed its call; Vietnam War protests surged. An array of personal emancipations (sex, drugs, rock and roll) and social demographics (baby boomers entering adolescence) combined to create a climate where his ideas could flourish. Civil disobedience was the most obvious Thoreauvian lesson, but more profound, his celebration of individuality inspired a generation of American students. (N.d.)

Tauber wonders how Thoreau appears to his present [2000s] students for whom *Walden* is on their Philosophy of Nature course reading list. He writes about how 'Thoreau both fascinated and baffled them … who could go from musings on a diving loon to the cost of building a house in a matter of sentences. An erudite laborer, a mystical pencil-maker, a poetic surveyor…' (ibid.). In his essaying of the relevance of Thoreau across generations, Tauber concludes:

> I suggest we regard Thoreau as a mirror of ourselves. By studying his life, we learn the limits of our own choices, to heed the moral imperative of establishing and then asserting our own values, and finally, to dream the dream of fulfilling them. Thoreau lived an American odyssey, not to the promise of the West, but rather to the frontier of self-knowledge and a life guided by moral concerns. A fecund lesson for our students to consider, and a nagging challenge for their teachers to ponder. Is Thoreau a man for our times or a relic of a discarded romanticism? A Johnny Appleseed sowing virtue or a Don Quixote flailing at windmills? He demands a judgment, for better or worse. In making it, I surmise we will more fully understand our own choice. (Ibid.)

This interpretive malleability makes the individualist romantic figure of Thoreau an attractive touchstone for any generation, or its eccentrics, to cling to in sourcing a radical, although authorised, tradition in which to locate a model. Yet, as we saw in chapter two, Penn's politics proffer a pre-1968 participatory left, of active citizenship, in the case of McCandless, at a variance to the familial and communitarian forces that he encounters in his travels, an individualistic mode based on the tenets derived from London and Thoreau. In this way Thoreau's persona in *Walden* provides an important intertext for the interpersonal account of McCandless in Krakauer's book and Penn's outsider cinema.

Leo Tolstoy

The third major figure that McCandless and Krakauer draw on is the turn of the twentieth-century author Leo Tolstoy. The opening of chapter three, 'Carthage', of *Into the Wild* includes epigraphs from Tolstoy's early short story 'Family Happiness' (1859) and Wallace Stegner's *The American West as Living Space* (1988). The quote from Tolstoy is prefigured by the words 'Passage Highlighted in One of the Books Found with Chris McCandless's Remains'. It reads:

> I wanted movement and not a calm course of existence. I wanted excitement and danger and the chance to sacrifice myself for my love. I felt in myself a superabundance of energy which found no outlet in our quiet life. (Quoted in Krakauer 1998: 15)

Like Thoreau and London, Tolstoy is utilised and put into play by Krakauer and Penn through their quotation, to facilitate an understanding of McCandless's journey and death. 'Family Happiness' is a first-person account of the courtship and marriage of the naïve Masha to her rural neighbour and family friend, Sergey. Played out between the city and the country and across the seasons, the melodrama of Masha and Sergey's relationship, as Edward Wasiolek points out, has been mistaken for 'communicating the vacuous truth that the country is good and the city bad' employing the 'natural seasons as an analogue to the movement of emotions' (1978: 41). For example, Masha's loneliness and grief over the death of her mother in the early parts of the story are set when 'the weather was cold and so windy that the snowdrifts came higher than the windows; the panes were almost always dimmed by frost, and we seldom walked or drove anywhere throughout the winter' (Tolstoy 2005: 1). Later as emotions lighten, when the couple fall in love, it is spring and later again, as their love wanes, it is a return to winter. Similarly, and more pertinently to the way in which Tolstoy has been highlighted by McCandless and quoted by Krakauer and Penn, the bustle of the city of St Petersburg compared to the stasis of country life could be seen as a marker of Masha's life, as the quote from Krakauer seems to suggest. However, Wasiolek argues:

> The narrative is in large part a fictive tracing out, one might even say a testing, of such subtleties – what happens to love when it is naturelike, that is, when it changes, grows; and what happens to it when it is unnatural, that is, fixed into something unchanged and unchanging. The novel begins with emotions that have become unnatural in the sense that they have become immobilized. (1978: 42–3)

For Wasiolek, Tolstoy is offering a critique of grief as a social convention, an emotion that misleads Masha: 'She mourns the passing of her mother, but she also mourns the passing of the delights the trip [to St Petersburg with her mother] had promised. (1978: 41). The sense of 'excitement and danger and the chance to sacrifice myself for my love' highlighted by McCandless and Krakauer is, in this way, a simplistic, misreading of the complexities of Tolstoy's work. Masha's own misreading 'in which false thinking, and even will can replace what is naturally given' (Wasiolek 1978: 46). Wasiolek compares the courtship in the city with the courtship of Sergey:

> The courtship of Masha by Sergey is characterized by the sense of newness and change at every moment, and what characterizes the unreal courtship is habit, sameness, and boredom. What had appeared to be excitement and variety to Masha, become, even to her at the end, habit and repetition ... Masha's estrangement from real life and from her husband begins in the country, and what estranges her in the country leads her to seek the city and sophistication and not the other way around. (Ibid.)

In McCandless's worldview, adopted by Krakauer and Penn, the reliance on a city/country dichotomy delimits the fuller appreciation of the sophistication of Tolstoy's melodramatic imagination, which employs an extended understanding of environment to include any surrounding influences on the human condition.

In examining the ways that London's representation of a wild Alaskan figure, of how Thoreau's persona has resonated out of *Walden*, and of a selective reading of Tolstoy's melodrama of bourgeois values, it is perfectly understandable why Penn would have been attracted to Krakauer's rendering of McCandless, particularly given the kinds of outsider figures we have already discussed in Franky Roberts from *The Indian Runner*, Freddie Gale from *The Crossing Guard* and Jerry Black from *The Pledge*.

Intersubjective Triad

As alluded to above, Penn's adaptation of Krakauer's book flows on from the manner in which Krakauer involves himself in the fiction of Christopher McCandless, identifying with him, understanding McCandless, the outsider adventurer in relation to the figure that Krakauer makes of himself in his previous book, *Into Thin Air* (1997). Amongst stories about comparative adventurers such as Gene Rosselini, John Mallon Waterman and Carl McCunn, and accounts of McCandless's relationships with the likes of Jan Burres and her boyfriend Bob, Ronald Franz, Wayne Westerburg, the latter grouping appearing as characters in Penn's film, Krakauer includes first-person passages recalling his own adventures in his youth and passages devoted to his encounters with McCandless's family. In the 'Author's Note' to *Into the Wild* he writes:

> I won't claim to be an impartial biographer. McCandless's strange tale struck a personal note that made a dispassionate rendering of the tragedy impossible. Through most of the book, I have tried – and largely succeeded, I think – to minimize my authorial presence. But let the reader be warned: I interrupt McCandless's story with fragments of a narrative drawn from my own youth. I do so in the hope that my experiences will throw some oblique light on the enigma of Chris McCandless. (1998: x)

Despite his confidence in his own ability to control the measure of his own subjectivity, Krakauer's presence is notable in the book. In two later chapters of *Into the Wild*, both entitled 'The Stikine Ice Cap', prefigured by epigraphs from John Menlove Edwards' 'Letter From a Man', Thoreau's *Journal*, John Muir's *The Mountains of California* and Donald Barthelme's *The Dead Father*, Krakauer diverts onto a recollection of his own 'willful, self-absorbed, intermittently reckless, moody' disposition in his youth (1998: 134) as a way into understanding McCandless's death as 'a terrible accident' rather than the possibility of suicide that had been speculated upon (ibid.). Krakauer then goes on to write about his obsession with climbing an Alaskan mountain called the Devil's Thumb. In a mirror to his account of McCandless, Krakauer mentions his 'literary diet overly rich in the works of Nietzsche, Kerouac and John Menlove Edwards' who 'climbed not for sport but to find refuge from the inner torment that framed his existence' (1998: 135), his own obliviousness to extreme natural danger as well as high career expectations from his own father. Written in the first-person, this intersubjective figuration continues the hall of mirrors from Thoreau and London to McCandless, to Krakauer and on to Penn.

As alluded to in the epigram to this chapter, Penn and Krakauer appeared together in the Sundance Channel's *Iconoclasts* (2007), a series that, according to its website, 'pairs up innovators from film, literature, architecture, fashion, food, music and business who respect and admire each other'. It is in this episode of *Iconoclasts* that it is possible to see a cementing of this intersubjective relationship. In the opening montage sequence it is apparent that both Krakauer, shown on an Alaskan glacier, and Penn, climbing an ice-covered cliff while wielding an ice-pick, understand each other in a lineage that McCandless also belongs to. Krakauer says: 'Alaska is more my element than his, but that guy [Penn] is a source [sic] of nature. He does what he wants, when he wants, the ways he does it and doesn't give a rat's ass what anyone else thinks.' Penn says, 'Krakauer is something else. I mean he's one of those people who puts themselves right there in the lion's den and reports it humanly, personally'; and later: 'My Jack London was Jon Krakauer.' These notions of extraordinary individuals encountering extraordinary, primordial (recalling London) landscapes dovetails with the ways in which they have both represented McCandless and his adventures.

In an interview for IGN Penn said:

I read [*Into the Wild*] when it came out. I read it twice in a row. I started to get the rights to it the next day. The impression that Jon Krakauer's book made on me and Chris McCandless's story made on me was the movie that I made. That's what I read and then was embellished by my collaborators later. But the structure, the skeleton of this thing, was [that] Jon had me 75 per cent of the movie that you saw already, and I had 25 percent of making cinematic what he'd made in literature and to do that with my partners. I can answer the question in boring length, but the movie should answer it for me. This is what I intended to make. (Penn 2007)

Despite the excision of Krakauer's presence as a subjective voice in Penn's film, the director adopts the multivalent structure of Krakauer's book and non-chronological narrative replacing the author's presence with that of McCandless's sister, Carine (Jena Malone) who not only appears as a substantial presence in the film but acts as a narrator and a reader of letters between Chris and herself.

The use of multiple social characters from Krakauer's book as fictional ones in Penn's film, including the narration by Carine at once leavens the variety of documentary voices in the novel into the performative realm as well as complicating the documentary/historical reality divide apparent in the film. This is particularly the case with Carine's narration. When asked by IGN about the nature of the 'bond between the sister and brother and hav[ing] her narrate the story when he never contacted her throughout his journey', Penn responds:

Because I knew it to be so from the letters that he had written her previously, from memory. Letters that are not copied in either the movie or the book, things that remain private. But it's not an idle claim that it in my view represents what the relationship was. I think that the answer is in the film. I think that she in the narration answers it, but it seems to me that that was the closest I could get to the truth of what that relationship was. (Ibid.)

Emile Hirsch and the Method

In the production reports and interviews surrounding the release of *Into the Wild* much was made of the choice of Emile Hirsch for the role of Christopher McCandless. According to Charles McGrath, Penn had initially wanted Leonardo DiCaprio to play McCandless, alongside Marlon Brando as Ronald Franz, when the project was first mooted some ten years earlier. In an interview with *Slash Film*, Hirsch claimed to have lost 26 pounds 'to get in shape for the film' and then lost another 13 pounds for the Alaska episode of the film, totaling nearly one quarter of his body weight in two phases. McGrath writes about the physical demands made on Hirsch including being asked to

> shoot rapids in a kayak, something he had never tried before; float naked in a freezing stream; and not flinch when an enormous grizzly passed within inches of him. (The bear was supposedly trained, but there were sharpshooters on the set just in case.) Besides physical stamina, Mr. Hirsch brings to the part a kind of loopy charm, in one scene talking directly to an apple he's eating, and the performance suggests that Mr. McCandless might have been less of a weirdo than an innocent, even a secular saint of sorts, who had a transforming effect on the people he met in his wanderings. (2007)

Later in his article McGrath takes this physicality further pointing to the scene on the rapids of the Colorado River as one that Penn 'cared a lot about' and decided to exchange a kayak for the canoe that the real McCandless used. According to McGrath, Penn decided that images of the inexperienced McCandless (Hirsch) tackling white water rapids 'would demonstrate the character's feeling of exhilaration and adventure, his almost mystical belief in his own abilities'. In a strange extension of the intersubjective relations between London, Thoreau, Krakauer and Penn, McGrath points out how Penn demonstrated what he wanted from the young actor:

> That Mr. Hirsch had never done such a thing and was scared half to death only made it better. To reassure Mr. Hirsch that he wouldn't drown, and perhaps to

Christopher McCandless's (Emile Hirsch) 'mystical belief in his own abilities' in *Into the Wild* (2007)

assert his own physical self, Mr. Penn shot through the rapids first, even though he too had never done it before. Describing this part of the filming over dinner, he made it sound a lot like Outward Bound. (Ibid.)

Sean Penn, in identifying an actor for the role of McCandless, recalls his choices of a young Viggo Mortensen or David Morse, for *The Indian Runner* rather than the experienced or even iconic Jack Nicholson or Ernest Borgnine in *The Pledge* or 'U.S.A.'. Instead of surrounding himself with experienced actors, Penn's choice of a young Hirsch for a role that Penn may have undertaken himself twenty years earlier, sees the director in the role of mentor. In the interview with IGN, Penn describes Hirsch's attraction to him for the role:

He's got a lot talent. You used to be able to get some pretty intriguing brooders, you know, out of the young generation or whatever that was, and then today you can get the clever and the witty and the sexy and the charming and the this and that, but none of those things happen to be the proper tool for this kit. I needed somebody who had a talent and a mug and a will – and also to photograph somebody going from boy to man, so you're catching somebody on that cusp. So it was all those things that Emile had that I don't know another who has. (2007)

In a further strengthening of the intersubjectivity between Penn and Emile Hirsch, the former came across Hirsch in Catherine Hardwicke's biographical drama *Lords of Dogtown* (2005), based on the same cultural milieu that gave rise to the Stacy Peralta-directed *Dogtown and Z-Boys* which Penn narrated four years earlier. In *Lords of Dogtown* Hirsch plays the role of Jay Adams, a contemporary, as we have seen, from the same milieu that produced the character Jeff Spicoli in *Fast Times at Ridgemont High*, as well as the actor who played him.

The City

This dichotomy between the city and country environments is played out explicitly in narrative and stylistic terms in Penn's film by contrasting between the images of what it understands to be natural images and those of the city. This is done through the inclusion of a distinct episode, recalling the isolated, stalled temporality and spatial confines of the Nebraska of *The Indian Runner* as well as the Los Angeles of *The Crossing Guard*, where McCandless ventures to Los Angeles by rail. What becomes a significant episode in Penn's film is derived from a conflation of two small fragments in Krakauer's book. The first is an entry from McCandless's journal where he goes to Los Angeles 'to get an ID and a job but feels extremely uncomfortable in society now and must return to road immediately' and another where the young man wrote that '[his nom de plume] Alexander [Supertramp] buried his backpack in the desert on 2/27 [February 27] and entered Las Vegas with no money and no ID (Krakauer 1998: 37). McCandless's journal, where he wrote in the third person, is quoted by Krakauer:

He lived on the streets with bums, tramps, and winos for several weeks. Vegas would not be the end of the story, however. On May 10, itchy feet returned and Alex left his job in Vegas, retrieved his backpack, and hit the road again... (Ibid.)

In Penn's film this slight entry becomes a lengthier diversion to provide scenes of contrast with the larger elegiac landscape images of the rest of the film.

After crossing back into the United States from Mexico, McCandless jumps a freight train at night and journeys to Los Angeles, in a montage sequence accompanied by Roger Miller's 'King of the Road'. The initial images of the city's downtown we see are through razor wire, over McCandless's shoulder, alongside the railroad tracks. He exits the train and the railway yards before emerging from a stormwater drain into the Los Angeles river. The film cuts to the clean lines of downtown skyscrapers and the scruffy, unkempt visage of McCandless with his backpack and soiled clothes. These images are followed by a short sequence of him walking the streets, with location sound, asking a passerby for the time. There is a sudden cut to nighttime and blurred neon lights before focusing on an urban neighbourhood and then on a line of men, including McCandless, in front of a Los Angeles Mission sign in a yellow light. McCandless is then at a counter of the Mission where he speaks with an attendant about an ID. After taking a bed McCandless wanders the nighttime streets of downtown Los Angeles, including the ubiquitous 2nd Street Tunnel in the Bunker Hill region; a Mexican cantina where he eats; and a series of trendy bars where he envisages himself superimposed into a yuppie's persona. Immediately following this sequence the film cuts to his backpack being unloaded from his locker in the Mission and him returning the key to the attendant followed by time-lapse imagery of bleeding car lights, city buildings and the San Pedro freeway sign (another nod to Bukowski and his world) illuminated at night with his face close-up in the foreground. And another image of McCandless reframed by the blurred lights from the opening of the sequence.

This sequence is prefigured by a nighttime scene at the Mexican border where McCandless is attempting to cross back into the US. A border guard questions him because he doesn't have a passport. As McCandless waits for the border guard to complete the process, we cut to a close-up of President George H. W. Bush's televised declaration of war in the Gulf (1990) – 'Some may ask, "why act now, why not wait". The answer is clear. The world can wait no longer' – before we cut to McCandless boarding the freight train. This brief scene sets up at least two intertexts. First, in a

Christopher McCandless outside the Los Angeles Mission in *Into the Wild*

scene situated on the US/Mexican border which the protagonist is crossing, it is a reintroduction to the prevailing mores of his country, at a time when it is about to go to war in the Gulf, a world away from the individualist pilgrimage he has been making down the length of his country, including the poverty and homelessness he is about to experience in the metropolis. Second, and an extension of the first, the words used by Bush in this scene raise the spectre of the same individualist, radical, pragmatic principles at the heart of American democracy which we have traced back to London and Thoreau. In this way the use of Bush's speech in this context can be understood as both an affirmation and betrayal of the worldview on which McCandless has based his journeying.

Penn's rendering of 'Nature'

The majority of *Into the Wild*'s *mise-en-scène* was constructed in concert with art directors John Richardson and Domenic Silvestri and director of photography, Eric Gautier. Gautier brought to the film a wealth of experience in French art cinema including work on the films of Agnès Varda (*One Hundred and One Nights*, 1995), Leo Carax (*Pola X*, 1999), Olivier Assayas (*Irma Vep*, 1996; *Clean*, 2004), Alain Resnais (*Wild Grass*, 2009), Raoul Ruiz (*Savage Souls*, 2001), as well as Walter Salles (*The Motorcycle Diaries*, 2004; *On the Road*, 2012). According to Gautier (2008), in an interview for *Variety*, it was Salles's *The Motorcycle Diaries* that Penn 'loved' and that 'both Walter Salles and Sean Penn were expecting [him] to bring something from the French films, something very intimate and close to the characters'. As Hirsch is often pictured alone in wide shots of the land, this intimacy within these broader images was important so that characterisation wouldn't be lost amongst the wide angles, at the same time as the film seeks to embed, to have McCandless amongst the landscape.

Much of *Into the Wild* is devoted to the landscape. Following the use of aerial shots, as we have seen, across his oeuvre, from some simple transition shots from the air in *The Indian Runner*, to the shots attempting a more expressive, mystical, 'angelic' representation of the lakes, forests and isolation of Jerry Black in *The Pledge*, Penn has given full rein to the aerial shot in *Into the Wild*.

The film opens on a framed photograph of Emile Hirsch as McCandless with a muffled 'Mama, mama, help me' before going out of focus, then back into an interior shot in which Marcia Gay Harden, as Chris's mother Billie, sits up in bed in response to a masculine voice asking 'What is it?' She says, 'I wasn't dreaming Walt, I didn't imagine it, I heard him, I heard him, I heard Chris, I heard him, I didn't imagine it,' before she breaks down and is held by Walt McCandless (William Hurt). This opening represents an immediate recalling of melodrama conventions we have seen at work in Penn's previous films. The use of interiors, particularly the bedroom, family photographs such as we saw in *The Crossing Guard*, the use of out-of-focus images, canted and cluttered framing, unable to contain the broken bonds of bourgeois life, all preface the singular, expansive and epic landscape images that are to follow.

This opening scene fades to black before the film's guitar-picking theme arrives and we witness a montage sequence of cluttered images taken in and out of a train hurtling through countryside: of the side of the train curving around a bend; a canted shot of the words 'Alexander Supertramp April 1992' in chalk on a steel beam; an ice flow obscured by bridge supports; a close-up on a 'No Trespassing' sign at the entrance to a tunnel. Scrawled text in yellow appears on the screen: 'Wayne. Greetings from Fairbanks!' There is a second montage sequence: of smalltown buildings; a thumb stretched out hitchhiking; a truck on icy roads and the blurred back of a backpack; a slushy road; an out-of-focus shop interior with the words 'Picked up a new book on the local flora and fauna' like a handwritten journal entry across the screen; a shot of a snowy landscape divided by a wire fence with 'I'm prepared and have stocked all necessary comforts to live off the land for few months' across the screen, as the shot cuts to a distant building with 'Creamers Dairy' on the roof; another shot of cars outside a Gold Hill Liquor, Gas, Groceries; and a third shot of an Alaskan Prospectors store before the journal text 'It might be a very long time before I return south' over a shot of a Downunder Guns store sign. The sequence then cuts to images of snow-covered land and pine trees alongside a road and the text 'Just wanted to let you know, you're a great man' followed by a white 'Closed for Winter' sign. This fades over an image of a green 'Stampede Rd' sign before an abrupt cut to a stilled image of a snow-bound plain with two lines of sparse vegetation marking out a pattern down the left hand side and across the near top of the frame with a snow-capped mountain along the very top of the frame. This shot is held for approximately ten seconds before the 'Paramount Vantage and River Road Entertainment present' title appears and the image ever-so-slowly begins to tilt downwards, as it emerges as an aerial crane shot, to where a grey pickup truck rolls into the lower left of the frame before a chain fence across a snow covered road appears and the title song ends. We hear a voice say, 'You left all your shit on my dash' and the reply 'Keep it.' 'Well, suit yourself' from the first and 'Thanks again' from the second voice. As this extraordinary shot holds, a small figure emerges into the frame as a voice calls 'hold on a minute!' The figure then walks back towards the truck. This shot lasts more than one minute and four seconds and is mostly silent. We then cut to an extreme close-up of a hand inside a truck lifting a pair of boots, before cutting to the truck's exterior and the walking figure with a backpack turned towards the camera is handed the boots out the truck window as a man says, 'Here take these. They'll keep your feet dry.' A shot from the truck's interior framed by the side of the man's face and the figure's shoulder with the white snow in between. 'If you make it out alive give me a call. My number's inside the boots.' The close-up of the man in the truck holds as the figure replies 'thanks' and takes the boots. We then cut to a close-up of the truck driver, in heavy jacket and cap with a beard and weathered face contemplating the figure off-screen before he starts the truck and reverses back around on the road. The figure with the backpack is shown walking away from the camera as the truck sounds fade and we cut back to the aerial shot for another six seconds as the figure walks across the lower frame right. We then cut to the same figure walking in silence in long shot mid-frame in snow-bound plains as the words 'I now walk …' are written on the screen followed by a cut to an extreme long shot similar to the long-held one as the title 'INTO THE WILD' appears in the same scrawled yellow text which modulates into a more formal green script, with the figure shrinking even further

The extreme shot of McCandless setting out in *Into the Wild*

before cutting to an image of a large mountain range accompanied by wind whistling on the soundtrack.

The following main title sequence, where the Eddie Vedder song 'Long Nights' emerges in full, is a series of epic images of mountains shrouded in mist, clouds in a sun-filled sky, a pan across and down mountain peaks, a Bald Eagle soaring in the sky, and a long tilt down a snow-covered mountain side to a medium shot of Emile Hirsch as McCandless with wild hair and full beard, lugging the backpack up a steep incline just as Vedder's baritone, rough-hewn vocals commence: 'Have no fear, for when I'm alone, I'll be better off, than I was before / I've got this light, I'll be around to grow, who I was before, I cannot recall / Long nights allow me to feel, I'm falling, I am falling/ The lights go out. Let me feel I'm falling / I am falling, safely to the ground.' This song accompanies a sequence of epic shots of McCandless in solitude, often shot from below with the sky as his backdrop, or trudging across the snow with the mountains in the background as the camera pans, placing a woollen hat on a bare branch or in extreme long shot crossing a plain toward a running stream, crossing the stream and hunting with a rifle, cooking his kill and pictured amongst forest foliage in a Zen-like repose, followed by a cut to a zoom in on a picturesque image of a mountain peak layered in clouds as the song ends.

These two sequences, which follow and can be seen in relation to those featuring McCandless's traumatised parents in the melodramatic scenes that open the film, seek to affirm Chris McCandless as a masculine individual. This is particularly the tenor of the extreme temporal length of the mostly stilled frame into which the figure of Chris McCandless moves as he is dropped off at the roadside as the 'alone', 'better off', 'around to grow' figure recalling London, Thoreau, the real-life McCandless and Krakauer.

Eddie Vedder

Much of *Into the Wild* relies on this balance between montage sequences and characterisation, due to Hirsch, in the main, being the only character on screen, as well as the film's assertions about Nature motivated by the Byron quote that prefigures the film. Much of this sequencing is accompanied by Vedder's music, specifically written and performed for the film. Charles McGrath asked Penn about his ideas for the music-image relationship in the film:

'I deliberately underwrote parts of the script because I felt that the music and the lyrics would tell part of the story,' he said. 'I liked a lot the way that works in *The Graduate* [1967] and in Hal Ashby movies like *Harold and Maude* [1971].' (2007)

Eddie Vedder is a figure who emerged from the late 1980s Seattle grunge music scene fronting the band Pearl Jam. Grunge was a musical movement, as Catherine Strong in *Grunge: Music and Memory* tells us, located somewhere between, on the one hand, the West Coast post-punk attitudes of bands such as Black Flag, Minutemen and Minor Threat and, on the other, the Thrash Metal of the likes of Metallica, Slayer and Anthrax (2011: 17–18):

Musically grunge has a 'dirty' sound to it (possibly where the name grunge came from) especially in the early days when low recording budgets, lack of expertise and money, and a deliberate lack of professionalism affected the recording process. The music was quite visceral with the bass low and guitars alternating being roaring and quiet. The form of grunge that eventually gained commercial success also had a strong melodic aspect to it. (2011: 18)

In this sound, and lyrics that Strong describes as being 'about failed, boring, doomed or destructive relationships' in tandem with the image of long hair, loose clothing and a certain impassivity, grunge music was designed as an alternative to the then contemporary music scene (2011: 19). In opposition to the rampant commercialism of the early 1990s, Eddie Vedder and Pearl Jam projected an earthier bohemianism born of a slacker/surfer attitude wedded to an activist persona. Vedder developed an intensity and rage in his singing and performance in music and in his grass roots approach to politics. Vedder's activism can be seen in his insistence in 1994 when Pearl Jam, then one of the most popular acts in the world, insisted that the corporate giant Ticketmaster donate $1 from every concert ticket sold to charity. Ticketmaster agreed, then added $1 to every ticket price, resulting in the band taking Ticketmaster to court, losing and then cancelling the tour, resulting in more litigation. Nevertheless, this established Pearl Jam's alternative and activist credentials.

The music of Pearl Jam (slang for semen) is a strong masculine sound, embodied in part by Vedder's baritone voice. This, combined with the already mentioned bohemian, surfer, activist components, seems an appropriate fit for the soundtrack to Penn's *Into the Wild*. Vedder had previously been associated with Penn having contributed to the soundtrack of Tim Robbins' *Dead Man Walking* and Jessie Nelson's *I Am Sam*, both of which starred Penn.

Vedder's music is a significant element of the film, overlain as it is over many of the montage sequences to which Penn devotes much of his film. Penn said to Rebecca Murray in a press conference for the film:

I'd written a script to be, in part, told by song. So I'd left out narrative in those transitional sequences, knowing just the seed of what I needed from the songs to close those gaps. It was about halfway through shooting, really, through Emile's performance that I started feeling, 'This is it. This is Eddie's voice. This is the musical soul, the voice of what Emile was bringing.' I asked, and then I'll let him take it from here. (Murray n.d.)

As suggested above, the accumulation of natural settings, a rendering of the place of Alaska in terms of the historical and the intersubjective figure of Christopher McCandless are further strengthened by Vedder's music which, while it includes certain 'message' lyrics ('as I walk, the hemisphere, got my wish, to up and disappear'), it is in the solemnity of Vedder's voice quality, bringing with it the surrounding figural qualities, that further extends the lineage of London, Thoreau, McCandless, Krakauer and Penn.

Over this masculine lineage Penn lays three feminine narrations, as well as a series of narrational vignettes and recitations belonging to Chris. One of these is Jena Malone's characterisation of Chris's sister, Carine McCandless, another to the real-life Carine McCandless and another to poet Sharon Olds. These voices provide an intriguingly complicated layering of the story of McCandless in relation to the familiar forces which are understood to be the source of some of his anguish as well as providing a divergence from the adaptation of Krakauer's book.

Penn's striving to get at this truth with these voice-overs recalls Terrence Malick's use of an unreliable narration in his films *Badlands* and *Days of Heaven*, but in particular *The Thin Red Line* (1998), in which Penn acted. In his book *The Thin Red Line* Michel Chion discusses Malick's use of what Chion terms an 'inner voice' to describe the ways in which narration works in these three films (2004: 53). Comparing Malick's narrations with those in David Lynch's *Dune* (1984) Chion sees the adaptation of the 'characters' streams of consciousness' appearing as italics in Herbert's book emerging in Lynch's film as the inner voice which is 'the equivalent of the theatrical and operatic aside found in Moliere or Mozart: it is usually a reaction to the situation in which the characters find themselves, a deliberation before action' (ibid.).

McCandless's own narration and words to himself and the use of on-screen titles, function to comment on the action, and lack thereof, in the scenes in Alaska but also on the recalled images of his life with his parents such as in the sequence around McCandless's graduation:

I see them standing at the formal gates of their colleges. I see my father strolling out under the ochre sandstone arch, the red tiles glinting like bent plates of blood behind his head. I see my mother with a few light books at her hip, standing at the pillar made of tiny bricks with the wrought-iron gates still open behind her, its sword-tips black in the May air. They are about to graduate. They are about to get married. They are kids. They are dumb. All they know is they are innocent, they would never hurt anybody. I want to go up to them and say, 'Stop! Don't do it. She's the wrong woman. He's the wrong man. You are going to do things you cannot imagine you would ever do. You are going to do bad things to children. You are going to suffer in ways you've never heard of.

'The broken bonds of bourgeois life'; Billie (Marcia Gay Harden) and Walt McCandless (William Hurt) in *Into the Wild*

You're going to want to die.' I want to go up to them there in the late May sunlight and say it. But I don't do it. I wanna live. I take them up like male and female paper dolls and bang them together at the hips like chips of flint as if to strike sparks from them. I say, 'Do what you were going to do. And I will tell about it.'

Over time, this 'narration' turns out into a recital. As the montage sequence develops a narrative with McCandless, at first walking beside and then arriving in a car with his sister Carine, he completes this monologue and we switch to location sound as she asks, 'Who wrote that?', to which he replies, 'It could have been either one of us, couldn't it?' This narration/recitation is a quotation from Sharon Olds' 'I Now Go Back to May 1937' from her *The Gold Cell* (1987). Penn described the inclusion of Olds:

> When I started to write, the poem had probably been in my head for about five years. But the book had been [for] about 10 years. When I started writing it, I got to about page three and that poem just jabbed me, so it was a way into something early in the picture. [...] I'd written the narration already but by that time but I knew I was going to want a woman's touch, and in particular, that woman's, if I could get it. So we made an overall deal with Sharon. I finished the script and then came back at the end when I'd recorded all of my original narration with Jena [Malone] prior to shooting, with timings and so on. Then I got Jena and Carine McCandless and Sharon and myself in a recording studio in San Francisco and we did our final kind of spin-around. Got it to be better and more with a woman's voice. (2007)

In Penn's film the female narrations, alongside McCandless's, operate along the lines of feminine 'inner voices' that, at the same time provide a link back to the familial relations which have set McCandless off on his journey, delineating the deceit in the family melodrama, at the same time as they comment on his intentions and raison d'être. Jena Malone as Carine McCandless:

> Chris measured himself and those around him by a fiercely rigorous moral code. He risked what could have been a relentlessly lonely path, but found company in the characters of the books he loved from writers like Tolstoy, Jack

London and Thoreau. He could summon their words to suit any occasion, and he often would. I forgot to ask what quote he'd have picked for his graduation dinner, but I had a good idea of who the primary target would be. It was inevitable that Chris would break away. And when he did, he would do it with characteristic immoderation.

Following Chion, *Into the Wild*'s inner voices, as distinct from the recitations belonging to McCandless, seek to articulate the backstory of the film. Chion's comparison of Malick's interior monologues with silent cinema is instructive here. While Malick's usage is 'short, fragmented', like the titles in silent cinema, Penn's is more utilitarian, a way to broaden characterisation as well as provide a relationship between McCandless's search for himself and his physical journey, in an existential manner, as well as better articulate the melodramatic structures which are the hallmark of this film and his cinema more generally.

In the conclusion we will take up this notion of melodrama as it relates to the critical aspect of Penn's cinema, derived as it is from the New Hollywood cinema, two seemingly opposed traditions which meld in his oeuvre.

CONCLUSION

Places of Hope

In the previous chapters we have seen how each film in the cinema of Sean Penn to date is definitely placed as it sits amongst a network of intertexts. These films are mostly about the personal worldview of a person born into a left-wing Hollywood and theatre background, who has accumulated a litany of friends and associates to whom he can turn for the figures who populate his filmic worlds. His oeuvre is replete with scores of quotations and references, figures in themselves, that bring to bear an idiosyncratic, serious and single-minded way of being in the world, to the stories of outsiders working at understanding themselves in relation to the worlds they find themselves in. In this way, these worlds are vaguely familiar, often overwrought, and sometimes unformed in the traditional ways we use that judgement. The films are also critical accounts of American culture, drawing on the traditions in literature that emerged out of the Transcendentalist movement and worked its way into left politics in the immediate post-World War II generation. As we have seen, it is possible to see this critical edge to representation re-emerging in the spirit of the New Hollywood cinema of the late 1960s and early 1970s, a signal period in film history for Penn.

Furthermore, Sean Penn's directorial work straddles the tradition of New Hollywood as it leads into US independent cinema. In 'Sequelizing Hollywood: The American "Smart" Film', Claire Perkins draws on Robert Kolker, '(asking the reader to suppress chronology for the sake of imagining the relation of the fictions) observ[ing] how Gene Hackman as Harry Moseby survives *Night Moves* [Arthur Penn, 1975] only to emerge "older, more frightened, and even more lonely, as Harry Caul in ... Francis Ford Coppola's 1974 *The Conversation*"' (2010: 95). For Perkins, Kolker enables her to further extend his imagining on to Hackman's other roles such as in Jerry Shatzberg's *Scarecrow* and onto to her principle interest, Wes Anderson's *The Royal Tenenbaums* (2001) as emblematic of how 'Hackman's performances gestures toward the way in which the anxiety-based attitudes that are largely stamped out of studio-based filmmaking in the late 1970s and through the 1980s reemerge in the 1990s smart film (ibid.).

Following Perkins, I'd suggest that the cinema of Sean Penn exists in a similar yet peculiar relation to New Hollywood and bears comparison. Perkins describes this shift:

> Where the Renaissance films tend to cast their apathetic protagonists as unattached drifters or obsessive loners, the similarly anxious figures of the smart film are securely tethered to a family, house, and career; generically, the shift can be broadly determined as a move from the road movie to the family melodrama. (2010: 96)

In these terms it is possible to understand this relationship less in terms of a shift *from* the road movie to the family melodrama than as a combination of the two. Just as Penn's films are both in and out of place they are also road movie melodramas where the masculine protagonists Franky, Freddie, Jerry, L'Homme and Christopher McCandless are all obsessive loners, constantly on the move, restless in the confines of place in which they find themselves, experiencing a crisis of identity in relation to disintegrating familial relations and faltering social circumstances casting these films in melodramatic proportions. At the same time, Penn's cinema is a reversal of the concomitant shift that Perkins observes Jeffrey Sconce discerning:

> He suggests that the critique of bourgeois taste and culture that the anxiety in both cycles represents is borne out in essentially different terms: in his estimation, the shift is from an activist emphasis on the social politics of power in 1960s and 1970s 'art cinema' to an ironic concentration on the personal politics of power, communication and emotional dysfunction in the later, smart cycle. (2010: 95)

In comparison, in the main due to his use of intertextual networks, Penn's cinema harks back, possibly in a nostalgic mode, to the New Hollywood, drawing not only on that cinema's key figures (Nicholson, Hopper, Stanton, Cassavetes, *et al*) but also it's activist, progressive and critical mode.

In all this Penn's works are distinctly located, communitarian, and concerned with people's relationships with their surroundings. Penn, again and again, utilises environmental factors to narrate small, intimate, often suffocating, mostly familial relationships at the same time as they open out in epic proportions onto the largest of humanist concerns; masculinity, environment, politics, culture. Invariably implicated in these relationships is the figure of the child, acting as a symbol of hope, of regeneration, against which the adult world is measured.

In *The Indian Runner*, the violent birth of Franky of Dorothy's child, is intercut with the murder of Caeser. In *The Crossing Guard*, Emily, Freddie and Mary's daughter, killed by John Booth, haunts both men until Emily, in her grave, reconciles the two, in relation to the metropolis of Los Angeles. Jerry's obsessive hunting of the killer of Ginny Larsen and other young girls in *The Pledge*, leads to his abuse of Lori and Chrissy, bringing about his own mental disintegration. 'U.S.A.' reconfigures this image of hope into a rebirth in terms of light and the growth of flowers emerging out of the darkness following the collapse of the Twin Towers. *Into the Wild* understands Chris McCandless's journey to selfhood as a response to the deceit he locates in his mother and father's marriage, an image of the corruption and limitations placed on self-realisation. In these ways, Penn's often oppressive, violent, uneasy, mixed-mode cinema culminates in a hopeful criticism, an image of America that correlates with Richard Rorty's proposal in 'American National Pride':

> We raise questions about our individual or national identity as part of the process of deciding what we will do next, what we will try to become. (1998: 11)

FILMOGRAPHY

Music Videos
'Eardrum Buzz' – Wire (1989)
'Kings Highway' – Joe Henry (1992)
'North Dakota' – Lyle Lovett (1992)
'Dance With The One That Brought You' – Shania Twain (1993)
'You Were Meant For Me (Juan Patino Radio Mix)' – Jewel (1995)[1]
'Highway Patrolman' – Bruce Springsteen (2000)[2]
'The Barry Williams Show' – Peter Gabriel (2002)

Features
The Indian Runner (1991)
The Mount Film Group in Association with MICO/NHK Enterprises Presents
Music Supervisor – Danny Bramson
Music by Jack Nitzsche
Edited – Jay Cassidy
Production Designer – Michael Haller
Director of Photography – Anthony B. Richmond B.S.C.
Line Producer – David S. Hamburger
Executive Producers – Thom Mount, Stephen K. Bannon, Mark Bisgeier
Co-Produced – Patricia Morrison
Produced – Don Phillips
Inspired by the song 'Highway Patrolman' by Bruce Springsteen
Written and Directed by Sean Penn

Cast
Joe Roberts – David Morse
Frank Roberts – Viggo Mortensen
Maria – Valeria Golino
Dorothy – Patricia Arquette
Randall – Jordan Rhodes
Caesar – Dennis Hopper
Mrs Roberts – Sandy Dennis
Mr Roberts – Charles Bronson
Mr Baker – Harry Crews
Mrs Baker – Eileen Ryan
Lady at Carwash – Kathy Jensen
Hotel Manager – Annie Pearson
Man at Del Mar – Phil Gould
Indian Runner – Kenny Stabler
Circus Dwarf – Neal Stark
Bearded Lady – Elaine Schoonover
Kid on Highway – James Intveld
In Loving Memory of Hal Ashby, Frank Bianco & John Cassavetes.

Music
'Feelin' Alright' –Performed by Traffic, Written by Dave Mason, Courtesy of Island Records LTD.
'Comin' Back To Me' – Performed by Jefferson Airplane, Written by Marty Balin, Courtesy of the RCA Records Labels of BMG Music.
'Fresh Air' – Performed by Quicksilver Messenger Service, Written by Jesse Oris Farrow, Courtesy of Capitol Records Inc.

By Arrangement with CEMA Special Markets.
'Couch' – Performed by Eric & Brett Haller & Craig Levitz, Written by Eric Haller.
'Red Texas Sunset' – Performed by Paulette Tyler, Written by Bud McGuire, Courtesy of All Nation Productions, Inc.
'Caballito Chontaeno' – Perfoermed by Grup 'rio Rojo' (Esteli), Written by Camilo Zapata, Courtesy of Aid to the Arts of Nicaragua.
'Green River' – Performed by Creedence Clearwater Revival, Written by John C. Fogarty, Courtesy of Fantasy Inc.
'Brothers for Good' – performed by Eric & Bret Haller, Written by Eric Haller.
'Summertime' – Performed by Janis Joplin & Bog Brother & the Holding Company, Written by George Gershwin and Du Bose Heyward, Courtesy of Columbia Records By arrangement with Sony Music Licensing.
'I Shall Be Released' – Performed by The Band, Written by Bob Dylan, Courtesy of Capitol Records Inc. Br arrangement with CEMA Special Markets.
'Rio Grande' – Courtesy of Republic Pictures Corporation.
'Gilligan's Island – Provided by Turner Entertainment Co.
1968 Democratic Convention/Demonstration New Footage - Sherman Grinberg Film Libraries.

The Crossing Guard (1995)
Miramax Film Presents
Casting – Don Phillips
Costume Designer – Jill Ohanneson
Music Supervisor – Randall Poster
Music – Jack Nitzsche
Edited – Jay Cassidy
Production Designer – Michael Haller
Director of Photography – Vilmos Zsigmond A.S.C.
Executive Producers – Bob Weinstein, Harvey Weinstein, Richard N. Gladsten
Produced – David S. Hamburger & Sean Penn
Written and Directed – Sean Penn
Production Manager – David S. Hamburger
1st Assistant Director – Brian W. Cook
Choreographer – Russell Clark
Set Decorator – Derek R. Hill
'Missing' Written and Performed by Bruce Springsteen, Courtesy of Columbia Records.
Score Produced by Michael Hoenig
Score Performed by Bradford Terrence Ellis
Featured Soloist on Tenor and Alto Saxophone – Sonny Fortune
Additional Music – Joseph Vitarelli
Music Editor – Richard Whitfield
The Producers with to Give Special Thanks to Art Linson, Bruce Springsteen, Michael Fitzgerald Patricia Morrison and Mother Against Drunk Driving and their many devoted volunteers.
Cast
Freddy Gale – Jack Nicholson
John Booth – David Morse
May – Anjelica Huston
JoJo – Robin Wright
Helen Booth – Piper Laurie
Stuart Booth – Richard Bradford
Verna – Priscilla Barnes
Peter – David Baerwald
Roger – Robbie Robertson
Bobby – John Savage
Mia – Kari Wuhrer
Jennifer – Jennifer Leigh Warren
Tanya – Kellita Smith
Sunny Ventura – Richard Sarafian
Coop – Bobby Cooper

Silas – Jeff Morris
Buddy – Buddy Anderson
Eddie – Dr. Edward L. Katz
Joe at Bar – Joe Vitterelli
Woman in Shop – Eileen Ryan
Jefferey – Ryo Ishabashi
Hank – Leo Penn
Production Manager – David S. Hamburger

Music
'Room At The Top' – Performed by Adam Ant, Written by Adam Ant, Andre Cymore and Marco Pirrone, Coutesy of MCA Records.
'Ubiquitous Mr. Love Groove' – Performed by Dead Can Dance, Written by Lisa Gerrard and Brendan Perry, Courtesy of 4AD by arrangement with Warner Special Products.
'Hopping to Health' – Performed by Sophia L. Cassidy
'Born A Cowboy' – Written and Performed by David Baerwald, Courtesy of A&M Records.
'Unspoken' – Written and Performed by David Baerwald, Courtesy of A&M Records.
'I Want a Little Sugar in My Bowl' – Performed by Hadda Brooks, Written by Nina Simone.
'Kings Highway' – Performed by Joe Henry, Courtesy of Mammoth Records.
'Herida De Amor' ('Love Hurts') – Performed by YNDIO Written by Boudleaux Bryant, Courtesy of Mexican Fontana by arrangement with Polygram Special Markets.
'Whatta Man' – Performed by Salt N' Pepa, Written by Herby Azor, Cherly James, Dave Crawford, Courtesy of Next Plateau/London Records.
'Emily' – Written and Performed by Jewel, Courtesy of Atlantic Records.
'Good Ship Lollipop' – Performed by Shirley Temple, Written by Richard A. Whiting & Sidney Clare.

The Pledge (2001)
Franchise Picture presents a Clyde is Hungry Films/ Michael Fitzgerald Production
Casting – Don Phillips
Costume Designer – Jull Ohanneson
Music – Hans Zimmer and Klaus Badelt
Edited – Jay Cassidy
Production Designer – Bill Groom
Director of Photography – Chris Menges
Executive Producer – Andrew Stevens
Produced – Michael Fitzgerald, Sean Penn, Elie Samaha
Based on the book by Friedrich Dürrenmatt
Screenplay – Jerzy Kromolowski & Mary Olson-Kromolowski
Directed – Sean Penn
Associate Producer – Brian Cook
Production Manager – Richard A. Bullock
First Assistant Director – Brian Cook
Second Assistant Director – Andrew Robinson
Art Director – Helen Jarvis
Set Director – Lesley Beale
Additional Music – Michael Brook and Craig Eastman, Heitor Pereira, Martin Tillman, Vocals – Alison Moynihan

Cast
Margaret Larsen – Patricia Clarkson
Rudy – Beau Daniels
Toby Jay Wadenah – Benicio Del Toro
Strom – Dale Dickey
Resort Owner – Wendy Morrow Donaldson
Sheriff – P. Adrien Dorval
Stan Krolak – Aaron Eckhart
Bus Driver – Shawn Henter
Ginny Larsen – Taryn Knowles

Hank – Nels Lennarson
Monash Deputy – Costas Mandylor
Real Estate Agent – J.J. McColl
Criminologist #1 – Gordon May
Deputy #3 Gardinar Millar
Doctor – Helen Mirren
Deputy #1 – Adam Nelson
Jerry Black – Jack Nicholson
Gary Jackson – Tom Noonan
Duane Larsen – Michael O'Keefe
TV Anchorman – Tony Parsons
Lori – Robin Wright Penn
Prisoner – Robert Popoff
Annalise Hansen – Vanessa Redgrave
Flea Marker Sales lady – Nicole Robert
Jim Olstad – Mickey Rourke
Chrissy – Pauline Roberts
Jena – Eileen Ryan
Alma Cage – Lucy Schmidt
Helen Jackson – Lois Smith
Eric Pollack – Sam Shepard
Floyd Cage – Harry Dean Stanton

'U.S.A.' *11/09/'01-September 11* (2002)
A Film Written and Directed by Sean Penn
With Ernest Borgnine
Executive Producer – Jon C. Scheide
–CIH Shorts Production
Director of Photography – Samuel Bayer
Editor – Jay Cassidy (ACE)
Music by Hector Pereira
Artistic Producer – Wendy Samuels
Costume Design – Jill Ohanneson
Filmmaking – Cathy Gesualdo, Jon C Scheide, Jill Frank, Joe Stafford, Sato Masuzawa, Hilary Momberger
Production Department – Sophia Cassidy, Cynthia Gates Fujikawa, Stephen Scheide, Nicholas Minkler, Bea Rembeczy, Diana Lui, Christina Graff, Adam Harris

Image – Mike Thomas, Eric Treml, Heimo Ritzinger, David Auerbach, Rob Baird, Michael May

Into the Wild (2007)
A Square One C.I.H./Linson Film production
Casting by Francine Maisler
Music by Michael Brook with Kaki King and Eddie Vedder
Original Songs by Eddie Vedder
Costume Design by Mary Claire Hannan
Edited by Jay Cassidy A.C.E.
Production Designer – Derek Hill
Director of Photography – Eric Gautier A.F.C.
Executive Producers – John J. Kelly, Frank Hildebrand, David Blocker
Produced by Sean Penn, Art Linson, Bill Pohlad
Based on the book by Jon Krakauer
Screenplay and Directed by Sean Penn
Cast
Chris McCandless – Emile Hirsch
Billie McCandless – Marcia Gay Harden
Walt McCandless – William Hurt
Carine McCandless – Jena Malone
Rainey – Brian Dierker
Jan Burres – Catherine Keener
Wayne Westerberg – Vince Vaughan
Tracy Tatro – Kristen Stewart
Ron Franz – Hal Holbrook
Jim Gallien – Jim Gallien
Unit Production Manager – John J. Kelly
First Assistant Director – David Webb
Second Assistant Director – Dylan Hopkins
Additional Narration– Sharon Olds, Carine McCandless, Jena Malone

Notes

1 This music video was made for the initial release of 'You Were Meant For Me (Juan Patino Radio Mix)' which was never released commercially. The song was re-recorded and released with a music video directed by Lawrence Carroll

2 This music video was made for the *Bruce Springsteen Video Anthology 1978–2000* DVD release. It seems Penn re-edited *The Indian Runner* for this release

BIBLIOGRAPHY

Beale, Lewis (1985) 'Gut-Level Evil: Sean Penn Films a Bizarre Crime Story', *Chicago Tribune*, 21 July. Web. Accessed 4 April 2015.
Bergfelder, Tim (2004) 'Popular Genres and Cultural Legitimacy: Fassbinder's *Lola* and the Legacy of 1950s West German Cinema', *Screen*, 41, 5, 21–39.
Bingham, Dennis (1994) *Acting Male: Masculinities in the Films of James Stewart, Jack Nicholson and Clint Eastwood*. New Brunswick, NJ: Rutgers University Press.
Blackwelder, Rob (n.d.) 'Z-Boys are Back in Town'. [Interview with Stacy Peralta and Tony Alva] SPLICEDwire. Web. Accessed 17 October 2010.
Boyd, Blanch McCrary (1984) 'The Natural', *American Film*, October, 22–6 & 91–2.
Buell, Lawrence (1973) *Literary Transcendentalism: Style and Vision in the American Renaissance*. Ithaca, NY: Cornell University Press.
____ (2001) *Writing for an Endangered World: Literature, Culture, and the Environment in the U.S. and Beyond*. Cambridge, MA: Belknap Press.
Burke, David (2011) *Heart of Darkness: Bruce Springsteen's Nebraska*. London: Cherry Red Books.
Campbell, Duncan (2002) 'Eleven Short Films about 9/11', *The Guardian*, 13 December. Web. Accessed 31 May 2015.
Carroll, Noël (1982) 'The Future of Allusion: Hollywood in the Seventies (and Beyond)', *October*, 20, 51–81.
Chion, Michel (2004) *The Thin Red Line*. London: British Film Institute.
Cook, Pam (1995) '*Outrage* (1950)', in Annette Kuhn (ed.) *Queen of the B's: Ida Lupino Behind the Camera*. Westport, CT: Praeger, 57–72.
Connelly, Christopher (1991) 'Sean Penn Bites Back', *Premiere*, 5, 2, 60–6.
Crews, Harry (1979) 'The Knuckles of Saint Bronson', in *Blood and Grits*. New York: Harper and Row, 101–26.
____ (1992) *Scarlover*. New York: Poseidon Press.
Denning, Michael (1997) *The Cultural Front: The Laboring of American Culture in the Twentieth Century*. London and New York: Verso.
Dickenson, Ben (2006) *Hollywood's New Radicalism: War, Globalisation and the Movies from Reagan to George W. Bush*. London, I.B. Taurus.

Dimendberg, Edward (2004) *Film Noir and the Spaces of Modernity*. Cambridge, MA: Harvard University Press.

Dobozy, Tamas (2001) 'In the Country of Contradiction, the Hypocrite is King: Defining Dirty Realism in Charles Bukowski's *Factotum*', *Modern Fiction Studies*, 47, 1, 43–68.

Dürrenmatt, Friedrich (2006a) *The Pledge*: Trans. Joel Agee. Chicago: University of Chicago Press.

Elsaesser, Thomas (1972) 'Tales of Sound and Fury: Observations on the Family Melodrama', *Monogram*, 4, 2–15.

Evil, Pierre (2009) 'Making the Invisible Visible: Dennis Hopper, an Aesthete in a Subcultural Environment', in Matthieu Orléan (ed.) *Dennis Hopper and the New Hollywood*. Paris: Flammarion/Cinémathèque Française, 158–63.

Frankel, Martha (1991) '... But Not Too Close', *American Film*, August, 18–25.

Gautier, Eric (2008) Interview with Ryan Mottesheard. '10 Cinematographers to Watch: Eric Gautier', *Variety*. 1 December. Web. Accessed 23 May 2015.

Guimond, James (1991) *American Photography and the American Dream*. Chapel Hill, NC: University of North Carolina Press.

Haithman, Diane (1997) 'Their Son, the Producer', *The Los Angeles Times*, 21 September. Web. Accessed 4 April 2015.

Hayden, Dolores (1997) *The Power of Place: Urban Landscapes as Public History*. Cambridge, MA: MIT Press.

Hines, Geoffrey (2007) *Born in the USA*. New York: Continuum.

Hirsch, Emile (2007) 'Interview: Into the Wild Star Emile Hirsch', *Slash Film*, 21 September. Web. Accessed 20 May 2015.

Humphreys, Reynold (2008) *Hollywood's Blacklists: A Political and Cultural History*. Edinburgh: Edinburgh University Press.

Iampolski, Mikhail (1998) *The Memory of Tiresias: Intertextuality and Film*. Trans. Harsha Ram. Berkeley, CA: University of California Press.

Iconoclasts. Episode 1: Sean Penn and Jon Krakauer. Sundance TV, tx 25 October 2007.

James, David E. (2005) *The Most Typical Avant-Garde: History and Geography of Minor Cinemas in Los Angeles*. Berkeley, CA: University of California Press.

Johnson, Ben. 'Penn's Pontifications.' *FrontPageMagazine*. Tuesday 3 June 2003. Web. Accessed 3 June 2015.

Kelly, Richard T. (2004) *Sean Penn: His Life and Times*. New York: Canongate US.

Kiesling, Scott F. (2004) 'Dude', *American Speech*, 79, 3, 281–305.

Kouvaros, George (2004) *Where Does it Happen?: John Cassavetes and Cinema at the Breaking Point*. Minneapolis, MN: Minnesota University Press.

Krakauer, Jon (1993) 'Death of an Innocent', *Outside*, reprinted in *The Independent*. Web. Accessed 27 August 2015.

____ (1997) *Into Thin Air: A Personal Account of the Mount Everest Disaster*. New York: MacMillan.

____ (1998) *Into the Wild*. London: Pan Books.

Lawson, Terry (2001) 'Behind the Camera', *Star News*, 23 January. Web. Accessed February 2009.

Lehane, Dennis (2001) *Mystic River*. London: Bantam.

Leigh, Danny (2006) 'Harry Dean Stanton: Last of the Dharma Bums', *Sight and Sound*, 16, 8: 50–4.

Loder, Kurt (n.d) 'The Rolling Stone Interview: Bruce Springsteen on "Born in the U.S.A."', *Rolling Stone*. Web. Accessed 16 October 2013.

London, Jack (1987) *The Call of the Wild, White Fang and Other Stories*. Ed. Andrew Sinclair. New York: Penguin.

Madigan, Andrew J. (1996) 'What Fame is: Bukowski's Exploration of Self', *Journal of American Studies*, 30, 3, 447–61.

Malick, Terrence (1975) 'Malick on *Badlands*: Interview with Beverly Walker', *Sight and Sound*, 44, 2, 82–3.

Martin, Adrian (2007) 'The Misleading Man: Dennis Hopper', *Film International*, 5, 1, 32–44.

Maupin, Amistead (n.d.) 'Gus Van Sant', *Interview*. Web. Accessed 4 April 2015.

McGrath, Charles (2007) 'Mother Nature's Restless Sons', *The New York Times*, 16 September. Web. Accessed 21 May 2015.

Menounos, Maria (n.d.) *Access Hollywood*. Web. Accessed 22 March 2013.

Moore, Jack (1983) 'The Land and the Ethnics in Crews' Works', in David K. Jeffrey (ed.) *A Grits Triumph: Essays on the Works of Harry Crews*. Port Washington, NY: Associated Faculty Press, 46–66.

Mortensen, Viggo (1995) 'Missing Sandy Dennis', in John Boorman, Tom Luddy, David Thomson and Walter Donohue (eds) *Projections 4: Filmmakers on Filmmaking*. London: Faber and Faber, 313–17.

Moss, William M. (1983) 'Postmodern Georgia Scenes: Harry Crews and the Southern Tradition in Fiction,' in David K. Jeffrey (ed.) *A Grits Triumph: Essays on the Works of Harry Crews*. Port Washington, NY: Associated Faculty Press, 33–45.

Murray, Noel (2003) 'Cameron Crowe, Rock Journalist', *The Dissolve*, 15 July. Web. Accessed 7 August 2013.

Murray, Rebecca (n.d.) 'Sean Penn and Eddie Vedder Team Up To Talk About *Into the Wild*', *About Entertainment*. Web. Accessed 11 June 2015.

Naremore, James (1988) *Acting in the Cinema*. Berkeley, CA: University of California Press.

Nash, Roderick (1967) *Wilderness and the American Mind*. New Haven, CT: Yale University Press.

Neale, Steve (1986) 'Melodrama and Tears', *Screen*, 27, 6, 6–23.

Nelson, Scott (2005) 'Who Was John Henry?: Railroad Construction, Southern Folklore, and the Birth of Rock and Roll', *Labor: Studies in Working Class History of the Americas*. 2, 2, 53–79.

Orléan, Matthieu (2009) 'Photography, Writing, Acting ... Movie-Making Had Everything in One Package', in Matthieu Orléan (ed.) *Dennis Hopper & The New Hollywood*. Flammarion, Paris, 124–43.

Peberdy, Donna (2012) '"Politics Is Theater": Performance, Sexuality, and *Milk*', in Timothy Shary (ed.) *Millenial Masculinity: Men in Contemporary American Film*. Detroit,MI: Wayne State University Press, 52–65.

Penman, Ian (1998) 'Harry Dean Stanton: The Trouble With Harry', in *Vital Signs: Music, Movies and Other Manias*. London, Serpent's Tail, 39–50.

Penn, Sean (1991) Interview with Julian Schnabel. [Photographs by Dennis Hopper]. *Interview*, September, 95–9.

____ (2002) 'An Open Letter to the President of the United States of America', *The Washington Post*. October 19. Web. http://www.peace.ca/seanpenn.htm. Accessed 3 June 2015.

____ (2004) 'Commentary/2nd Act – A Year Later, Sean Penn Returns To Iraq And Files A Personal, Candid Report From The Front', *The San Francisco Chronicle*, 14 January. Web. Accessed 3 June 2015.

____ (2007) 'Interview: Sean Penn', *IGN*, 19 August. Web. Accessed 15 May 2015.
____ (2008) 'Conversations with Chávez and Castro,' *The Nation.*, 15 December. Web. Accessed 3 June 2015.
Perkins, Claire (2010) 'Sequelizing Hollywood: The American 'Smart' Film', in Carolyn Jess-Cooke and Constantine Verevis (eds) *Second Takes: Critical Approaches to the Film Sequel.* Albany, NY: State University of New York Press, 87–104.
Pramagiorre, Maria (2010) 'The Global Repositioning of the City Symphony: Sound, Space, and Trauma in *11'09'01–September 11*', *Jump Cut: A Review of Contemporary Media,* 52. Web. Accessed 30 May 2015.
Pulver, Andrew (2001) 'The Revolution Starts Here', *The Guardian*, 28 August.
Rhodes, John David and Elena Gorfinkel (eds) (2011) *Taking Place: Location and the Moving Image.* Minneapolis, MN: University of Minnesota Press.
Rich, B. Ruby (2009) 'Ghosts of a Vanished World', *The Guardian*, 16 January. Web. Accessed 7 August 2013.
Rochlin, Margy (1986) 'The Two Faces of Sean Penn', *American Film*, April, 20–5 & 27–8.
Roffman, Peter and Jim Purdy (1981) *The Hollywood Social Problem Film: Madness, Despair and Politics from the Depression to the Fifties.* Bloomington, IN: Indiana Universtiy Press.
Rorty, Richard (1998a) 'American National Pride: Whitman and Dewey', in *Achieving Our Country: Leftist Thought in Twentieth-Century America.* Cambridge, MA: Harvard University Press, 3–38.
____ (1998b) 'A Cultural Left', in *Achieving Our Country: Leftist Thought in Twentieth-Century America.* Cambridge, MA: Harvard University Press, 75–107.
____ (1999) *Philosophy and Social Hope.* Harmondsworth: Penguin.
Rosenbaum, Ron (1986) 'Acting: The Method and Mystique of Jack Nicholson', *New York Times Magazine*, 13 July. Web. Accessed 6 June 2009.
Rowe, Nicolette (2008) 'Centrifugal Bostons and Competing Imaginaries in *Mystic River*', *Journal for Cultural Research*, 12, 1, 81–97.
Sánchez Vera, José Joaquín (2013) 'Thoreau as Mirror for Jon Krakauer's *Into the Wild*', Diss. Karlstads University. Web. Accessed 14 May 2015.
Salvi, Delia Nora (1969) 'The History of the Actors' Laboratory, Inc. 1941–1950'. PhD dissertation, University of California, Los Angeles.
Schemo, Diana Jean (1994) 'Even in Her Own Words, A Woman of Convictions', *The New York Times*, 27 December. Web. Accessed 25 April 2015.
Shafrazi, Tony (2011) 'Double Standards: An American Education', in Tony Shafrazi (ed.) *Dennis Hopper: Photographs 1961–1967.* Cologne: Taschen, 58–66.
Shelley, Peter (2014) *Sandy Dennis: The Life and Films.* Jefferson, NC: McFarland.
Slide, Anthony (1999) *Actors on Red Alert: Career Interviews with Five Actors and Actresses Affected by the Blacklist.* Lanham, MD: The Scarecrow Press.
Smith, Gavin (1991) 'Sean Penn At Close Range', *Film Comment*, 27, 5, 58–68.
Sounes, Howard (1998) *Charles Bukowski: Locked in the Arms of a Crazy Life.* New York: Grove Press.
Sontag, Susan (1984) 'America, Seen Through Photographs, Darkly', in *On Photography*, Harmondsworth: Penguin, 27–48.
Strong, Catherine (2011) *Grunge: Music and Memory.* Guildford: Ashgate.
Studlar, Gaylyn (2013) '"The Corpse of Reprieve": Film Noir's Cautionary Tales of "Tough Guy" Masculinity', in Andrew Spicer and Helen Hanson (eds) *A Companion to Film Noir.* Malden, MA: Wiley-Blackwell. 369–86.

Tauber, Alfred (n.d.) 'Henry Thoreau as a Mirror of Ourselves', *Thoreau Reader*. Web. Accessed 14 May 2015.

Thomson, David (1990) 'A Bit of a Coyote, a Hell of a Woman', *American Film*. November, 26–32 & 50.

____ (2004) 'The Decade When Movies Mattered', in Thomas Elsaesser, Alexander Horwath, Noel King (eds) *The Last Great American Picture Show: New Hollywood Cinema in the 1970s*. Amsterdam, Amsterdam University Press, 73–82.

Tiusanen, Timo (1977) *Dürrenmatt: A Study of the Plays, Prose, Theory*. Princeton, NJ: Princeton University Press.

Tolstoy, Leo (2005) *Family Happiness and Other Stories*. New York: Mineola.

Walsh, Keri (2010) 'Why Does Mickey Rourke Give Pleasure?', *Critical Inquiry*, 37, 1, 131–62. Web. Accessed 2 March 2015.

Wasiolek, Edward (1978) *Tolstoy's Major Fiction*. Chicago: Chicago University Press.

Walt Whitman (1984) 'Democratic Vistas', in *The Portable Whitman*. Revised and Enlarged Edition. Ed. Mark Van Doren. London and New York: Penguin.

Ziolkowski, Theodore (n.d.) 'Durrenmatt's Fiction: Introduction', in *Friedrich Durrenmatt*. University of Chicago Press website. Web. Accessed 14 April 2015.

INDEX

About Schmidt 85
Academy Awards 19–20
activism 6, 14–18, 20–2, 30, 61, 88, 102, 121, 126
Actors Studio 10, 46, 50
Alder, Loretta 17
American Dream (magazine) 38
American imagination 103–4, 110
American Photography (magazine) 38
Americans 18–19
Americans, The (tv series) 37–8, 46
American West as Living Space, The (book) 111
Andersen, Hans Christian 77, 86–7
Anderson, Wes 125
Apocalypse Now 14, 44–5
Arbus, Diane 32, 38–40, 45
As Good as It Gets 55, 85
Ashby, Hal 13, 37, 121
Asphalt Jungle, The 59
Assassination of Richard Nixon, The 10, 20
Assault on Precinct 13 4
Assayas, Olivier 118
At Close Range 6, 10, 25–6, 50
auteur cinema 14

'Back off Mary Poppins' (*Two and a Half Men* episode) 92
Bad Day at Black Rock 99
Badlands 13, 33–4, 122
Ball, Alan 9
Barfly 75, 89

Beat movement 37–8, 76, 88; poetry 45; post-Beat 44
Best Years of Our Lives, The 11, 13, 46
blacklisting 6, 10, 11
Blackout, The 45
Blackwelder, Robert 24–5
Borgnine, Ernest 7, 95, 97–100, 116
Born in the USA (song) 35
Bowling for Columbine 9
Brando, Marlon 46, 48–51, 92, 115
Brat Pack 89, 92
Breakfast Club, The 89
Breakheart Pass 43
Brecht, Bertolt 55
Brigand, Alain 7, 95–7
Bronson, Charles 6, 32, 33, 42–4, 50–2, 52n.5, 54
'Brothers Under the Bridge' (song) 35
Buell, Lawrence 1–3, 109–10
Bukowski, Charles 5, 7, 53, 75–6, 117
Bush, George H. W. 9, 15–17, 100, 117–18

Cahiers du cinéma 4, 64
Call of the Wild, The (novel) 105–7
Carax, Leo 118
Carpenter, John 4, 99
Carroll, Noël 4–5
Cassavetes, John 5, 7, 37, 53, 61, 64–6, 68, 72, 74, 126
Cassavetes, Nick 61
Cat on a Hot Tin Roof 11, 76n.1
Chahine, Youseff 96

Chandler, Raymond 68
Chayefsky, Paddy 7, 98
Chicago Seven 15
Chinatown 7, 54–5, 59–61, 68, 74
Chion, Michel 122, 124
Civil Disobedience 110
Civil Rights movement 110
Claim, The 3
Clifton, Elmer 12
Clinton era 9
Close Encounters of the Third Kind 4
Cockfighter 92–3
Cold War 10
Colors 6
communism 10–11; anti-communist 10–11; sympathisers 11
Comolli, Jean-Louis 64–5
Conference of Studio Unions (CSU) 10
Conversation, The 125
Coppola, Francis Ford 45, 89, 125
Couturié, Bill 6, 14
Cradle Will Rock 9
Crews, Harry 5–6, 32–3, 40–1, 43, 52n.4, 75, 90
Cronenberg, David 48
Crossfire 12
Crossing Guard, The 1, 5, 7, 10–11, 27, 32, 37, 50, 52n.2, 53–76, 78, 83, 85, 90–1, 95, 101, 113, 116, 118, 126; and Bruce Springsteen 52; and *Chinatown* 60, 68; and masculinity 55–6; and melodrama; and Jack Nicholson 5, 7, 50, 53–4, 60–1, 72, 78, 85, 95; and New Hollywood 53; see also place/locations/Los Angeles and *The Killing of a Chinese Bookie*
Crowe, Cameron 23–4

Dardenne Brothers 3
Days of Heaven 88, 122
Dead Man Walking 20, 121
Dean, James 46, 48, 50, 54
Dear America: Letters Home from Vietnam 6, 14
Dennis, Sandy 6, 33, 50–2, 54, 69
Depression 13, 37
Dillinger 93
Dmytryk, Edward 12
Dogtown and Z-Boys 24, 116

Dogville 9
Dune 122
Dürrenmatt, Friedrich 7, 78–89, 93
Dylan, Bob 88

Earp, Jeremy 17
East of Eden 48
Eastwood, Clint 5, 9, 28–30, 50
Easy Rider 27, 44, 46, 54, 75
Edinburgh Film Festival 8
11/09/'01-September 11 7, 95–7
Elsaesser, Thomas 73–4
Emerson, Ralph Waldo 104, 107, 109
English Romanticism 108
Escape From New York 99

Faces 64–6, 72
Fagan, Myron C. 11
Fahrenheit 9/11 9
Fall Guy 11, 46
Fantasia 4
Far from Vietnam 97
Fast Times at Ridgemont High 6, 23, 24, 116
Fast Times at Ridgemont High: A True Story (book) 23
Fellini, Federico 3
feminine inner voices 123
film noir 4, 7, 13, 53, 56, 60, 67–8
Foley, James 10, 25
Fonda, Jane 15–16, 54
Ford, John 3, 34, 42
Forman, Milos 91
Foucault, Michel 21
Frank, Robert 32, 37–40, 46, 113
French New Wave 97
From Here to Eternity 99
From This Day Forward 13

Gautier, Eric 118
Gazzara, Ben 65–6, 76n.1
Genova 3
Gentlemen's Agreement 13
German New Wave 97
Germany in Autumn 97
Ginsberg, Allen 37, 88
Godard, Jean-Luc 97
González Iñárritu, Alejandro 96
Grapes of Wrath, The 34, 37
Grifters, The 58–9

Grimm Brothers, The 86
Guardian, The (newspaper) 8
Guthrie, Woody 13, 34–7

Hackman, Gene 42, 125–6
Hardwicke, Catherine 116
Hawks, Howard 4
Hayden, Tom 6, 15–16
Heckerling, Amy 23–4
Hellman, Monte 4, 11, 93
Highway Patrolman (song) 6, 26, 32–6, 52n.1n.2
Hirsch, Emile 7, 30, 103, 115–16, 118, 120
History of Violence, A 48
Hoffmann, Nico 80
Hollywood 10 12
Hollywood Reporter, The (magazine) 11
Hopper, Dennis 4–6, 26–8, 32–3, 44–52, 54, 75, 90, 92, 99, 126
House Un-American Activities Committee (HUAC) 6, 10
Huston, Anjelica 7, 53–5, 57–65, 68, 90, 99
Huston, John 34, 58–60

I am Sam 10, 20, 121
Iconoclasts (tv series) 8, 114
Imamura, Shôhei 96
In Country 33, 35
Indian Runner, The 1, 5–6, 9–11, 14, 22–3, 25–6, 31–76, 78, 83–5, 87, 90, 98, 100–3, 113, 116, 118, 126; and Bruce Springsteen 6, 32–6, 52n.2; and New Hollywood 14, 33, 53; Terrence Malick 32–4; and Viggo Mortensen 6, 32–3, 39, 44, 48–51, 116; see also place/locations Nebraska
International Alliance of Theatrical Stage Employees (IATSE) 10
intertextual networks 126
In the Electric Mist 78
Into the Wild 1, 5, 7, 32, 100–1, 103–24, 127; and Emile Hirsch 7, 103, 115, 118, 120; see also place/locations/Alaska and wilderness and Christopher McCandless
Into Thin Air (book) 113
Iraq War 15–18
Irma Vep 118

It Happened in Broad Daylight 7, 79–85
It Happened in Broad Daylight (1997) (tv movie) 80
Ivena, Joris 97

Jacoby, Hans 79–80
Jameson, Fredric 21, 48, 68
Jarrico, Paul 12
Joffe, Mark 9
'John Henry' (song) 6, 33, 36, 40–2
Johnstown Flood 32, 36
Judgement in Berlin 10, 11

Kaufman, Philip 88
Kazan, Elia 11, 13, 46, 76n.1
Kerouac, Jack 37, 113
Killing of a Chinese Bookie, The 53, 61, 64–8, 76
Klein, William 38, 97
Kolker, Robert 125
Kouvaros, George 64–5
Krakauer, Jon 7, 103–4, 106–16, 120, 122
Kristeva, Julia 5
Kromolowski, Jerzy 78, 83

landscape 3, 33, 40, 77, 83–4, 114, 117–19; American 45; wild 109
Last Detail, The 37, 54–5
Last Movie, The 44
Lee, Spike 6, 16–17
left-wing 6, 11–12, 88, 90, 108, 111, 125; American left culture 6; Hollywood 8, 20–2, 125
Lehane, Dennis 28–9, 78
L'Homme 97–101, 116
liberalism 9; Hollywood 9
Loach, Ken 96
London, Jack 7, 104–7, 111, 113–15, 118, 120, 122, 124
'Long Nights' (song) 120
Lords of Dogtown (book) 116
Lupino, Ida 11–12
Lynch, David 18, 50, 122

MADD 63–5
Malick, Terrence 4, 13, 20, 32–4, 88, 122, 124
Malone, Jena 114, 122–3
Mann, Delbert 7, 98

Man Who Sued God, The 9
Marty 7, 46, 98–9
masculinity 42–3, 52, 54–7, 94, 126; American 73, 92; construction of 57; in crisis 47, 102; naturalness of 55; *noir* 13
M*A*S*H (tv series) 16
Mason, Bobbie Anne 35
McCandless, Carine 122–3
McCandless, Chris/Christopher 7, 22, 103–18, 120, 122–4, 126–7
McCarthyism 13
McGuane, Thomas 93
McHale's Navy (tv series) 99
melodrama 50, 58, 65, 68–75, 112, 118, 124; and family 7, 68–75, 123, 126; road movie 126
Men, The 13
Menlove Edwards, John 113
Method 32, 46, 48–50, 54, 89; Emile Hirsch and the 7, 115–16; Method Acting Foreign Policy 18
Milius, John 93
Milk 19–20, 30–1
Milk, Harvey 19–20, 23, 30–1
mise-en-scène 4, 30, 42, 84, 87, 118
Monsieur Verdoux 13
Moore, Michael 8–9
Morse, David 6, 32, 42–4, 50–1, 53–5, 74, 116
Mortensen, Viggo 5–6, 32–3, 39, 44, 46, 48–51, 54–5, 116; as Franky in *The Indian Runner* 5, 26, 32–4, 36, 39–52, 85, 113, 126
Mothers Against Drunk Drivers *see* MADD
Motorcycle Diaries, The 118
Mueller, Niels 10
Murder My Sweet 68
Mystic River 6, 9, 17, 20, 28–30, 50

Nabokov, Peter 32, 35
Nash, Roderick 105–9
Native American 6, 35–6, 44
naturalism 46–7
Nebraska (album) 6, 33–7, 52n.1; *see also* Bruce Springsteen
Nelson, Jessie 10, 121
Network 98

New Hollywood 4–6, 8, 13–14, 20, 33, 50, 53–5, 60, 91–2, 124–6
Nicholson, Jack 5, 7, 9, 50, 53–7, 58–62, 65–6, 68–9, 72, 74, 77–9, 83–5, 89–95, 99, 116, 126; as Freddie Gale in *The Crossing Guard* 53–4, 56, 60–1, 95, 113; as Jerry Black in *The Pledge* 9, 77, 83–9, 90–1, 93–4, 113, 118; and masculinity 54–7; *see also The Indian Runner*
Nietzsche, Friedrich 21, 113
Night Moves 125
9/11 97; post-9/11 15; World Trade Center (WTC) 9, 15, 95–7, 100; and Twin Towers 7, 100–1, 127
92 in the Shade 93
Not Wanted 11–12, 46

Oates, Warren 92–3
Odets, Clifford 13
Olson-Kromolowski, Mary 78, 83
One Flew Over the Cuckoo's Nest 91
One Hundred and One Nights 118
On the Road 118
On the Waterfront 46, 48–50
Ouedraogo, Idrissa 96
Outside (magazine) 103
Outsiders, The 89

Paramount 10
Paris, Texas 88, 92
Parker, Trey 8
Pat Garrett and Billy the Kid 92
Pearl Jam 121
Peckinpah, Sam 99
Penn, Arthur 92, 125
Penn, Leo 6, 10–13, 44, 76n.1
Peralta, Stacy 24–5, 116
Pinky 13
place/locations: Alaska 1, 7, 22, 32, 103–4, 107, 113–15, 119, 122; Columbus 38, 40, 54; Los Angeles 1, 7, 10, 13–15, 26, 28, 31–2, 53–4, 60–3, 66, 68, 75–6, 116–17, 127; Maine Woods 108–9; Manhattan 1, 7, 95–6, 101; Mexico 42, 96, 117; Nebraska 1, 6, 14, 25, 31, 33–5, 40, 46, 51, 54, 116; Nevada 1, 7, 32, 77, 75, 103; Omaha 1, 54, 64

Pledge, The 1, 5, 7, 9–10, 32, 68, 75, 77–95, 100, 101, 113, 116, 118, 127; and Jack Nicholson; *see also* place/locations/Nevada and Cinton era
Pledge: Requiem for the Detective Novel, The (novel) 78
Pola X 118
Polanski, Roman 54, 60
Poseidon Adventure, The 99
Pretty in Pink 89
Prizzi's Honor 58–9
Problemfilms 80

Raiders of the Lost Ark 4
Rebel Without a Cause 44, 46, 48, 50
Red Channels 11
Redgrave, Vanessa 78, 86, 88
Renaissance films 126
Resnais, Alain 97, 118
Richardson, John 118
Right Stuff, The 88
Rio Bravo 4
Rio Grande 100
Ripley, Arthur 34
road movie 27, 93, 126
Robbins, Tim 5, 8–9, 20, 28, 121
Rohmer, Eric 3
Roosevelt, Franklin D. 13, 37
Rourke, Mickey 7, 75, 78, 89–92, 95
Rowlands, Gena 72
Royal Tenenbaums, The 125
Ruiz, Raoul 118
Ryan, Eileen 6, 10, 25, 40, 54
Ryan, Steve 11–12

Salles, Walter 118
Sanders Peirce, Charles 5
San Francisco Chronicle (newspaper) 17–18
Sarandon, Susan 8, 18
Saroyan, William 15
Sarris, Andrew 4
Saussure, Ferdinand de 5
Savage Souls 118
Sayles, John 8–9
Seeger, Pete 42
Shattuck, Kathrun 11
Shepard, Sam 78, 88–9, 92
She's So Lovely 61
Silvestri, Domenic 118

Six Feet Under (tv series) 9
Sixteen Candles 89
Solomon, Norman 6, 16–18
Sontag, Susan 38
Spielberg, Steven 4
Splendour in the Grass 50
Springsteen, Bruce 6, 32–7, 41, 52n.2
Stanislavski, Konstantin 46, 54
Stanton, Harry Dean 5, 7, 78, 91–5, 126
Stegner, Wallace 15, 104, 111
Strasberg, Lee 46, 54
Sturges, John 99
Sunshine State 9

Tanovic, Danis 96
Taps 89
Tavernier, Bertrand 78
Team America: World Police 8
That Cold Day in the Park 50, 52
Thin Red Line, The 20, 122
Thomson, David 14, 59–60
Thoreau, Henry David 5, 7, 104, 107–11, 113–15, 118, 120, 122, 124
Thunder Road 34
Till the End of Time 12
Times of Harvey Milk, The 19, 30
Tolstoy, Leo 7, 104, 111–13, 123
Trotskyist Workers' Revolutionary Party 88
24 Hour Party People 3
Two and a Half Men (tv series) 92
Two Lane Blacktop 92–3

Undercover Man, The 11
'U.S.A.' 1, 5, 7, 32, 95, 96–102, 116, 127; *see also* L'homme
US independent cinema 125
US/Mexican border 118

Vajda, Ladislas 7, 79–81, 86
Van Sant, Gus 19, 30–1
Varda, Agnès 97, 118
Variety (magazine) 118
Vietnam War 14–17, 22, 32, 33, 35, 44, 46–8, 51, 97, 100–1, 110; Hollywood 14; movies 6, 45; post-Vietnam 21; veterans 34–5
Vedder, Eddie 120–4
Versprechen, Das (The Pledge) (novel) 80–3
von Trier, Lars 9

Walden (book)   108–111, 113
War in the Gulf   117–18
War Made Easy   17
'We Got the Beat' (song)   24
Welcome to Sarajevo   3
Wenders, Wim   88, 92
West German Cinema   80
When the Levees Broke: A Requiem in Four Acts   6, 16
White Fang (novel)   106–7
Whitman, Walt   8, 20–2, 107
Who's Afraid of Virginia Woolf?   50, 52
Wild Bunch, The   99
wilderness   7, 104–9; condemnation of 104; cult   105–6; physical   108; savage 108; civilisation   109

Wild Grass   118
Wild One, The   46, 48
Winterbottom, Michael   3
With or Without You   3
Wonderland   3
Wong, Kar Wai   3
World War II   13, 15, 99, 125; post-World War II   5, 10, 12, 46
Wright Penn, Robin   61, 74, 77
Wyler, William   11

Zinnemann, Fred   99

GPSR Authorized Representative: Easy Access System Europe, Mustamäe tee 50, 10621 Tallinn, Estonia, gpsr.requests@easproject.com

www.ingramcontent.com/pod-product-compliance
Lightning Source LLC
Chambersburg PA
CBHW051403290426
44108CB00015B/2132